Love, Lust, and Longing in the White House

Love, Lust, and Longing in the White House

THE ROMANTIC RELATIONSHIPS OF AMERICA'S PRESIDENTS

Webb Garrison

Cumberland House
Nashville, Tennessee

Published by Cumberland House Publishing, Inc., 431 Harding Industrial Drive, Nashville, Tennessee 37211

Cover design by Karen Phillips
Page design by Mike Towle

All photos and illustrations not otherwise credited are owned by the author.

Library of Congress Cataloging-in-Publication Data is available.
ISBN: 1-58182-081-X

1 2 3 4 5 6 7 8 9 — 05 04 03 02 01 00

Contents

Preface

Forty-one Men, Their Mates, and Their Paramours

Our presidents, their wives, ex-wives, and lovers (and even the wives' and ex-wives' ex-husbands) are a remarkable bunch. They comprise a fairly representative cross-section of America from 1789 until the twenty-first century. Practically every conceivable type of male and female is represented. Other books have dealt with either chief executives only, their wives and/or first ladies only, or a single husband-wife pair. This work offers a glimpse, and often more, of all known and many suspected relationships involving all chief executives and their mates.

Virtually all reference works dealing with chief executives list Grover Cleveland as having been both our twenty-second and twenty-fourth president, since he is the only man ever to win nonconsecutive terms as the nation's chief executive. This usage has therefore been followed here.

Names by which men and women were most widely known to relatives, intimates, and the general public are used in chapter headings. A glance at the table of contents reveals that our first seven presidents—and some successors—were treated with a certain sense of formality. No chief executive was universally known by a nickname or an abbreviated name until Andy "Old Hickory" Jackson left his beloved Rachel behind and went to Washington to assume power. Subsequently, it became a common but not universal practice to use informal designations for men at the helm of the nation. John Quincy Adams could have been widely known as JQA, but he was not. Use of a cluster of initials in lieu of a name didn't come into vogue until the Great Depression, and even then presidential initials have become household names just three times—with FDR, JFK, and LBJ.

This gradual modification of nomenclature to a more informal tone points to an even more sweeping change. Our early presidents were regarded as the closest thing this country has ever had to a monarchy. Hence, they were almost universally treated with deference or respect. Again, a change took place during the Andy Jackson administration. He was the subject of numerous satirical and sometimes biting cartoons, and that opened the door for all presidents to become targets of satirists and political cartoonists. Revered as he is today, Abraham Lincoln probably received more bad press in the form of cartoons than did any other man who occupied the White House prior to the twentieth century.

Yet, even with the growing informality inherent with the use of nicknames and poisonous pens, presidents remained pretty much immune to having the dirty laundry of their marital infidelity washed in public until Warren G. Harding came along. Harding, unfaithful in his marriage to the ever-compliant but bossy Flossie, was skewered before being roasted over a slow fire. Since Harding's administration, the numbers have been six of one, a half dozen of another—six have escaped damaging revelations about their private lives; a half dozen have been cooked over hot coals. The lid blew off after revelations about presidential candidate Gary Hart and his goings-on forced him out of the presidential sweepstakes in 1987.

It is possible, but not certain, that many early chief executives and their wives bear up well under scrutiny because they really were exemplary persons. However, had they been subjected to microscopic examination by investigative reporters, some of them might not have come up smelling like a rose.

Factual information as well as the accompanying dirt about unbridled lust in the White House has been largely concentrated in the twentieth century. Before the term *gay* gained today's connotations, James Buchanan was widely regarded as being interested only in a male companion, but remarkably little was said in print about this matter. Many of his contemporaries surely must have noticed Abraham Lincoln's keen interest in young men, but no one took potshots at the pilot who was guiding the ship of state through the bloodiest war in our nation's annals.

Bill Clinton came along 130 years after Lincoln and found himself the target of an intense legal investigation surrounding his alleged affair with a flirtatious White House intern. He also was the butt of barnyard humor and the subject of tales that made headlines even before such tales had been investigated. Since no earlier president was caught with his fly unbuttoned or his zipper down, the man from Arkansas has been widely regarded as the most lascivious of all chief executives. Whether or not that dubious honor will remain attached to him permanently, only time will tell. Whatever secrets relating to love, lust, or longing future aspirants may try to hide, their private lives will surely come under intense scrutiny the minute they set out for a move to 1600 Pennsylvania Avenue.

Love, Lust, and Longing in the White House

1

George and Martha Custis Washington

George Washington, twenty-six years old and regarded by all who knew him as an up-and-comer in the world of politics and power, called on the widow Custis some time in March 1758. He was enamored with another woman at the time, but found in Martha a great deal that he liked. They spent an evening getting acquainted, and the widow probably had her three-year-old son Jackie and his young sister Martha brought by a slave to meet George.

Martha Custis provided accommodations for the night. After a hearty breakfast the next morning, Washington rode off to Williamsburg, the colonial capital of Virginia to attend to pressing business. One week later he was back at Martha's home, White House in New Kent County on the Pamunkey River. After a brief stay, he again rode off. This time, however, he was a different man. He was engaged to be married to the wealthiest widow in the colony after having spent all of twenty to twenty-two hours in her presence. Mutual acquaintances were not surprised when they heard that a marriage ceremony would be held a few months later in Williamsburg.

Although decidedly plain in appearance and the recipient of only a smattering of education, Martha had certain assets not to be taken lightly. At age eighteen, Martha had married plantation owner Daniel Parke Custis, who was twice her age. She went on to bear him four children, two of whom died in infancy. At the time of his death in 1757, Custis was renowned as the manager of seventeen thousand acres of rich farmland producing an annual crop of tobacco worth a small fortune. Before he paid his first call to White House, ambitious young Washington knew that the widow—only five feet tall and a year his senior—was probably the wealthiest marriageable woman in the entire colony.

Their wedding, attended by the royal governor, was one of the gala affairs of the 1758–59 social season. The Reverend Peter Mossum, who officiated, is said to have blinked in astonishment when he saw the bridegroom resplendent in blue and silver, with red trimmings and gold knee buckles.

11

Yellow dominated the attire of the twenty-seven-year-old bride, who knew that as soon as legal formalities were completed her husband would take control of her entire estate. Members of the plantation aristocracy remarked to one another that the ceremony clearly marked a marriage of convenience. Martha needed a competent man to look after her affairs, and, in turn, George jumped a few rungs up the ladder when he said, "I do." He later wrote numerous letters to the wife he sometimes called "my agreeable Consort," but these documents lacked the fire and ice sprinkled through some of his letters to another woman.

Martha Dandridge Custis before her marriage to George Washington. (Adapted from the John Wollaston painting that is held by Washington and Lee University)

THERE IS NO EVIDENCE that the pair ever quarreled seriously for any length of time during forty years of marriage. Mrs. Washington probably knew perfectly well that she was not her mate's first choice, but she seems to have taken precautions to be sure she was his last.

Nearly a decade before George and Martha decided to tie the knot, he probably would have married Betsy Fauntleroy—if she would have had him. Her social standing was a bit above that of the twenty-year-old suitor, who grew up in comfort but not in luxury. As the daughter of a Richmond County justice and burgess, Betsy would have given George entry into social and political realms not otherwise available to him. He seems to have pressed his suit rather persistently, but the sixteen-year-old object of his affection never wavered in her unwillingness to enter into a commitment.

After he had given up on Betsy as a lost cause, the young male, by now making a name for himself as an entrepreneur, took an enforced trip to Boston by way of New York. In the fast-growing city he met and was intrigued by Mary Philipse, who reputedly owned about fifty thousand acres of the thing George most cherished—land. Mary later became Mrs. Roger Morris and joined her husband in wholehearted opposition to the Colonial revolt whose military phase was headed by Washington.

Abundant evidence, based almost entirely upon letters that Washington wrote and did not know were being preserved, indicates that he couldn't keep his eyes off the eighteen-year-old bride of his close friend and neighbor, George William Fairfax. Young Mrs. Fairfax, the former Sarah Cary, universally known simply as "Sally," was attractive, vivacious, extremely well educated, and an incurable flirt.

Although Sally Fairfax is invariably identified as the one passionate love of Washington's life, it is likely that he was chiefly infatuated with her opulent lifestyle and social standing as daughter-in-law of the great Lord Fairfax. Whatever the case, he was drawn to her more strongly than steel is drawn to a magnet. They exchanged many letters. George destroyed Sally's letters to him, but she carefully preserved his.

It is apparent he first wrote to Sally immediately after meeting her for the first time at the Belvoir mansion in which she and her husband lived. Two more of his letters soon went to Belvoir, but she did not reply. Distraught and perplexed, George wrote to both Sally's brother and her sister and requested each of them to intercede on his behalf.

Inevitably, Sally's sister-in-law got wind of what was taking place, and she dashed off a letter to Washington. In it, she voiced a warning that additional letters from him to Sally might bring trouble to both of them. Although he was too intelligent not to know that the warning should be heeded, he ignored it and continued to write to Sally. In one of the letters that she preserved without his knowledge, he told her that a few lines from her pen would serve to make him "happier than the Day is long."

On the heels of learning that he had become engaged to Martha Custis, Sally broke her lengthy silence and sent George a letter of congratulations. His reply, written at Fort Cumberland on September 12, 1758, came as close to being passionate as anything he ever penned. Framed within twenty-four hours after having received Sally's response to the news that he would soon take another woman as his wife, Washington's letter, with additional paragraph breaks added, said:

> How joyfully I catch at the happy occasion of renewing a correspondence which I feared was disrelished on your part, I leave to time, that never failing expositor of all things, and to a monitor equally faithful in my own breast, to testify. . . . Tis true I profess myself a votary of love. I acknowledge that a lady is in the case, and further, I confess that the lady is known to you. Yes, Madame, as well as she is to one who is too sensible of her charms to deny the Power whose influence he feels and must ever submit to.
>
> I feel the force of her amiable beauties in the recollection of a thousand tender passages that I could wish to obliterate, till I am bid to receive them . . . You have drawn me, dear Madame, or rather I have drawn myself, into an honest confession of a simple fact.

Misconstrue not my meaning; doubt it not, nor expose it. The world has no business to know the object of my love, declared in this manner to you, when I want to conceal it . . . I dare believe you are as happy as you say. I wish I was happy too.

George Washington married Martha three months after pouring out his feelings to Sally. George wrote to Martha, too, but when read from the perspective of many generations his letters to his wife seem formal and perfunctory. Seven months into their marriage, during which period he had been away from Mount Vernon much of the time, he penned to his bride a letter that she preserved. Its final word is extremely revealing, for he said:

We [Maj. George Washington and men of the Virginia militia under his command] have begun our march for the Ohio [in order to confront the French and their Indian allies]. A courier is starting for Williamsburg and I embrace this opportunity to send a few words to one whose life is now inseparable from mine. Since that happy hour when we made our pledges to each other, my thoughts have been continually going out to you as another self. That an all-powerful Providence may keep us both in safety is the prayer of your ever faithful and affectionate friend.

Throughout her life, Martha Washington had other friends in addition to the man to whom she entrusted her estate and her children. Only a few of her letters survive, and these reveal that she lacked what today would be called a grade-school education. That did not, however, prevent much-younger and better-educated women from forming a close attachment to her.

An ardent but inarticulate advocate of more rights for women, Martha advised young female relatives to seek and to exercise all independence that circumstances permitted. Writing to a niece in 1794, she urged her to do something that the wife of Washington could not do under Virginia law—that is, "exert yourself in the management of your estate." She then added from five years of personal experience that, "A dependence is, I think a wretched state."

For his part, her husband did not know how wretched a life a stepfather could lead until Jackie and Martha became adolescents. At age twelve Martha's daughter Patsy experienced a violent seizure that marked the beginning of recurrent episodes that folks of that period called simply "fits." If she suffered from epilepsy, as seems to have been the case, physicians consulted by her mother were unable to help.

Jackie must have been a charming child when he was first escorted by a slave to meet the visitor who would soon become his stepfather. He was given advantages that Washington never had. Christmas toys were ordered

George, Martha, and her children. (Edward Savage painting, held by the Philadelphia Museum of Art)

for him from London, and by the time he was eight years old he had a tutor. The Reverend Jonathan Boucher, a rector of the Church of England who headed an exclusive boarding school in Caroline County attended by Jackie, clearly had his fill of young Custis by the time he was sixteen or seventeen years old. Writing to Jackie's stepfather, Boucher said: "I never did in my life know a youth so exceedingly indolent or so surprisingly voluptuous: one would suppose Nature had intended him for some Asiatic Prince." Washington gave the note only perfunctory attention. His time and energy were almost totally devoted to his numerous business ventures, his speculation in land, and his growing apprehension that long-simmering complaints of colonists might lead to a rupture between England and her North American colonies.

UNDER WASHINGTON'S SUPERVISION, FIVE distilleries built at Mount Vernon eventually turned a tidy profit by producing about a thousand gallons per month. He grew tobacco in large quantities during his first two years as a married man, but failed in later seasons and ultimately decided he was not suited to be a tobacco farmer. He built a gristmill, operated a fishery for which he bought a brigantine of some size, bought into a speculative venture involving the drainage of the vast Dismal Swamp, and erected a sawmill.

Although George put time and money into these and other ventures—some of which cost him everything he invested in them—his chief passion was land acquisition. Marriage to Martha gave him control of at least six thousand fertile acres and one hundred slaves, in addition to the sixty or so he already owned. Management of the Custis plantation and estate didn't satisfy his hunger for land, it only whetted his appetite for more. Earlier, he had been a major backer of a venture known as the Ohio

Company, which had received a grant of two hundred thousand acres from King George only to lose control prior to the American Revolution. By the time Virginia's House of Burgesses finally validated claims of the company, three years after the outbreak of the Revolution, much of the best land had been claimed by squatters who then refused to vacate their relatively small tracts.

He made several trips to what was then the far West and usually came home with his saddlebags crammed full of property deeds. His insatiable hunger for more and more square miles was so great that he investigated and probably invested in ventures as distant as Florida and Georgia's western land that bordered the Mississippi River.

Even in his later years, Washington enjoyed nothing so much as mounting one of his spirited horses and taking a personal look at some of his land.

Scanty and inaccurate records fail to reveal precisely how much land George Washington had accumulated when he preceded Martha in death. He could have been possessor of as much as forty-eight thousand acres—or as little as twenty-five thousand. Extremely wealthy, regardless of the precise size of his holdings, the man whose first big acquisition came at the marriage altar was far more interested in land than in women.

Although he was disappointed that Martha bore him no children, there is no evidence that he ever engaged in a sexual liaison with another woman. Had he even wanted to do so during seemingly hopeless years of the colonists' revolution against the mother country, he probably couldn't have pulled it off. During much of the time he spent away from Mount Vernon as the commander of Colonial forces—the dreadful winter at Valley Forge included—faithful Martha slept by his side every night.

Numerous commentators on the life of the man whose wife eventually came to be known as Lady Presidentress have come to a single conclusion. According to these analysts, the former widow Custis and George Fairfax knew about everything that went on between George and Sally. Secure in that knowledge, they acted as though they knew nothing. Hence, the two spouses spent their mature lives surrounded by creature comforts, respected by all with whom they came in contact—and untainted by scandal.

2

John and Abigail Adams

S he lacked some essential social graces; she did not sing, dance, or even play cards. This probably had something to do with her having been reared as a minister's daughter. But her father was not responsible for how she walked in a queer, pigeon-toed fashion. To top the matter, her hair—perhaps tousled from too much time spent reading and writing—resembled a tangle of bulrushes.

These comments paraphrase the exact words penned by John Adams in his voluminous diary soon after he began to notice that a neighboring clergyman's daughter was becoming a woman. When he put some of his observations into a letter to her, she gently responded by requesting that he stop looking at her dark side. There, she admitted, "no doubt you discover many Spots—which I rather wish were erased, than conceal'd from you."

The young attorney in whom Abigail was becoming interested as a male and not simply an acquaintance later had the temerity to put into writing his reflections concerning what he called "her Spotts." In the light of such candor, it seems incredible that the two should have married and lived happily together for many years.

Adams himself tried to describe the alchemy between them. He lived in an era when Benjamin Franklin's lightning experiments were still regarded as marvelous by folks who did not know that the real marvel lay in the fact that the Sage of Philadelphia *survived* his tests. In what John Adams called "electrical experiments," this unseen force often serves to pull together two quite dissimilar things, such as lint and a freshly laundered black blouse or a pair of trousers. A tug of this sort "between Glass and feather" is clearly too great to be resisted, he pointed out. Years later in France, he said that this force operates much like that of a magnet, by whose power "when a pair approach within striking distance they fly together like the needle to the pole [of the magnet]."

Not fully realizing what he was doing, the future president accurately analyzed the bond that linked him with Abigail. Entirely dissimilar in a great many respects, they were pulled to one another by a force or forces they did not attempt to analyze. Both of them accepted the fact that they seemed to have little in common—yet neither could resist the pull toward the other. This "unseen but unbreakable bond" resulted in their marriage which, unlike unions of many couples who seemed to have nearly everything in common, was never severed or even seriously damaged.

JOHN BECAME ACQUAINTED WITH Abigail when she was a spindly youngster of about fifteen, but at that time he had no interest in her. Always popular with girls, he described himself in his autobiography as being amorous—that is, "fond of the society of females"—beginning at the age of ten or eleven. Because his father had issued stern warnings about the dangers of venereal diseases, he

"The pigeon-toed Smith girl," who at age twenty-two protested that she "was as thin as a rail." (Original held by Massachusetts Historical Society)

never attempted to engage in sexual conquests, however. When well past middle age, he could honestly congratulate himself—as he actually did—that "My children may be assured that no illegitimate brother or sister exists or ever existed."

His unwavering decision to stay away from flesh pots didn't mean that he was immune to attraction, though. On the contrary, not long after launching his career as an attorney, he became enamored with Hannah Quincy—a brunette he categorized as glamorous and intriguing. She seems to have been ready to become Mrs. Adams, but John kept his priorities clearly in sight. To him, financial stability was more important than marriage. He went to the extent of fantasizing about Hannah—whom he called Orlinda—but simultaneously tried to keep from touching her. She tired of his hesitancy and married another man.

A mutual friend, Richard Cranch, brought John Adams and Abigail Smith together in the aftermath of Adams's breakup with Hannah. Deeply interested in Abigail's older sister, Mary, Cranch had spent many hours with the younger girl. Her father had until that point been her only teacher, and his own education was not the best. Cranch sensed "an intense eagerness to learn" in the adolescent, so he lent her novels by a then-noted author and taught her the rudiments of French.

Abigail's avid interest in learning and the large store of knowledge inside the head of a girl largely self-taught caught John's interest before he began to look at her hair, face, and body in a more-than-casual fashion. Although his background put him well beneath hers in the estimation of those who knew them both, he was so impressed by her hunger for learning that he, too, began to bring books to her. Together they had thumbed through only a few before he suddenly realized that she had become an attractive young woman.

John was still far from ready to think seriously of marriage: It took years for most fledgling attorneys to begin to earn enough to support a family. But he soon began to make Abigail his only love—and she reciprocated quietly but strongly. When he started to sense danger signals, he did what hardly any other suitor would have done. He put his ideas on paper—and delivered a letter to Abigail. In it he urged: "Patience my Dear! Learn to conquer your appetites and Passions!" Writing as though he had neither appetites or passions, he stressed to his beloved that, "The Government of one's own soul requires greater Virtues than the Management of Kingdoms."

John could have saved his paper and ink; Abigail's mother was strongly opposed to accepting him as a son-in-law. Abigail was descended from one of the most distinguished families of Massachusetts; even though her suitor was a great-great-grandson of Pilgrims John and Priscilla Alden, he had absolutely no other claim to distinction. Abigail was the daughter of a revered Unitarian minister, so she occupied the top echelon of folks who lived in and around Braintree, Massachusetts. John's father was a mere farmer, a vocation belittled in a regional proverb that, to the effect, says, "Not that there is anything against farming, for we all have to eat, but farmers are so very gauche, you know."

Mother Smith's frequent and strongly expressed views may have prolonged the courtship somewhat, but other factors were involved. John was still on a subsistence income, and throughout his life considered himself incapable of making enough money to avoid worry about the future.

One time the sweethearts did not see each other for six weeks because he had been inoculated from smallpox and had to stay in isolation in Boston. Not knowing in those days how the malady spread from one person to another, health authorities forbade the transmission of letters written by an inoculated person unless they had been thoroughly smoked. This practice may have made John and Abigail the first courting couple on record to exchange frequent and voluminous letters, half of which reeked of smoke produced from inside John's "pest house."

LONG BEFORE THEY MARRIED, John and Abigail adopted the habit of calling one another by classical names as a sign of enduring affection. To the struggling attorney, Abigail was occasionally Miss Adorable. More frequently, however, she was Aurora or "my Diana," and to the minister's daughter he became Lysander. Diana and Lysander wrote and talked about many things. They gravely exchanged ideas about the ruinous state of the Colonies and the increasing tension with the mother country. They discussed the traits and strengths of men standing for public office. They even spent an evening wondering about how best to cultivate beans, and what *physick*— or home remedy—was best for upset stomach.

They weren't coldly unemotional toward one another: On the contrary, both yearned for the physical union that neither was willing to enter into before marriage. About a month before he finally decided that, somehow, they could eke out a living on his income, John wrote to Abigail:

> You shall polish and refine my sentiments of life and manners, banish all the unsocial and ill-natured particles from my composition, and form me to that happy temper that can reconcile a quick discernment with a perfect candor.

She used less ponderous and more pointed language. After registering delight that their long courtship would soon lead them to the altar for a ceremony performed by her father, staid prose could not express her emotions. Waxing poetic, Abigail's words rushed over one another as she told her beloved:

> Should I see thee,
> Were I imprisoned e'en in paradise
> I should leap the crystal walls.

His contemporaries described John as being "a lump of a man with a pigeon's breast" whose protruding eyes made many of them uncomfortable. Abigail, who took his enumeration of "her Spotts" in stride, saw him as handsome and courtly. Years later, when he constantly shook with palsy and talked with a lisp because he refused to wear dentures, she still regarded him as her knight in shining armor.

Some biographers labeled their union as a political marriage. Although this characterization of their middle and latter years is valid, it certainly was not the unseen but powerful force that drew them together when he was twenty-eight and she was barely nineteen years old.

Neither of them attached significance to the fashion in which they arrived at a mutually satisfactory conclusion within a few years. Already

John Adams in mid-life.
(Independence National
Historical Park Collection)

hankering for public office, John mused that if he should enter an election and win, it would require him to be in Boston or Philadelphia for long intervals. He did not then imagine that he would be a delegate to Continental Congresses, a diplomat forced to spend a full decade in Europe and England, vice president, and then president of the United States.

Abigail, who refused to speak in public and who preferred her own hearth to any marble fireplace in the western world, firmly, positively, and finally told him to go into the world and make his mark. She would, however, remain at home as much as possible.

As HUSBAND AND WIFE, they were elevated from near-impoverished obscurity by the fact that Abigail encouraged John to defend British soldiers who had been charged with grievous crimes in the aftermath of the Boston Massacre of March 5, 1770. Both of them were well known as ardent opponents of British tyranny, so it surprised and shocked their circle of friends to learn that John would appear in court on behalf of Captain Thomas Preston and seven subordinate Redcoats.

When the accused were brought before the Superior Court of Judicature, witnesses for the prosecution testified that unprovoked soldiers had fired into a mass of citizens quietly going about their business. John produced witnesses who said that civilians were the aggressors and begged jurors to consider how they would have behaved had they been struck to the ground by clubs and then stomped upon by the heavy rough shoes that were then standard wear. To the astonishment not merely of Boston and of Massachusetts, but of every city and every colony, jurors acquitted six soldiers and ruled that the other two were guilty of manslaughter instead of murder.

John's legal fee was not big enough to pay for his meals and lodgings while he defended men widely considered to be indefensible, but his courageous actions made his name familiar everywhere. Abigail nodded knowingly when she heard the outcome of the trial: She had long been convinced that her John was destined for greatness.

It would have taken her completely aback to be informed that she would eventually stand shoulder to shoulder with him in the esteem of multitudes. Today she is properly revered as one of the first Americans openly, articulately, and ardently to espouse the rights of women. Here the pair perpetuated their separate roles as "Glass and feather," for they were poles apart in their thinking, but they never lost their love and respect for one another.

During four years as a member of the Massachusetts legislature, John spent a great deal of time away from home. Consequently, the pile of letters written to him by Abigail grew thicker and thicker. From Boston he went to Philadelphia, where he helped frame legislation that led to American independence. Most of a decade was then spent as a U.S. emissary abroad. During this period, along with Benjamin Franklin and John Jay, Adams hammered out the vital 1783 Treaty of Paris. Abigail remained at Braintree, except for an interval during which she and her husband were together in London.

John had barely returned home when members of the electoral college chose him as George Washington's vice president. Abigail rarely saw him during the period in which New York served as the nation's capital and visited him only occasionally when the center of political power was shifted to Philadelphia. He was an inevitable candidate for the presidency in 1796, but shrewd and sharp-tongued Abigail didn't want him to take the post.

To the surprise of the new nation, internationally known Charles C. Pinckney garnered just one electoral vote—and Adams of Braintree received seventy-one. When his election was fixed and final, Abigail reluctantly made plans to join him. They were the first to reside in the largely unfinished mansion in Washington City that was then called the President's House. It was a very poor place in which to live, she said many times, but it had one valuable feature—clothing that had been washed could be hung to dry in the large "audience room."

Abigail was fond of Martha Washington, but refused to follow her near-imperial example. Before her husband took his oath of office, she made it crystal clear that she had no desire to become a second Lady Presidentress. Two centuries before the nation and the world rocked and reeled for months while a special counsel and an army of attorneys tried to pin a crime upon a president, Abigail showed almost uncanny foresight. Retirement to some peaceful place, she mused to the chief executive to whom she had given wise advice for decades, "would be a much more eligible situation than to be fastened up hand and foot and tongue, to be shot at as our Quincy lads do at the poor geese and turkeys."

Since Grover Cleveland's nonconsecutive terms cause him to be counted twice, forty-one men have served as forty-two presidents. The stories of these males and their mates are as varied as those of the American people at large. Too many of them are tarnished and some are downright sordid, but accounts of some husbands and wives who went to the White House enlarge our appreciation for marriage as it is practiced in a democracy.

Abigail and John Adams were not the only two genuine lovers who were transported to Pennsylvania Avenue by circumstances. They stand, however, close to the top of the list of mere mortals whose union has remained a source of inspiration for many generations.

3

Thomas and Martha Jefferson, and Company

Literally, not figuratively, Thomas Jefferson looked down on most of his contemporaries except George Washington. At six feet, two inches, the first president was barely half an inch shorter than his minister to France and secretary of state who would become his vice president in 1796. Washington was the heavier of the two by quite a lot, however. "Long Tom," as many of his intimate acquaintances called him, was thin and angular.

Some of Jefferson's major interests were considered to be feminine; few males of the day were good violinists who also sang well, with or without invitation. He clearly had a generous dose of libido, however, and until some twentieth-century presidents topped him, he was the chief executive who evoked the most commentaries about his goings-on with members of the opposite sex.

There's no documentary evidence to support the tale that nineteen-year-old Jefferson was sexually involved with sixteen-year-old Rebecca Burwell—but that was not because he failed to show signs of being ready and willing. She was interested in him, but not inclined to become his lover or his wife, so she jilted him in order to become Mrs. Jacques Ambler. Her decision quashed his plans to buy a vessel he called "a full-rigged flat," name it *Rebecca*, and use it to "visit England, Holland, France, Spain, and Italy." Presumably he hoped that the girl for whom he planned to name his ship would be aboard it with him, but in writing of his plans he said nothing about her. Instead, he stressed that in Italy he hoped "to buy a good fiddle."

When Long Tom heard that Rebecca was engaged, he wrote a letter to a friend in which he waxed philosophical about the woman he had been calling his "dear Belinda." After sharing the news that she was no longer fair game for him, he ended his account by writing, "Well, the Lord bless her! I say." Neither he nor she then knew that her husband would become treasurer of the Old Dominion.

Jefferson's second bout with uncontrollable panting was anything but discreet. A glimpse of Mrs. Betsy Walker, who lived not far from him, sent Long Tom into "heavy sweats" that did not subside readily. Years later her husband, John, published a story according to which his close neighbor tried for years to seduce his wife. Whether John was scrupulously accurate or bent upon smearing a neighbor who had become a major political figure is anybody's guess. Yet it is a matter of record that Walker challenged Jefferson to a duel, and they were restrained from resorting to pistols at dawn only when James Madison intervened. Of this phase of his life, the president of the United States said only that "When young and single, I offered love to a handsome lady, and I acknowledge its incorrectness."

His undisputed third heartthrob other than Mrs. Martha Wayles Skelton, who was mistress of Monticello mansion for a full decade, was Mrs. Maria Hadfield Cosway. Jefferson, who met her in France a few years after Martha's death, was so imposing a dignitary that her husband seems to have looked the other way. Maria, sixteen years younger than the U.S. minister who lived in Paris, was widely described as having been a raving beauty. An eye-catching photograph in which she snuggles against her husband often evokes a double take when seen. Although Maria was decidedly the smaller of the two, Richard Cosway is as pretty and as fashionably dressed as the woman who made the heart of widower Jefferson leap and bound.

Maria affected him so strongly that in her presence he forgot that he was close to entering what in the 1780s was considered old age and so acted like a young buck whose horns were not fully grown. Attempting to show Maria his agility, he tried to jump over a fence but didn't make it and from the subsequent fall suffered a permanent injury to his right hand. If that cooled his ardor, however, his letters to her do not reveal it. Richard Cosway took his wife from Paris in 1787, but the celebrated American who lived there continued to correspond with Maria for some time.

Some persons who have tried to analyze one of the most complex and gifted men who ever headed this nation attribute his interest in Maria (but not Rebecca or Betsy) to his passionate devotion to the wife who died after just ten years of marriage and left him to care for two motherless girls. Martha, the older girl whom he called Patsy, had her father's slim figure, auburn hair, and angular features. She lived with him in Paris for about five years, then married a second cousin who eventually became governor of Virginia. Mary, whom Long Tom called Polly, was six years younger than Martha and spent only a few years in Paris under the watchful eye of slave Sally Hemings. Like her mother, she died very early in the aftermath of childbirth.

Hemings's eighteen-month stay in the residence of the U.S. minister to France contributed mightily to a puzzle. That enigma—whether or not

Jefferson despised formality, especially in clothing. (Library of Congress)

an aging Long Tom fathered children by a lovely young slave—is not likely ever to be solved to the satisfaction of dyed-in-the-wool Jeffersonians, the general public, or scientists who use DNA as a key to unlock closed doors of the past.

ALTHOUGH JAMES CALLENDER WAS *not* a biological ancestor of the contemporary purveyor of innuendo who turns out the Drudge Report, he would have been big on the Internet had it existed at the turn of the eighteenth century. For Long Tom at age fifty-eight—practically a patriarch in the brand-new nineteenth century—Callender turned out to be the tar baby of southern folk lore. Figuratively speaking, Jefferson earlier picked up the political propagandist and embraced him for his cutthroat verbal attacks upon John Adams. Once he had his hands on the fellow, the master of Monticello was stuck to him and couldn't get loose.

During much of his career, Callender poured his venom on the heads of Jefferson's political opponents. Through one of his pamphlets, "The Prospect Before Us," he helped cause Adams to lose to Martha's widower in what was already the quadrennial scramble for top political power. When the pamphleteer caused his readers' eyes to bulge in 1802 from being informed about goings-on between Thomas Jefferson and Sally Hemings, the chief executive issued a thunderous denunciation of the meddler into the lives of other persons.

Almost certainly as a favor to his friend, James Monroe went on public record as saying that Jefferson had no part in the writer's earlier attacks on Federalists that had helped to boost the prestige of Republicans. On the heels of the official statement issued by the governor of Virginia, Callender provided newspaper editors with copies of letters written earlier to him by Jefferson. The letters demonstrated beyond a shadow of a doubt that regardless of whether the Hemings story was true, the Republican President had been less than honest about "The Prospect Before Us." Matter of fact, Callender gleefully produced documents to show that Jefferson had praised the pamphlet and may have helped to pay for its publication.

Jeffersonians who fail to see in their idol anything resembling "the Spotts" that John Adams discerned in Abigail before they married, insist that Long Tom denied the Hemings story—once. The passage to which they point occurs in a private letter. For the public record, the third president of the United States said only that he refused to answer "calumnies of the newspapers." That was his way of avoiding a denial or an acknowledgment of a male-female and master-slave relationship that Fawn Brodie believed to have been love—not conquest—that persisted for more than thirty years.

Regardless of whether culpable human nature or cunning malice is at the heart of the Callender story, it was revived with enthusiasm during America's Centennial of 1876. After that spate it lay low for a few decades, then like the fabled Phoenix took on another life in recent decades—with renewed vigor. This fresh mushroom growth from spores that should have been dead long ago prompted Dr. Eugene Foster and other European geneticists to mount a scientific study for the truth. Scrupulous tests were made of DNA samples from descendants of Jefferson's uncle and nephew, plus descendants of Hemings. Writing in the scientific magazine *Nature*, scientists said that their molecular findings point to the probability that Long Tom is the ancestor of some present-day Hemingses. This conclusion failed to deal with the fact that several of his relatives had "the Jefferson DNA" and some of them spent a lot of time at Monticello, too.

That does not mean the Jefferson-Hemings story was concocted without foundation and can be dismissed as slander directed toward the master of Monticello. On the contrary, the basic account is completely believable. It is consistent with master-slave relationships that abounded in Colonial times and later. It is strengthened by the fact that Sally was the half-sister of

Martha. But believability is a far cry from proof; incontrovertible evidence that Sally bore children who were sired by her owner simply does not exist.

IT IS CLEAR THAT Jefferson was sometimes interested in other females. However, it seems equally certain that he loved Martha much more ardently than the first president loved his spouse. Like Washington, Long Tom teamed up with a widow. Unlike George, Thomas picked a woman who was widely described as being both beautiful and vivacious. She did have one important thing in common with Mrs. Martha Dandridge Custis, however. Like Washington's bride, she was filthy rich.

At age seventeen Martha Wayles had married Bathurst Skelton, whose death two years later put her in possession of 135 slaves plus forty thousand or so acres of land. Admirers literally swarmed around the home of Martha's father, for in addition to being extremely wealthy she was described as tall and queenly—topped by beautiful hair that belonged to the same family of colors as Jefferson's. Unfortunately, no authentic likeness of her exists.

The master of Monticello (then under construction) knew Martha was a gifted musician, an important attribute to Thomas. Tradition has it that he was strongly attracted to her by her skill on the harpsichord before he learned anything about her background. A story that has long made the rounds in Virginia has it that music cemented their growing fondness for one another and then led them to the altar.

According to a tale that was published long ago, numerous courtiers made their way to Martha's home, the Forest, located in Charles City on the James River. Two ardent swains are supposed to have arrived at her place at the same time, so they decided to go to the door together. "There they suddenly paused," according to an account that is two centuries old.

"From within they heard the sound of voices singing to the music of the harpsichord and the violin—and the voice of the performer on the violin was that of Long Tom." Reputedly smiling at one another "in a forced and melancholy manner," the unidentified pair knew that they were licked, so they didn't even knock on the door. Thomas and Martha soon became man and wife in a ceremony held in the home of her father on the first day of 1772.

They spent their two-week honeymoon in the Forest, after which they set out for Monticello in a two-horse carriage. At first their journey was delightful, as both sang without instruments upon occasion. Well short of their destination, however, the weather turned brutal. When their carriage bogged down in snow, Long Tom unhitched the horses and helped his bride onto one animal. He mounted the other, and they arrived on horseback at the one-room brick cottage built for use until Monticello was completed.

To all intents and purposes, the marriage was idyllic—except for the frequency of Martha's pregnancies. If she lost a fetus or two by spontaneous abortion, no record of such a matter was kept. But after having been pregnant more than half of her life as Mrs. Jefferson, delivery of her seventh full-term baby left her so weak that she never regained her strength. Two years after her mother's death, the little girl who was her last child also died. During the more than ninety days Martha spent in a hopeless struggle to recover from her last delivery, she reputedly exacted from her husband a solemn vow that he would never again marry.

Some persons eager to advance what they see as evidence to support the Hemings story underscore the importance of the pledge Long Tom is believed to have made to dying Martha. These persons are also quick to point out that Hemings was the daughter of John Wayles. As half-sister of Martha, she may have resembled her enough to fan her owner's interest in her as a woman rather than as a slave.

Except for those school children whose history books have been altered so as to downplay major events in order to include racial and ethnic personalities, every boy and girl learns that Jefferson wrote most of the Declaration of Independence. It was this document, rather

Martha Randolph Jefferson, named for her mother. (J. Serz engraving)

than the Constitution of the United States, to which our sixteenth president turned with reverence when he was faced with the crisis of secession. One curiosity of the Constitution is that as originally ratified, it stipulated that for purposes of representation in Congress, a resident of a state whose skin was black should be counted as three-fifths of a person.

It is less widely known today that Jefferson's famous Declaration originally included a passage in which King George III of England was castigated for permitting his subjects to engage in the slave trade. Some scholars dismiss Jefferson's indictment of slavery in his original draft of the Declaration as being of no significance. Others see the man, who was simultaneously a

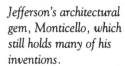
Jefferson's architectural gem, Monticello, which still holds many of his inventions.

skilled architect, inventor, musician, and political leader, as having been far ahead of most of his contemporaries in his views about slavery. During his second term in the President's House, which was located in Philadelphia, the master of Monticello signed into law a bill that forbade the importation of slaves after 1807.

JEFFERSON PERPETUALLY SPENT MORE money than he received, even during the years after Martha's estate enriched him. Slaves accounted for most of his wealth, and although he stopped buying new ones he retained old ones until his death. His will provided for the emancipation of five slaves at various intervals—all of them were male members of the Hemings family. By this time a woman beyond fifty years of age, Sally remained a slave. Persons who passionately deny that she had more than a slave-master relationship with Jefferson point out that gossip would have been renewed had he freed her.

Regardless of whether he swore never to marry a second wife, he vowed to uphold the Constitution and to do his best to foster the growth and prosperity of our nation. In this respect, he stands head and shoulders above most chief executives. Measured by any standard, the master of Monticello was a bold risk taker. Whether or not he figuratively thumbed his nose at dignified society by years of cohabitation with a yellow-skinned girl who bore more than a superficial resemblance to Martha remains an insoluble question.

4

James and Dolley Madison

A book entitled *Presidential Sex—from the Founding Fathers to Bill Clinton* purports to tell all. Don't turn to the 1998 revised edition, however, if you expect Wesley O. Hagood to enlighten you concerning doings of the fourth president and his wife. Although twenty-six pages are devoted to his predecessors, James Madison doesn't rate a single page. He and his wife receive only brief mention in connection with other persons.

It's a temptation to toy with the notion that Hagood may have been influenced by Madison's strenuous 1806 efforts to enforce the act of Congress that's known as the Non-Intercourse Act. You're right, though—this legislation had absolutely nothing to do with the bedroom of the president or anyone else's. The act sought to cut off U.S. trade with England and France in order to persuade them to bargain about hot issues of the decade.

James and Dolley may have been practically ignored by Hagood and others because they slept in separate bedrooms, and nothing remotely scandalous was known about the fourth president until recent times. A major reason for using two marital beds rather than one stemmed from the fact that the twice-married bride had a small son who demanded a place next to his mother in bed. It's arbitrary to downgrade the childless president as having been asexual just because he was less than wildly enthusiastic about being a nightly member of a threesome. So let's take a peek at some of the activities of James and Dolley that didn't result in legislation, as well as a hasty glance at a few of their lasting achievements.

Paul Jennings, a slave whose station in life was thinly camouflaged by calling him a body servant, was closely and intimately linked with Madison during nearly all of his owner's life. When he dictated his recollections to a scribe, Jennings stressed that the two-term president "always dressed wholly in black—coat, breeches, and silk stockings, with buckles in his shoes and breeches." At least one full-length portrait by a skilled artist supports the Jennings summary.

James contributed vastly to shaping our democracy, despite the fact that he wore black silk stockings. When he conversed for any length of time with Long Tom Jefferson, which was often, he must have had severe muscular pains in his neck. Tilting your head for a long session with a fellow eight and a half inches taller than you can make you wish you knew a good masseur. Diminutive as he was, though, Madison constituted an even one hundred pounds of human dynamite.

According to his own voluminous notes about his activities, at about age twenty the man destined to succeed Jefferson as president contracted a first-class case of love fever. He was then a student at the College of New Jersey—now Princeton—where he met and became enamored of Mary Freneau and lost his heart to her. He recovered, however, and seems to have made no effort to become her husband.

Matters took a different turn a few years later. Madison never had to work for a living. He had filled one political office after another, always moving up. His father, who had inherited an estate in Orange County, left everything he had—including about a hundred slaves—to young James. The Madison estate didn't include lots of land although some of it was just right for growing tobacco—until 1801. After that the annual yield was just enough to support a comfortable lifestyle but not enough to give real financial independence. As a result, James, whose attitude toward slavery was ambivalent, was for life welded to the Old Dominion's long-famous plantation-plus-slavery economic base. Jennings, who described his owner's attire, emphasized that he never owned more than one suit.

WHILE A DELEGATE TO the Continental Congress, with sessions held in Philadelphia, he lodged at the home of Mrs. Mary House and ate many of his meals there. Another semipermanent guest of the place, Catherine Floyd, didn't attract much attention from the Virginian when he first saw her at age thirteen.

By the time Catherine was as old as Mary Freneau had been when she stole his heart, Madison was willing and eager to get married and didn't think it mattered that he was a trifle more than twice the age of the juvenile he called Kitty. They agreed to become man and wife and set the date for their union six months or so in the future—following the adjournment of Congress.

The detailed story of the second time James had his heart broken didn't come out for many decades. Biographer Irving Brant dug up enough material about the man whom many folk called "Dolley's husband" to fill eight volumes. In the process he spent days poring over old handwritten documents. Page after page produced by James Madison had been heavily censored by using a heavy coating of ink to blot out words, phrases, and sentences.

Much of that ink had faded during the course of well over a century. Brant noticed that symbols used in a simple code that the writer probably

Our fourth president. (Gilbert Stuart paint-ing—original held by Bowdoin College Museum of Art)

devised for his personal use lay beneath many spots effectively blacked out. He was able to find enough symbols that had remained hidden for decades to put them together, decipher their code, and come up with radical new findings about James.

Martha Bland, wife of a Vir-ginian who was a delegate to the Continental Congress, called Madison "the most unsociable creature in existence." He cer-tainly was not unsociable while with much younger females. He lost his heart to Kitty and never went anywhere without wearing around his neck a chain from which dangled an ivory miniature that depicted the face of his beloved fifteen-year-old. Kitty wore a locket that was outwardly similar to his—but hers held an ivory miniature of the male eager to become her husband.

Partly because he was totally dependent upon the income from a plantation that was cultivated by slaves, James vacillated toward the mar-riage altar. Kitty must have been as strong-willed as she was attractive and intelligent. During the six months between their engagement and the time set for their marriage, she changed her mind. As a result she bid James adieu and soon married a graduate of Philadelphia's medical college. Madi-son's best friends—who never had an opportunity to peek at his diary entries before he tried to obliterate many of them—probably didn't know that he carried the torch for Kitty long after she dumped him.

Clearly, the rising politician from Virginia knew the meaning of wanting a female. His eleven-year wait between Kitty and the young widow Todd of Philadelphia may have stemmed from the fact that he didn't want to risk getting his heart cut out and stomped on for the third time.

MADISON WAS ATTRACTED TO a woman seventeen years his junior the first time he saw her. Having lost her first husband in a yellow fever epidemic, Dolley Payne Todd was in no rush to remarry; she was almost pathologi-cally absorbed with her small son. The breach between her and prospective suitors was widened by the fact that she was a faithful member of the Society of Friends, which probably would have expelled her had she married outside the faith.

When James found out that Dolley was well acquainted with Aaron Burr, the man who in 1804 had killed Alexander Hamilton in a duel, he persuaded Burr to arrange for him to meet Dolley. Soon after the meeting set up by Burr, the diminutive political leader from Virginia began devoting most of his time to courtship. As a guest of Dolley's sister, he spent weeks with her at elegant Harewood Plantation, where their opportunities to be alone were limited.

After two or three months, James diffidently slipped on her finger a gold ring set with small diamonds and begged her to become his wife—immediately, if not sooner. Dolley didn't reject his proposal, but she avoided forthright acceptance of it. "Give me time to look after my little boy," she demanded.

It took several weeks for her to set up a trust for the education and support of small Payne Todd, so her lover was forced to return to his plantation accompanied only by hope. Dolley developed an undiagnosed illness that made her bedfast for a time, and she refused to write more than perfunctory notes to James until she was back on her feet. As a result, her long letter saying that she was willing to become Mrs. Madison did not reach his Montpelier plantation until July 1894, about eighteen months after his proposal.

Dolley wrote that the middle of September would be a good time for a wedding ceremony, and she stressed that she wanted it to be held at Harewood—a good seventy-five miles from Montpelier. Her letter made James deliriously happy, but his exuberance diminished a bit when he learned that she would spend part of the intervening period visiting relatives instead of going with him to Saratoga Springs.

During months of enforced waiting, the future president told a friend that he dreamed of his bride-to-be every night, and sometimes he involuntarily called out for her by name during his sleep. His "Flame" burned with such intensity, he said, that he feared he would "shortly be consumed" out of dread that Dolley's heart might not be "callous to every other swain but himself."

Adopting a more restrained tone in a letter sent to Harewood, he labeled a note from her as a "precious favor" that gave him unspeakable joy. He then used what today seems to have been stilted language to stress that he didn't want to experience—for the third time—a woman's change of mind. "I hope you will never have another deliberation," he told her. Then he added that, "If the sentiments of my heart can guarantee those of yours there can never be a cause for such." By this time, he had an additional reason for concern: He had received positive word that if Dolley married him she would, indeed, be expelled from membership in the Society of Friends.

On the heels of the wedding for which he had waited so eagerly, Madison took his bride to her sister's plantation for a two-week visit. Before it came time for them to leave, Dolley was hit by a fresh bout of the malaria from which she had suffered at periodic intervals for years. When she recovered, they hurried to Philadelphia because urgent business was facing political leaders. Representatives of the thirteen colonies were deeply divided on so many issues that Mr. and Mrs. Madison did not take up residence in his Montpelier mansion until almost three years later.

By then Dolley had made many a tongue wag in the city where the Declaration of Independence and the Constitution were framed. She really was booted out of the tight-knit circle of Quakers among whom she had spent her life until her marriage to an outsider. Once she herself became an outsider, she began wearing rouge and didn't feel properly dressed unless she had on the latest French style.

Abigail Adams was among many strait-laced ladies of the era who thought that Dolley and those who aped her ways were becoming "an outrage upon democracy." In one of her famous letters, the wife of the second president castigated Dolley's new fashion of dress that was becoming increasingly common. More and more women, she said, were showing themselves in public wearing clothes of such nature that a viewer could literally see through them. Abigail described such an outrageous costume as being:

> A satin petticoat of certainly not more than three breadths, gored at the top, nothing beneath but a chemise . . . The arm naked almost to the shoulder and without stays or bodice. A tight girdle round the waist, and the rich luxuriance of nature's charms fully displayed.

In closing her denunciation of the decadence to which female attire had fallen, Abigail observed that, "Most ladies wear their clothes too scant upon the body and too full upon the bosom. Not content with the show which nature bestows, they borrow from art and literally look like nursing mothers."

The description penned by Abigail was accurate, as revealed in the famous Gilbert Stuart portrait of the wife of the fourth president. Even without benefit of the painting, Abigail's commentary is sufficient to cause twentieth-century females and males to liken Dolley Madison to widely heralded country-music singer Dolly Parton.

Later adopting a turban as her identifying symbol, Dolley Madison probably didn't blink her violet eyes when she learned what Abigail thought of the latest French fashions. She and her husband, whose preference for separate bedrooms was not general knowledge at the time, did

Dolley Madison, still a Quaker at heart but not dressed to take part in a meeting.

much more than blink, however, when she—rather than the president—became the target of gossip disseminated by word of mouth plus a few newspapers. The other man? Purportedly, none other than "Long Tom" Jefferson, Madison's intimate friend. Gossip said that in taking up residence in the President's House without a wife who would serve as official hostess, Jefferson turned to Dolley. Rumors about Thomas's relationship with Sally Hemings, coupled with the way in which his hostess "showed herself in public," led to talk about a liaison between Dolley and Thomas. Once this story got into circulation, fresh details were soon added.

Dolley had been oversexed all of her life, asserted her most violent critics. Matter of fact, she probably couldn't help it, because her sister Anna suffered from the same malady. Madison, who was unable to father a child, permitted his wife to be Jefferson's lover in order to boost his own political strength. Congressman Richard Cutts of Massachusetts allowed his wife, Anna, to accommodate European diplomats with the hope that she could bring about a reduction in international tensions.

Matters became so bad that editors of a Baltimore newspaper regaled their readers with a review of a nonexistent French-language book. One especially pointed segment of the bogus review dealt with a fake chapter in which an impotent husband was linked with a promiscuous wife.

Gideon Granger of Connecticut, who served as postmaster general under Jefferson, became a self-appointed champion of the besmeared women who before marriage were widely admired as "the Payne sisters." His protestations concerning their virtue seem to have had no effect upon persons eager for scandal. Granger achieved brief fame in legal circles a bit later, however. He was largely influential in persuading Connecticut authorities to stop the legal wrangling over whether or not Jefferson had shown lecherous intent with respect to the wife of his neighbor, John Walker.

Granger's language with respect to those who indulged in tongue-wagging about Dolley and Anna was so earthy that Congressman Samuel Hunt of New Jersey took personal offense. Never called a scumbag, but outraged at being labeled a scandalmonger, Hunt demanded satisfaction from Granger. The postmaster general didn't bother to reply to Hunt's challenge to a duel.

In spite of the fact that Madison's buxom wife later had many admirers, the whirlwind at which she was the center during Jefferson's presidency carried over into her husband's administration. The man from Montpelier rode out the storm with equanimity. Perhaps he turned in memory to a remark made by a French scholar decades earlier and copied into his notebook when he was launching his rise to fame:

People who are too tender of their reputations, and too deeply piqued by slander are conscious of some inward infirmity. A reputation based on true virtue is like the sun that may be clouded but cannot be extinguished. Having been slandered, Plato said simply that "I shall behave so that nobody will believe it."

Largely responsible for framing the Bill of Rights, James Madison had watched closely as political opponents and newspapermen tried to skewer his wife, her sister, and his friend whose Monticello mansion was close to his own plantation. Reflecting upon these matters, the man whose life was much more colorful than his drab garb offered a final word about the media of his era.

"To the press alone, chequered as it is with abuses," he observed, "the world is indebted for all the triumphs which have been gained by reason and humanity over error and oppression."

5

James and Elizabeth Monroe

$ 9,071.22.5
James Monroe had spent an entire afternoon preparing a detailed inventory and checking it twice. Since government money was involved, his total was figured to the half cent. When he announced it to his wife, she indicated token pleasure that he had finished a tedious chore. Elizabeth Monroe was not pleased, however, at having to part with all of her household gear and furnishings. Some pieces had been purchased in Paris at great bargains, and others could not be readily replaced at any cost.

She and her husband had been pushed into a corner unlike any that another first family before or since has occupied. A British force that landed on the shore of Chesapeake Bay had moved rapidly inland and had seized Washington City. Redcoats stayed only briefly—but long enough to burn as many public buildings as possible, including the President's House.

When they left, most of the mansion's walls stood and had suffered only minor damage. But the interior had been reduced to a pile of ashes plus charred timbers. One phase of rebuilding the mansion on Pennsylvania Avenue involved giving its exterior a glistening new coat of white paint—not whitewash, as sometimes reported. It was this highly visible change that led some persons to speak of the renovated structure as "the White House." This usage caught on gradually, however. Most or all of the thousands of documents that originated in it during Abraham Lincoln's administration were headed as coming from the Executive Mansion.

Col. Samuel Lane, commissioner of public buildings for the District of Columbia, had been allocated fifty thousand dollars for furnishing the huge structure, called by whatever name. Many things considered essential were missing as last-minute preparations were made for its occupancy. In this dilemma, Lane approached the president-to-be and offered to buy for the nation the things that Elizabeth Monroe had acquired during their years in Europe. Lane brought in experts and told them that their appraisals must be exact. As a result, an ornamented mustard pot was valued at $9.56 ¼ and a fish knife was listed at $10.46.

In later decades other first families had to occupy temporary quarters, then move into a renovated and sometimes enlarged White House. None of them, however, went into a structure that had been ravaged by fire, and none of them were urged to sell their personal possessions to the government. Thirty-four years had made the marriage bonds of the Monroes remarkably resilient. There is no record that either of them berated the other for the governmental dilemma that forced them to part with things they had treasured for years.

AT AGE EIGHTEEN JAMES Monroe dropped out of the College of William and Mary at Williamsburg in order to fight the British. As a lieutenant, he was among the body of Continentals who crossed the Delaware River at midnight in order to make a successful assault upon Hessians occupying Trenton, New Jersey. There the young adult, who was the son of a well-to-do but not wealthy Virginia carpenter and planter, was severely wounded. He might have bled to death had it not been for a New Jersey physician who joined the Continental force after it reached his state.

Jumped to the rank of captain, young Monroe became an aide-de-camp to Lord Stirling aka Gen. William Alexander and went with him to Valley Forge. On the heels of the brutal winter there, he became interested in a girl believed to have been a relative of Stirling. In a letter to a mutual acquaintance he protested that his sweetheart, who may have been Nannie Brown, was "entirely too over possessive for his taste." They parted company without having become deeply involved, and Monroe apparently showed absolutely no interest in another female for nearly a decade.

Back in the Old Dominion by 1780, Gov. Thomas Jefferson put Monroe in charge of state forces and made him a lieutenant colonel. His military record probably helped to make him a member of the Virginia Assembly at age twenty-four, and one of only eight lawmakers who comprised the Council of State. In time that would otherwise have been idle, he studied law in the offices of Governor Jefferson.

Almost certainly a Jefferson protégé, Monroe, beginning at age twenty-five, was sent to the Continental Congress for three successive terms. By this time Philadelphia had lost out to New York as the seat of deliberations. Many delegates, including Monroe, were initially awed by the biggest city in North America and by its wealthy and aristocratic citizens descended from Dutch pioneers.

One of these men was Laurence Kortright, a Tory who had been a British officer during the Revolution. The successful war waged by colonists cost him more money than most men of those times ever saw. Yet he managed to salvage a substantial fortune and in time became a major force in the movement by which the New York Chamber of Commerce was created. All three of his beautiful daughters made their debut, and when tall and stately Elizabeth was seventeen years old she caught the eye of James Monroe, then twenty-seven. He soon began calling her his "Smiling Little Venus" and must have begun talking of marriage very soon after they met.

Elizabeth Kortwright, from a likeness on ivory. (Dictionary of American Portraits)

Kortright was anything but pleased when he learned of what was taking place. Elizabeth's suitor came from a family that, while well above the poverty level, was far from wealthy and influential. To the New Yorker, it was very important that each of his daughters find a mate within their own social circle—and preferably within the ranks of their father's political allies.

The Congressman from Virginia knew of Kortright's views but ignored them. He escorted Elizabeth to a series of balls and parties interspersed with afternoons spent in reading poetry to each other. Their wedding ceremony was held in Manhattan's Trinity Episcopal Church shortly before the eighteenth birthday of the bride, who was described in newspaper reports as being strikingly handsome—a term then widely applied to females—in her regal wedding gown. Years later Mrs. John Quincy Adams noted that Elizabeth always dressed in the latest fashion and from a distance seemed to move about like a goddess.

Because Monroe tended to be staid and reserved, their love did not have the flair and élan that marked the union of John and Abigail Adams. It is certain that they sometimes disagreed strongly and occasionally exchanged biting words during a spat. However, there is no evidence that either of them ever so much as flirted with another member of the opposite sex after they exchanged vows on February 16, 1786.

Although outside observers didn't regard the Monroes' marriage as sparkling, James and Elizabeth were the first to exhibit true love as residents

The restored Executive Mansion in 1817—ready for occupancy by the Monroes, but practically bare of furniture. (White House Historical Association)

of the mansion well named as the White House. Characteristically, Monroe failed to record the birth date or name of their only son, who died at an unknown time before age two. Both of their daughters, Eliza and Maria, grew to maturity—and both played special roles during their father's later years.

JAMES WAS THE FIRST U.S. president to openly and publicly support the idea of moving most or all Native Americans out of established states of the Union. He didn't favor doing so by force, however; he considered such a course of action "revolting to humanity and utterly unjustifiable." He was sure that force wouldn't be necessary in order to get the aborigines out of the thirteen original states that had earlier been English colonies. His solution for "the Indian question" was as simplistic as his solution for the problem of how to deal with slaves who bought or were given their freedom. "Between the limits of our present States and Territories and the Rocky Mountains and Mexico," he wrote, "there is a vast territory, to which they [Indians] might be invited with inducements that might be successful."

Especially in parts of Europe, but also the United States, Monroe's wife was widely admired for an exploit she pulled off in Paris. In 1777 James had helped administer first aid to wounds received by the Marquis de Lafayette at Brandywine Creek, and they became lifelong friends. By the time the American became U.S. Minister to France, the French Revolution had caused Lafayette to flee the country, and he was imprisoned in Austria.

Madame Lafayette and her son, the Americans learned soon after reaching the post to which Jefferson had sent them, were confined in a Paris jail, and she was facing the likelihood of a trip to the guillotine. Monroe, who would never have dared risk his position by trying to interfere with French justice, approved heartily of his wife's proposed plan of action. At the suggestion of Elizabeth, he secured a carriage—a vehicle that had been outlawed by Revolutionary leaders—and put liveried servants upon it. They drove the diplomat's mate to the prison where Mme. Lafayette was confined and Elizabeth requested—or perhaps demanded—permission to see the imprisoned wife of her husband's friend. Functionaries, taken aback by the carriage and its imperious occupant, let her visit their distinguished prisoner. All Paris was soon agog at what *La belle Americaine* had done. As a result, the ruling Committee on Public Safety freed Lafayette's wife and son.

James Monroe about 1819, as depicted by Samuel F. B. Morse. (White House Historical Association)

During Monroe's two terms as chief executive, however, actions of Elizabeth and her older daughter brought constant criticism by persons living inside what is now called the Beltway. Elizabeth engaged in small-stakes gambling with Dolley Madison, since both of them were enamored of the card game Loo. That was as far as the daughter of a New York aristocrat would go in bending down to persons beneath the social and economic levels of her girlhood.

In striking contrast to Dolley's ways while she was hostess for Jefferson, Elizabeth preferred formality and insisted upon strict observance of diplomatic protocol. Along with this, she appointed her older daughter, Eliza, the presidential hostess for her husband's first term and much of his second.

Eliza was described as being "a tall, black-haired raving beauty" whose husband, George, became her father's secretary. She received most of her education at Madame Campan's exclusive school for girls in Paris. There she became an intimate friend of fellow student Hortense Beauharnais—the daughter of Josephine Bonaparte, later to become the mother of Napoleon III. Small wonder, therefore, that Elizabeth's daughter observed customs that were associated with European royalty, and therefore she came to be despised in the fast-growing federal city on the Potomac River.

JAMES AND ELIZABETH HAD no better financial luck than did Jefferson. The president's $25,000 annual salary fell far short of expenditures, with entertainment and clothing accounting for relatively large sums. When they left the White House, they were $75,000 in debt, and even after the sale of the Virginia property had to watch every dollar. After the death of his wife, the impoverished ex-president spent his last few months in the New York home of his younger daughter, Maria.

A significant part of Monroe's post-presidential financial troubles stemmed from a fracas that broke out when he thought such matters were behind him. As he and Elizabeth prepared to leave the White House, political foes produced evidence showing that purchases for the mansion during his administration were skimpy and sometimes faulty. According to a vociferous critic of the pair, it was impossible to account for the vast sum of $20,000 of the money appropriated for furnishing the mansion.

Both James and Elizabeth were furious—and both were determined to leave Washington with as few unanswered questions as possible. The furnishings James and Elizabeth had reluctantly sold as his administration started had received eight years of extremely hard use; some things had been destroyed or damaged beyond repair. "Never mind," they told one another, "we have to get these innuendoes behind us."

Anthracite coal was bringing less than $11 per ton at wholesale, and a hundred-pound sack of flour was worth only $5.13. In this economic climate the last official act of the Monroes was in the form of a purchase. They bought back from the government the badly abused furnishings they had provided eight years earlier and obligated themselves to pay to the U.S. Treasury the sum of $9,071.22.5

6

John Quincy and Louisa Adams

I am a man of reserved, cold, austere, and forbidding manners," John Quincy Adams wrote in June 1819. Then fifty-four years of age, he confessed to his diary that he was "a gloomy misanthropist." His political enemies rejected that label as too mild, and they castigated him as "an unsocial savage."

The most familiar full-length portraits of our sixth president show a man whose piercing eyes and grim mouth suggest that he was too strait-laced to permit foolishness from anyone. His all-black garb reinforces the brutally frank self-appraisal that went into his diary. That verbal description, combined with images by a photographer, lead to the conclusion that he must have been a lifelong puritanical and tyrannical zealot.

That appraisal is close to the mark if you consider the forty-eight months Adams spent in the White House. In his younger years, however, this grim-looking New Englander had been known to relatives and friends not as John Quincy but as Johnny. That nickname hints that he may have given his parents repeated doses of the kind of grief we associate with adolescents and young adults who are downright rebellious.

Johnny made some present-day rebels look tame. Abigail Adams—highly intelligent and exceptionally competent—has been the only woman to be both the wife of a president and the mother of a president. Her skills, combined with those of her husband's, barely enabled her to cope with Johnny. Like many contemporary parents, she and John had their hands full during the turbulent teenage and stormy young adult years of their oldest surviving son.

A drawing made at the Hague in 1783 depicts Johnny Adams as a decidedly saucy-looking teenager who served as secretary to the diplomat who was his father. Johnny's facial expression at age sixteen suggests that he might have been downright impudent on occasion. Regardless of whether that appraisal is accurate, by age fourteen his interest in the opposite sex was so consuming that he didn't try to conceal it.

His first infatuation was with a girl whose name he didn't know. As a member of the audience at the Bois de Boulogne near Paris, he was instantly smitten by a performer he judged to be about fourteen. Her appearance on the stage sent Johnny spiraling, but because he feasted his eyes on her while sitting by his mother he never had a chance to speak to her.

According to Johnny's diary, the little French girl he saw from a distance of about sixty feet regularly came close to him in his dreams—for years. Long after his visit to the Bois de Boulogne, he penned a painful confession meant for no eyes but his, in which he dealt with the vision of loveliness he glimpsed from afar. "Of all the ungratified longings that I ever suffered," he wrote, "that of being acquainted with her—merely to tell her how much I adored her—was the most intense."

By the time he was eighteen, Johnny's diary was liberally sprinkled with impressions of females he had seen or met. Perhaps he wanted to make sure that no one would ever be able to identify all of those he mentioned. On the other hand, his memory of even brief encounters may have been so keen that he didn't need to commit full names to writing. He wrote of a Miss Jarvis, whom he considered to be very fair but not a looker like Miss Ogden, whom he rated as "a beauty." Of five or six female siblings in a single family, only Sally received from him a descriptive adjective: "Handsome."

Johnny's father went to London in 1785 as the first U.S. Minister to Great Britain. Left behind in Massachusetts, the youngster had been placed at Haverhill as a boarder with the Rev. John Shaw. There he met fellow boarder Nancy Hazen, age seventeen, and was smitten by "her dazzling eyes" plus her figure—which had all the right curves in precisely the right places. Still, the French performer, about three years younger than Nancy, was visiting him regularly in his dreams. Hence, "young Mr. Adams" seems to have been content to look at Nancy and write an elegant poem for her before admitting to himself that his mother would never accept her as a daughter-in-law.

When he met sixteen-year-old Mary Frazier at Newburyport nearly four years later, he was reading law while constantly reminded by his mother that he was a long time away from earning an adequate income. Both Johnny and Mary were yearning to see if they could live on a young lawyer's fees, but Abigail put her foot down firmly and advised her son to avoid any lasting entanglement. Without mentioning Mary, she went so far as to hint that he might be wise to quit his present pursuit and look for a wealthy girl.

At age twenty-two Johnny confided to his diary that he didn't give a fig whether or not a girl had money as long as she was well endowed with other assets. Regardless of her money, he wanted nothing to do with a female who might be both fat and prudish. A poem he called "A Vision" was inspired by the girl to whom he gave the fake names of "Clara" and "Maria" in his musings to himself.

Many years afterward the poem was resurrected and published as the work of a future president. The former chief executive, who hadn't been called Johnny in decades, received a copy from a friend and found his mind spinning again. Lines of verse, he confided to his correspondent, were "portraits from life that were shaded by fancy." The poem, he said, was written as "the effusion of a genuine but not a fortunate passion."

His passion was unfortunate, his mother emphasized over and over, because he should never think of marrying beneath himself. After all, his middle name that he seldom used during this period was Quincy. Johnny's great-grandfather had been about as close to

John Quincy Adams, about 1795. (John Singleton Copley original held by the Boston Museum of Fine Arts)

nobility as anyone in the Massachusetts Bay Colony could be. He had been a member of the royal governor's council and speaker of the assembly—to say nothing of the fact that he was a lineal descendant of England's King Edward III.

To Abigail, that meant Mary wasn't good enough for Johnny. Neither was Nancy Hazen or two others in whom he became deeply interested. Catherine Jones may have been the enigmatic Clara whose name recurs repeatedly in his diary. Little is known about Sally Gray except that as a student at Harvard, Johnny was enamored of her.

STILL A BACHELOR AT age twenty-seven and still looking around very hard and very eagerly, John Quincy Adams became U.S. Minister to the Netherlands. His post was not demanding and England was nearby. Despite the fact that he was an outspoken and often cynical critic of everything and nearly everyone British, he made an occasional trip to London. On one of these excursions he met three of the older daughters of Baltimore-based merchant Joshua Johnson, who had taken up residence not far from the English capital.

All of the Johnson girls were talented and attractive, but Nancy was widely considered to be superior to her sisters. Louisa, who was younger, was twitted even by her parents as being haughty and proud. She acknowledged that the fun poked at her by family members probably contributed to her abnormal timidity and shyness. Caroline was closer than her two older sisters to Mary Frazier's tender age when a decidedly younger Johnny Adams had become enamored of her.

Still, John Quincy passed over Nancy and Caroline in favor of Louisa. He had been together with her only a few times when he wrote his mother that he was beginning to think seriously "of the duty incumbent upon all good citizens to have a family." By the time he returned to his post in Holland, he had put into writing a memorandum according to which his choice had been irrevocably made. That didn't mean he was about to hurry into a binding relationship; the salary level of minor diplomats was not adequate to support a family in comfort. JQA, as he had begun to be known, seems to have entered into a formal engagement with Louisa—warning her that she might have an extended wait.

His first and paramount obligation in life, he told his fiancée, was to his country. He warned her not to test his temper "by a formal and professed assertion of your spirit." Not once but several times he voiced dislike for some of the songs that she liked to sing. As an added premarital move that was characteristic of his then-prevailing attitude toward females, JQA drew up for Louisa a formal course of study. He presented it to her and urged her to get started upon it at once in order to repair deficiencies in an education that had been largely "imparted by governesses."

Numerous clues suggest that he was never so eager to make Louisa his wife as had been the case earlier with Mary. Yet he had made up his mind, and he firmly expected to return to England some time within the next seven years or so in order to take Louisa as his "companion for the remainder of the Journey or Voyage of life."

Abigail, and to a lesser degree her husband, again voiced doubts and her disapproval. Louisa had spent so much time abroad that she would find it difficult to adjust to life in America. She was a decade younger than JQA—still at so tender an age that her parents might decide they weren't ready to let her go. Her wealthy father moved in economic circles far beyond the reach of a lowly diplomat who would find himself miserable if long in their company . . .

For the first time in his life, JQA became so angry at his mother that he stormed at her in a letter. If he waited for all requisites to be met, he raged, he would "certainly be doomed to perpetual celibacy." Despite the fact that he customarily referred to Louisa only as "a highly valued friend," he let it be known that this time he was the decision maker who had already made up his mind.

Lovely Louisa had mastered both the pianoforte and the harpsichord. And she had spent almost as much time reading classical writers as had

JQA. Yet in writing to her fiancé, she protested that she had grown "so miserably dull, stupid, and wan" that she was being called the Nun.

Their lengthy wait ended late in July 1797. JQA did not preserve an account of his feelings on the fateful day or of the marriage ceremony that took place in All Hallows Church. Louisa, however, jotted down her reaction to the return of the man to whom she was pledged. "I met him with feelings of bitter and mortified affection," she wrote. Part of her negative reaction, she realized, stemmed from her realization that she would soon leave her parents.

On the eve of their wedding, Louisa thought they were immediately to go to Lisbon, Portugal. She was surprised and taken aback to learn that President Washington had changed his mind. JQA must at once start for Berlin to assume his duties as Minister to Prussia. An unforgettable moment of their four-year stay in Berlin stemmed from what her husband called her sallow complexion. Seeking to "relieve the dullness" of her face and attire, she used a bit of rouge given her by the queen of Prussia. Furious at such a display, JQA wiped off every trace of the rouge with a towel.

After four years in Berlin, they returned to the United States for a stay in Massachusetts twice as long as they had been in Prussia. Then it was off to Russia. Leaving their two older sons in America, they set out for the immense nation that had never received a U.S. minister. Their residence in Saint Petersburg came to an unexpected and abrupt end in 1814, however, when President Madison ordered the now-seasoned diplomat to become chief U.S. negotiator for a proposed treaty of peace with Great Britain. JQA left for Ghent so hurriedly that he had time only to direct Louisa to sell everything but his books and join him in Paris as soon as possible.

Louisa, subject to migraine headaches and fainting, became pregnant a dozen times in twenty years and suffered seven miscarriages. It was small wonder that she was typically described as sickly. Somehow, the woman who had endured disparagement before her wedding proved to be tough and resilient in an emergency. She dutifully packed JQA's books carefully, disposed of everything else they owned, and bought a huge carriage that could be equipped with runners for travel in heavy snow.

Accompanied only by an adolescent driver and her small son, Charles, Louisa set out on a thousand-mile journey through regions still in chaos because of the Napoleonic wars. At one point she had to rely upon her knowledge of French in order to persuade soldiers that she was a relative of Napoleon who was in haste to join him. Sometimes traveling for two or three days without food and sleeping wherever she could find shelter and straw, the "sickly" wife of the diplomat made it to Paris.

Lauded for having effected the Treaty of Ghent, JQA went on to become, in succession, minister to Great Britain, secretary of state, and

Louisa Adams, about the time she moved into the White House. (Charles Bird King)

president of the United States. Louisa despised life in the White House, which she termed "that great unsocial mansion." In it, their long-simmering disagreements over the role a wife should play came to a boil. JQA noted that both he and Louisa suffered from "frailties of temper." She compared marriage with hanging and did everything she could think of—even cultivating silkworms—to avoid having to spend hours of quarreling or boredom with her husband.

A barrage of newspaper attacks served to relieve the tedium at intervals. Louisa's aloof manner led editors to dub her "the Queen." JQA was the target of so much merciless abuse that he was often enraged by it. "Put some wool in your ears," his wife advised him tartly, "and don't glance at the papers." He nodded agreement, but couldn't resist reading stories that accused him of having procured an American woman for Czar Alexander I while in Saint Petersburg.

Andrew Jackson's followers played down the importance of the fact that the social highlight of the Monroe administration had been a ball given for him by JQA. Eager to take over the White House after the dull and colorless administration of our sixth president, Jackson's crew manufactured dirt when they could find none. Among their yarns was the falsehood that while being separated from one another by the English Channel, JQA and Louisa had indulged in sexual orgies during their long engagement.

Louisa and her husband were overjoyed to vacate the White House in favor of a modest home in Quincy, Massachusetts. Yet JQA had spent too many years in the service of his country to turn his back upon politics. He soon ran for the House of Representatives, and in an uncharacteristic moment he authorized Louisa to head his campaign. Her deft and dedicated management made him the only ex-president to serve as a U.S. representative—a post he filled for seventeen years and in which he became lauded as Old Man Eloquent.

With the total support of his wife, JQA took on the sensational and highly unpopular cause of slaves who had staged a mutiny aboard the Spanish vessel *Amistad*. Although he had limited experience as a practicing attorney, he managed to get the case heard by the U.S. Supreme Court—where he won the freedom of his pro bono clients.

Concern about the place of blacks in society helped convince JQA to re-think his views on the role of women. Instead of continuing to insist that a male should rule every roost, he made a stirring speech on the floor of Congress in favor of female activism. Responding to a fellow lawmaker who had said that women had no right to petition on political subjects, he said in part:

> Women are not only justified, but exhibit the most exalted virtues, when they depart from the domestic circle and enter on the concerns of their country, of humanity, and of their God. . . . So far from regarding such conduct as a national reproach, I approve of it, and I glory in it!

Time after time during her first thirty-two years with Adams, Louisa had wondered what led her to enter into so contentious a union. During their golden final seventeen years together, she rejoiced over and over. Although plagued with doubts, she had held her head high as she went with him to All Hallows Church in England—her girlhood in Quincy now but a dimming memory.

7

Andy and Rachel Jackson

I f you ever again associate my name with your wife's, I'll cut off your ears!"

Andrew Jackson's fiery threat came in response to an accusation of adultery. Lewis Robards of Kentucky believed his wife and Jackson were having an affair, and he said so in public—far underestimating the quick temper of his supposed rival.

When Jackson threatened to remove his ears, Robards had a warrant served against his rival. In court, the man destined to become our seventh president persuaded his personal guard to part with his hunting knife. Brandishing the long blade, he stared at Robards, who ran from the courtroom in a nervous panic. When the plaintiff disappeared, the magistrate quickly dismissed the case.

This was only one of many tumultuous episodes in the life of the Tennessean who became universally known as Old Hickory. As a young man, his life was punctuated with violence that began during the American Revolution. A military messenger at age thirteen, he was captured by the British and ordered to shine the boots of an officer. The boy defiantly refused, so a slash by a sword resulted in both a cut on the head and lifelong hatred of the British.

Later charges of sexual misconduct led him to spend much of his political career defending himself, his wife, and his friends against gossip and rumor. False charges, which abounded, threw him into an obsession that resulted in lifelong rage; his wife, who was cast in a gentler mold, felt continuous humiliation so keenly that it contributed to her failing health.

IF EVER THERE WAS a case of love at first sight, it was with Young Hickory—as he became known later—and Rachel Donelson. Their deep affection was much more than youthful fleeting passion. It continued throughout their long and successful marriage. Yet once the shadow of impropriety fell over them, it never disappeared.

Their tumultuous story began in a boardinghouse near the banks of the Cumberland River. Young Jackson had completed his training as a lawyer and was so successful that he became U.S. attorney general for the newly created Southwest Territory, which included much of present-day North Carolina and Tennessee. Having moved to Nashville from Jonesboro, North Carolina, he chose to reside at the rural boardinghouse of John Donelson's widow instead of living in the seat of justice in the western district of North Carolina.

Mrs. Donelson's daughter, Rachel, had married Lewis Robards of Kentucky when she was seventeen. Their union was plagued with insane jealousy on his part that soon led him to assume that Rachel was unfaithful. After a particularly violent argument, he ordered her to leave and never return. Her brother then brought her back home to work in her mother's place, just in time to meet the new boarder who had recently arrived from North Carolina.

Jackson was instantly smitten by Rachel's winning personality and beauty. Her dark, lustrous hair and eyes coupled with her dimples made a combination that to him was irresistible. As icing on the cake, she was widely known as an excellent dancer and skilled horsewoman.

Weeks after having been ordered to leave her husband's home, Rachel received a message asking her to return. She ignored it, so Robards came in person to fetch her and immediately became suspicious of her relationship with Jackson. When Jackson denied any impropriety, angry words were

Somewhat idealized, this portrait of Rachel Jackson conveys some idea of her youthful loveliness.

exchanged that included threats of a duel. Nothing came of that, but Jackson moved out of the boardinghouse run by Rachel's mother.

Rachel returned to Kentucky with her husband, but soon found that nothing had changed. Unable to tolerate the accusations and hot temper of her husband, she decided to leave again—this time of her own volition. Her mother thoughtlessly sent Andrew to bring Rachel to her sister's home.

After a period of time, rumors were that Robards was once more planning to come for her. Tiring of this upheaval, Rachel made plans to run away to Natchez in Spanish Florida. She knew a friend of the family, Capt. John Stark, who would give her passage on a flatboat. Before Rachel went aboard, Stark asked Jackson to come along for protection against Indians. Jackson accepted, seemingly without considering that travel with a married woman would be judged scandalous.

Rachel arrived at Natchez, Mississippi, on January 12, 1790. During the next few months, Jackson made many trips to see her as their affection grew. No one really knows what happened during these visits; both of the pair seemed oblivious to what people thought and to society's rules of propriety.

On one return trip to Nashville, Jackson heard that Robards was actively seeking to finalize his divorce, claiming that Rachel had deserted him and had committed adultery. Even though Jackson was a hothead, for once he restrained from retaliation. Instead he asked Mrs. Donelson for permission to marry her daughter.

Many scholars have questioned why Jackson, an attorney, never bothered to verify the finality of Rachel's divorce. To gain a divorce at that time, one had to file with the legislature. On December 20, 1790, the Virginia legislature gave Robards permission to sue for divorce; this action did not constitute legal dissolution of the marriage. Unbeknownst to Rachel and Andrew, Robards never followed through on the final steps; Jackson's failure to discover this brought a lifetime of problems to him and Rachel.

Believing herself free to marry Andrew, Rachel exchanged wedding vows with Old Hickory in August 1791. As Jackson's political enemies pointed out years later, the ceremony took place in Spanish territory, where Protestants were not allowed to marry. Nonetheless, they soon bought a farm and began their life together, not dreaming what the future held for them.

Nearly two years later, a court granted Lewis Robards his divorce on the grounds of adultery by his wife. Rachel Jackson was crushed; believing her divorce to be final, she had entered into new marriage vows. Technically, she had committed bigamy and adultery for the prior two years. Her awareness of public disgrace seemed far worse than death, but no amount of shame could change the legal record.

To rectify matters, Andrew and Rachel remarried in a legal and official ceremony on January 17, 1794. The Nashville community seemed to accept their explanations of their first marriage—but political enemies now had a lifetime supply of slander to spread.

Andrew Jackson was the center of attention at the lavish ball given for him by John Quincy Adams late in the Monroe administration.

Jackson made it his life's work to defend the honor of his beloved Rachel. Any mention of the supposed scandal threw him into a murderous rage. One of his accusers was John Sevier, his rival who won their race for the governorship of Tennessee. Sevier made the mistake of casting aspersions on Rachel's character in front of a crowd on the courthouse lawn in Knoxville, where Jackson was judge. He said, "I know of no great service you have rendered the country except taking a trip to Natchez with another man's wife."

Jackson shouted, "Great God! Do you dare mention her sacred name?"

A fight broke out and the two men were forcibly separated, after which Jackson challenged Sevier to a duel. When Sevier failed to appear at the appointed time, his challenger inserted in the *Knoxville Gazette* an ad that branded him as "a base coward and poltroon." That evoked action from Sevier, who asked for another date to be set and finally showed up with seconds and friends. He offered a formal apology, which prevented the duel from taking place.

Jackson's next opponent did not fare as well. In 1806 he got into an argument with Charles Dickinson over a horse race. Their dispute soon got out of hand. Some say that Dickinson had been drinking too heavily. Whether that was the case, when he made disparaging remarks about Rachel, Jackson's temper flared and another duel was arranged. But it could not be fought in Tennessee, where dueling had become illegal. So the famous Jackson-Dickinson meeting took place in Kentucky on May 30, 1806. An excellent marksman, Dickinson fired first and hit Jackson near his heart. The challenger's pistol did not discharge on the first shot, so he fired again—very deliberately. His bullet hit his opponent in the stomach and Dickinson died a few hours later.

JACKSON WAS BRANDED A murderer by many who didn't sympathize with his feeling that he had no choice but to avenge Rachel's name. The bullet from his own wound stayed lodged near his heart and caused discomfort as long as he lived. When he felt a twinge from the old wound, he treated it as an emotional reminder that he had done everything in his power to protect the honor of his beloved wife.

Andrew and Rachel enjoyed many years of happiness in spite of gossip and several miscarriages and infant deaths. They adopted an Indian child and lavished attention on their nieces and nephews. Their questionable first marriage ceremony ceased to be a major topic of conversation. Rachel, with no desire for life in the limelight, was content to be a wife and homemaker. She pleaded with Andy to stay at the Hermitage, their estate in Tennessee, and sometimes—but not always—she prevailed. He went to the House of Representatives and then to the Senate.

AS LONG AS SHE lived, Rachel really did like to smoke a corncob pipe or "segur" in the evenings. Grammar in her letters made her seem to be an ignorant, backwoods woman. On top of everything, Old Hickory's political foes had again dragged out the dirt about their marriage. John Quincy Adams's supporters had branded Jackson as a murderer and Rachel as an adulteress—even portraying his mother as having been a prostitute.

Rachel dreaded going to the inauguration so much that she contemplated staying at home. However, men destined to form her husband's cabinet pointed out that she should enjoy the victory. Staying away would mean the snobby Washington wives had gotten the upper hand. So she made plans to go and purchased a white gown for the occasion.

While on a shopping trip to Nashville, Rachel overheard some ugly gossip about herself in the parlor of the Nashville Inn. Some women were ridiculing her country ways and her so-called marriage. Her friends found her crying and on the border of hysteria, and she continued to cry on the journey home. Not many days later, she had a heart attack. She lingered briefly but died three days before Christmas at the age of sixty-one.

Old Hickory refused to believe his beloved Rachel was dead. He stayed with her body all through the night, waiting for her to revive. Servants finally convinced him to bury Rachel in her inaugural gown on Christmas Eve. Thereafter, he kept a locket around his neck with a portrait of his lifelong love. At night, he removed it and propped it beside his bed so he could see Rachel's image.

Broken-hearted and grieving, Jackson began his term as president. Soon he became embroiled in yet another sexual scandal—this time centering upon the wife of a cabinet member. In his fragile emotional state, he saw this as an extension of the persecution of Rachel.

One of Jackson's stalwart supporters and friends who had been picked for a cabinet post, John Eaton, had married the daughter of a Washington innkeeper. A raving beauty, Margaret ("Peggy") O'Neale had grown up among important men, and she enjoyed their company. Because she entered into discussions, laughed loudly, sang at the slightest invitation, and held strong opinions, members of the capital's high society said she had never learned her place as a woman.

Rumors were rampant about her alleged affairs with boarders and she did invite speculation by flirting. When she married John Timberlake, a sailor, she had many lonely periods at home. Timberlake's suicide at sea served as fuel for the fire of gossip; wagging tongues passed along the unfounded tale that he had killed himself in misery over his wife's unfaithfulness.

Eaton had been a close friend of Margaret's husband, so when Timberlake died he felt it was his duty to look after her. Soon they fell in love and ignored convention by becoming man and wife before her traditional year of mourning ended. When Peggy's second husband was picked by Old Hickory to become a member of his cabinet, members of the social upper crust turned up their noses. Imagine it—the daughter of a common innkeeper was to have a place at official dinners!

Many women and some husbands set out to make Peggy Eaton's life miserable. Rumors about her early years flourished, and several men

Peggy Eaton, who in many ways reminded the president of his deceased Rachel, was flirtatious but probably not promiscuous.

claimed she had been familiar with them. One rumor alleged that she had had children by John Eaton while her husband was at sea. Another insisted she miscarried a child of Eaton's, although records showed that her husband had been home on leave about the time the baby was conceived.

Mrs. John C. Calhoun of South Carolina, wife of the vice president, was among the first to snub Eaton's wife. At that time, there was strict etiquette about how to call upon people. Mrs. Eaton visited Mrs. Calhoun, left her card as was the custom, and expected Mrs. Calhoun to return the visit. Having heard all the wild rumors about Peggy's morals, Mrs. Calhoun decided not to return the call. One after another, wives of top governmental officials did likewise, and when Peggy appeared at social functions they refused to acknowledge her presence.

Jackson and his staff spent countless hours collecting evidence to prove that Peggy was innocent of all accusations. He spent the early months of his presidency defending her honor instead of tending to the affairs of state. Surely the most unusual cabinet meeting in history was held because of the innkeeper's daughter. Jackson called his cabinet together to present evidence of her innocence to them, but the session did not stop the gossip and snubbing.

With rumors running rife, Rachel's widower held individual meetings with cabinet members and requested cooperation from their wives that never was given. Finally, Martin Van Buren offered to resign to appease Jackson's enemies and put the controversy to rest. John Eaton quickly followed suit.

Jackson then shocked the nation by asking for the resignations of the remaining members of the cabinet, except his postmaster general. Never before had a president asked for mass resignations of cabinet members; Old Hickory had done so over what some dubbed "a petticoat affair." John Eaton threatened one cabinet member with a duel. Peggy called a cabinet member's wife "a first class dowdy" and termed another "a large, coarse brawling creature raised too suddenly into a position she little knew how to fill."

The Eatons finally retreated to Tennessee, where John waited without avail for a seat in the Senate that Jackson had promised him when he resigned. Jackson completed his term of office, at least as bitter and angry as he had been years earlier when the honor of his Rachel was challenged. During previous administrations it had been widely considered ungentle-manly to attack the private lives of one's opponents. This era of relatively polite politics had come to an abrupt end. The Petticoat Affair had opened a Pandora's box that cannot be closed.

Jackson retired to the Hermitage in Nashville, where he brooded over the loss of Rachel and decided to honor her memory by building a chapel dedicated to her. Today, hordes of visitors flock to the middle Tennessee site in order to pay tribute to Rachel and her husband, rather than to gossip about them.

8

Martin and Hannah Van Buren

Martin and Hannah Van Buren were the first presidential couple of which both were U.S. citizens at birth. Every previous first couple had been born as British subjects. To add to their distinction, the two Van Burens were of Dutch—as opposed to English or Scottish—ancestry. During their years together they often used the Dutch language in conversation, and Martin preferred to call his mate *Jannetje* instead of *Hannah*—her name's Anglicized version.

If these factors weren't enough to make a nearly forgotten man and wife stand out from the crowd of forty-one chief executives and their mates, personal worth was. Martin was financially poles apart from his predecessors, Jefferson and Monroe, who both died dead broke. Martin, on the other hand, left for his three living sons a two-hundred-acre farm on which stood a thirty-room brick mansion. This fine real estate was only a small part of his fortune, which at his death was estimated to be at least $225,000—an enormous sum at that time.

Martin, Jannetje, and their parents weren't recent arrivals from Holland. Jannetje's mother, Maria Quakenboss Hoes, was Dutch through and through, so it was natural for her to take a Van Buren as her second husband. Although neither of them cared much for genealogy, Maria's daughter and son-in-law could have traced their Dutch ancestry back to the seventeenth century or earlier. Martin's great-grandfather was known to have come to America from a Dutch province as an indentured servant. That meant the president's ancestor had to work for about seven years without salary, just to repay the person who furnished the money for his passage across the Atlantic Ocean.

Martin and Jannetje knew one another from early childhood. Both of them grew up in the totally Dutch village of Kinderhook, New York, on the Hudson River. Neither had enough of a formal education to make much difference in their lives. Little Mat, as he was known to relatives and friends in childhood, probably stayed in the tiny Kinderhook shed that doubled as a school a bit longer than did Jannetje. He was all of thirteen years old when he turned his back on education and set out to make his mark in the world.

Initially a delivery boy, he soon began making himself useful in his father's tavern. One of the regulars there was a distinguished gent by the name of Aaron Burr, whose visits to the Van Buren bar later led to a smear campaign directed at the son of the tavern keeper. Burr's example may have played a part in turning Little Mat on to politics very early. He actively campaigned for Thomas Jefferson at age eighteen and later won a seat in the Republican congressional caucus held in Albany. Burr's partner later took Martin into his law firm, a move that greatly strengthened the young Dutchman's ties with the noted political leader.

Jannetje Van Buren. (Library of Congress)

While still reading law, Mat—no longer "Little"—saw quite a bit of Jannetje, who was about a year his junior. They probably never experienced anything resembling courtship, but simply drifted together.

By the time they married early in 1807, when Jannetje was twenty-three years old, Mat was being groomed for his first public office—surrogate of Cumberland County. Months before they tied the knot, they had agreed on a basic issue. They'd never, ever spend money they could get only by borrowing, and they would try always to have at least a tiny nest egg laid aside. That early practice of frugality may help to explain Martin's great wealth in his old age.

LIKE JOHN QUINCY ADAMS, Martin knew before he entered the vocation that it would be tough to make a living as a fledgling attorney. Unlike Adams, he never went through a period of rebellion against his parents and never lived beyond his means. He and Jannetje discussed at length the advantages and disadvantages of living in New York or another big city and decided to hunt a smaller place. They eventually picked Hudson, a thriving town located on the east bank of the river for which it was named. It was located about fifteen miles from their childhood homes and seemed to be a good place to build his law practice.

The Van Burens had saved enough money to buy a home on Warren Street, and it is conceivable that they moved into one of the first prefabricated dwellings in North America. Shrewd builders in Providence and Nantucket had seen a booming market in fast-growing Hudson a few years before the Van Burens reached it. Numerous stout clapboard homes had been built in both of the larger centers. Dismantled, they were shipped by water to Hudson, where they were put back together so well that some of them were still occupied well over a century later.

By the time they were settled in Hudson, Martin and Jannetje had become proud parents of a son, now slightly more than a year old. Little Abraham eventually had three siblings, all of whom were male. No member of the family seems to have realized that frequent childbearing was taking its toll on Jannetje. She seems never to have complained about her pregnancies or anything else. Whatever suited her Martin was just fine with her. He took to politics like a duck takes to water, and at age thirty he was a New York state senator.

Van Buren had held that office for six years when he lost thirty-five-year-old Jannetje to exhaustion from childbirth, complicated by tuberculosis. When she knew that her end was near, she might have asked that he remain faithful to her for life. Whether or not she actually made that suggestion, he never remarried—but at least once he probably would have done so, had the lady been willing.

U.S. Senator Martin Van Buren of New York. (Engraving after a portrait by Inman)

Two years into life as a widower, Martin became a U.S. Senator and held office for seven years. He then ran for and won the New York state house for no other reason than a conviction that he might be able to help boost Andrew Jackson to the presidency. His influence swung the crucial New York vote, whose 42 electoral votes boosted the total of the Tennessean to 219. To the amazement of some observers, Van Buren received

189 electoral votes for the vice presidency. The office went to John C. Calhoun, although Van Buren bounced back to take it four years later.

Later, as our eighth president, the dyed-in-the-wool Dutchman from New York ran into plenty of trouble. Just two months after his inauguration, a group of major banks refused to give out gold and silver in return for paper currency. This precipitated the Panic of 1837, during which nearly one thousand financial institutions went under. The nation did not return to normalcy until Van Buren had been out of the White House for two years.

Unemployment plus scattered food riots helped create a climate in which newspaper writers and editors plus political rivals felt free to say anything they wished about the president. Opposition forces spread the story that the chief executive was known to have very early ties with Aaron Burr, the illegitimate son of the Revolutionary officer who nearly won the presidency in 1800.

Davy Crockett, a Tennessee congressman not yet lauded as "the king of the wild frontier," smeared Van Buren up one side and down the other. "He struts and swaggers like a crow in the gutter," Crockett said. "He is laced up in corsets such as women in town wear, and if possible, tighter than the best of them." He then said that were it not for the chief executive's excessively large red whiskers that were tinged with gray, "it would be hard to look at him and know whether he was a man or a woman."

Congressman Charles Ogle of Pennsylvania created a national sensation by delivering a speech in which he falsely charged that Van Buren was throwing away taxpayers' money by spending lavishly for the White House. He also insisted that the New Yorker had directed the building of pairs of mounds that were scattered across the lawn of the mansion. "Every set of these," insisted Ogle, "was designed to resemble an Amazon's bosom—with a miniature knoll or hillock at its apex to denote the nipple."

Only Van Buren's foes paid any attention to the absurd allegations of Crockett and Ogle. Yet his most faithful followers confessed that they were humiliated and somewhat hurt when they read a newspaper account of his dress. Written by Henry B. Stanton, it claimed to be an accurate description of the way the chief executive looked when he turned up for church one morning. Stanton said:

> His complexion was a bright blond and he dressed accordingly. On this occasion he wore an elegant snuff-coloured broadcloth coat topped by a velvet collar. His cravat was not made from cotton grown in the American South; it was fashioned of silk that had been tinted orange and to which lace tips had been attached. His vest and his silk hose were of the pearl hue, while his trousers were of white duck. He displayed Morocco shoes, yellow kid gloves, and a broad-brimmed beaver hat.

That description was probably exaggerated, but in an era when cross-dressing was seldom a subject of conversation, the president really did employ a great deal of lace on his clothing. When his son paid a visit to England and received a royal reception, newspapers fighting the president dubbed the young attorney Prince John—a nickname he heard at intervals long after his father left the White House.

BEFORE, DURING, AND AFTER his administration, Jannetje's widower was linked with a series of women. A granddaughter of Jefferson's, about twenty-four, reputedly was begged for marriage by the rapidly balding, middle-aged senator from New York. Significantly, Van Buren's unfinished memoirs refer to Ellen Randolph as "a very interesting young lady" despite the fact that these papers include no mention of his long-dead wife.

There is considerable evidence that at age sixty-nine he proposed marriage to the daughter of the attorney under whom he had studied decades earlier. Margaret Sylvester, who was forty years old, is thought to have given him a firm but not rude no. According to the story that is widely accepted, she told him that having been a spinster for four decades, she believed she'd stay in that category for the rest of her life. Even his most zealous political foes failed to suggest that there was anything approaching impropriety in his relationships with Randolph and Sylvester.

It would be strange if any dirt could be found concerning Van Buren's relationship with women. Jannetje's husband became aptly named when someone thought of calling the old Dutchman "the Red Fox of Kinderhook."

9

William Henry and Anna Harrison

William Harrison functioned as chief executive for only thirty-two days—barely long enough to form a cabinet that included Daniel Webster and Thomas Ewing, foster father of Gen. William Tecumseh Sherman. His inauguration attracted a huge and enthusiastic crowd, but Anna was not in it. She stayed in Ohio, planning to take up her duties as hostess in the spring, so it turned out that she was never an occupant of the White House.

Despite the brevity of their stay at the highest level, William and Anna stand out from the crowd of first families in many respects. No other president and his wife had ten children. And he might not have stopped there: He was accused of taking a Native American woman as his mistress, allegedly fathering children by her as well. William was the only president who studied medicine and was the last chief executive born as a British subject. Alone among his peers; he served as a territorial governor—and the last political office he held before the presidency was that of county clerk.

Anna was the only first lady born in New Jersey and was the first to receive a formal education. She was the only woman who was both wife of a president and grandmother of a president (Benjamin Harrison). No other wife of a president performed none of the official duties expected of her, yet she was the first widow of a president to receive a pension. Until Anna said yes to William, no future first lady had eloped in order to be married.

The lives of William and Anna were plenty colorful long before canny political leaders persuaded him to run for the presidency. He grew up on the Berkeley Plantation of his wealthy father, who had been governor of the Old Dominion and who had signed the Declaration of Independence. After attending college in Virginia for three years, he went to the College of Physicians and Surgeons in Philadelphia, where one of his teachers was the famous Dr. Benjamin Rush. After just one year in Philadelphia, however, he became a soldier and spent much of his early life fighting Indians.

Serving under Gen. Anthony Wayne, in 1794 the young officer fought at Fallen Timbers—named for a vast and tangled mass of huge trees earlier leveled by a tornado.

During a dozen years as governor of the Northwest Territory, Harrison negotiated numerous treaties with Indians, and in 1811 he led soldiers against the great Shawnee warrior Tecumseh. The struggle's final battle, fought at Tippecanoe, was a toss-up even though Tecumseh was killed there, probably by Richard Johnson. When Tecumseh's followers withdrew, the fight was hailed by the white men as a great victory. Nearly three decades later, it was as the winner at Tippecanoe that Harrison ran for and won the nation's highest office—boosted partly by publicity about Johnson's sexual indiscretions.

ANNA'S FATHER, JUDGE JOHN C. SYMMES, quit his post as chief justice of the New Jersey Supreme Court in order to move to Ohio and speculate in what was then western land. Educated at Mrs. Isabella Graham's exclusive boarding school for girls in New York City, Anna joined her father in Ohio soon after his holdings reached five hundred thousand acres.

When he noticed that William and Anna were more than just friends, Judge Symmes didn't take kindly to the notion of having a professional soldier as a son-in-law. Having been ordered by the judge to steer clear of any entanglement, the young lovers managed to hold their yearning for one another in check until Symmes left home on business. Taking advantage of his absence, they went to the North Bend, Ohio, residence of Dr. Stephen Wood, treasurer of the Northwest Territory. There they were married on November 25, 1795—by a justice of the peace.

Symmes was furious with his daughter. Although forced often to come in casual contact with his brand-new son-in-law, he refused to speak to him. At a farewell dinner for General Wayne, they were seated in such fashion that both realized one would have to begin a conversation. Anna's father, still boiling mad over the elopement, briefly mentioned their marriage before demanding: "How do you expect to support my daughter?"

Harrison, who enjoyed relating this experience in later life, said that he snapped a four-word reply: "With my sword, sir!"

Chosen by President John Adams to govern the Indiana Territory, Harrison continued to think of himself as a soldier. It was natural, therefore, for him to resign as governor in order to take command of the Army of the Northwest during the War of 1812. At the head of his troops, he drove the British from Detroit and soon clashed with them in the battle of the Thames. This time, unlike Tippecanoe, where he became nationally famous, he really did win a resounding victory.

Anna Harrison wanted nothing to do with political campaigns and used a minor illness as an excuse to stay away from her husband's inauguration.

When he again took off his uniform in order to supervise his estate from the mansion he had built there, Harrison said he would never leave it for any length of time. Anna, who called him Pah in spite of her boarding school education, didn't like it when he was persuaded to run for a seat in Congress.

After holding it for three years, he became an Ohio state senator and then a member of the U.S. Senate. Whigs persuaded him that he could win the presidency and pushed their nomination on him in 1836. Before election day, William privately conceded that he didn't think he had a chance against the Red Fox of Kinderhook—Martin Van Buren. He was right. Although he was not far behind the New Yorker in popular votes, he gained less than one-fourth of the electoral votes.

In defeat, Harrison had no idea that his opponent's vice president and his former military ally, Richard M. Johnson, would help boost him to victory four years later. Johnson hadn't been settled in Washington very long when it became known he had used a black concubine for years. His Julia Chinn died before he was elevated to high office, but throughout Kentucky it was public knowledge that Johnson looked after the welfare of their mixed-blood children. He picked another black female as Julia's successor and when she abandoned him in favor of a Native American he found a third female slave who suited him.

Anna Harrison, who wasn't interested in the goings-on of the vice president or any other political leader, was unhappy when William told her he had decided to make another run for the White House in 1840. Political opponents derided him as Granny and declared that a man of sixty-seven was far too old to win. Angry at being mocked, he responded by taking an ultra-radical step. Leaving Anna behind and breaking sharply with precedent, he hit the campaign trail and actively worked for his election.

Phrased in one fashion or another, most of his speeches included a ringing cry to the effect that a backwoodsman in a hunting shirt was the greatest of Americans. That made it easy to portray him as the "log cabin and hard cider" candidate of the common man who was pitted against aristocratic Van Buren. Not content with reciting the story of Johnson's sexual preferences, Harrison's followers spun a yarn according to which their candidate had been born in a log cabin. A composer dashed off what he called the "Log Cabin Waltz" and it became widely popular. Capitalizing on the mythical great victory at Tippecanoe, they handed out tiny bars of Tippecanoe Shaving Soap at rallies. With John Tyler as his running mate, "Tippecanoe and Tyler, too" made a great campaign slogan. Since females didn't vote, no Tippecanoe rose water was produced for them.

Indian fighter William Henry Harrison— "Pah" to his boarding-school-educated Anna.

Smelling victory and eager to put the spoils system to work in their favor, Whigs may have spent as much as $20,000 on the first razzle-dazzle presidential campaign. They had an enormous paper ball especially manufactured, then sent teams of men to pull it from place to place. Their accompanying slogan, "Keep the ball rolling!" became so widely familiar that it entered general speech. When her husband rolled to an easy victory with 80 percent of the electoral vote, Anna sighed heavily and said she wished his friends had left him where he was "happy and contented in retirement."

Despite his vaunted stamina, Harrison was worn out before the popular votes were cast. On March 4, 1841, he still had not fully recovered from the ordeal of the campaign trail. Refusing to wear an overcoat—which he believed onlookers might consider a sign of weakness and age—he rode to his inauguration on horseback. In the aftermath of eternally long outdoor ceremonies in bitterly cold weather, he showed up at three inaugural balls in succession.

Small wonder that the Log Cabin chief executive born in a plantation mansion contracted a severe cold that wouldn't go away. Exactly one month after having made the longest speech ever delivered by an incoming chief executive, the man who rose to fame by fighting Indians and the British breathed his last.

10

John, Julia, and Letitia Tyler

President John Tyler's right foot rested on the metal stairway that led to the deck of the USS *Princeton*. He began shifting his weight to start upward, then cocked his head and listened intently. Recognizing the voice of William N. Waller, the chief executive turned back as a gesture of courtesy. Three minutes later a mighty overhead blast set the warship to quivering. Cries of agony from the deck told persons below that tragedy had struck.

February 28, 1844, had been billed as a gala day in Washington. By noon about 450 persons had boarded the U.S. Navy's first steam-powered warship to be fitted with a screw propeller. Swedish engineer John Ericsson, who designed it, was later the principal builder of the first U.S. ironclad—the famous USS *Monitor*.

Capt. Robert P. Stockton, commander of the *Princeton*, was eager for influential men and women to experience his vessel's capacity to surge smoothly forward. He personally planned the Potomac River excursion that began at Alexandria and offered a good look at Mount Vernon as the vessel passed close to it. To Stockton, the highlight of the day was the planned firing of the world's most powerful naval gun—dubbed the Peacemaker and mounted in the bow of the *Princeton*.

As the mighty warship plowed along the Potomac River, the Peacemaker twice emitted a mighty roar and the *Princeton* shuddered briefly. A sumptuous collation was offered to distinguished guests and their friends, then the warship made a 180-degree turn and headed back toward its starting point. As Mount Vernon hove in sight for the second time, some of those who had finished eating wandered back on deck and suggested that Stockton have his immense gun fired as a salute to the memory of our first president.

Down below, everyone thought the entertainment had come to an end but popular singer Waller consented to render just one more tune. As he began to sing, the husband of Tyler's daughter Elizabeth Waller did not know that his melody would lead his father-in-law to pause out of respect—thereby saving his life.

A veteran of the War of 1812, had our tenth president made it to the deck, he would have been standing very close to the Peacemaker when the gun exploded at the breech. Spewed in every direction, heavy chunks of metal mowed down persons gathered around the piece. Secretary of State Abel P. Upshur, Secretary of the Navy Thomas W. Gilmer, the president's valet, a naval officer, a diplomat, and a wealthy New Yorker never knew what hit them. Miraculously, dignitaries who happened to have stepped behind the forward mast of the warship were shielded by it and were not even scratched.

Margaret and Julia Gardiner of New York, aboard as personal guests of the chief executive, fainted when a petty officer who had raced down the stairway made an announcement. All except six men were safe, he proclaimed, before reading the list of casualties that included the father of the two young women.

Rushing to Julia's side and calling for smelling salts, the president helped to revive her and then gently guided David Gardiner's sobbing daughter to a launch that took them to the landing used by White House personnel. Barely able to walk with assistance, the New Yorker nodded agreement when Tyler suggested that she should spend the night in the room that later gained special fame as the Lincoln Bedroom. When Julia woke up the following morning, the president, almost old enough to be her grandfather, was sitting patiently by her bedside with no reading matter or writing material in his hands.

Although Julia expressed gratitude and surprise at his presence, she probably would have been puzzled had he not been there. Three weeks earlier she had been in the White House for the first time as a dinner guest, along with her father. Tyler, who dearly loved a fast game of cards, expressed delight when he learned that the young New Yorker was a veteran player. Ignoring other guests, he led Julia to a table at which the two of them played for more than an hour.

Expressing surprise that so much time had passed so swiftly, Julia thanked her host for an unforgettable evening and rose to join her waiting father. Oral tradition has it that the president, whose period of official mourning for his wife Letitia had just ended, was practically panting by this time. Unconfirmed gossip includes the unlikely story that when he rose from his chair he chased his guest around the card table and tried to plant a good-bye kiss on her cheek.

Regardless of precisely what took place on the evening of February 7, 1843, everyone who knew the president intimately soon realized that he was head over heels in love with Julia. He begged her to marry him during the ball at which Washington's birthday was celebrated, but he got

Explosion of the Peacemaker, instantly killing Julia's father and five other men. (Nathaniel Currier lithograph)

nowhere. She later said that she blurted "No, no, no!" to him, simultaneously shaking her head repeatedly and "flinging the tassel" of the Greek cap she wore that evening "into his face with every move."

Tyler's comfort to the New York socialite a year later during her time of shock and grief over the sudden death of her father cemented a relationship that was already intimate despite her "No, no, no!" When she went home to weep with her widowed mother, Tyler wrote an emotionally charged letter every day.

Mrs. Gardiner quickly discovered that her daughter was toying with the idea of becoming the nation's first lady. Hence, she repeatedly warned her daughter that the Virginia native who was in the White House didn't have the resources necessary to support Julia in the style in which she was accustomed. Trying to look like she was indulging in casual small talk, the woman widowed by an explosion wondered aloud what it would be like "to become the stepmother of a man's full-grown children."

This allusion made Julia so angry that she stalked out of the mansion on Gardiner Island, adjacent to Long Island, and cooled off by walking about the premises for more than an hour. When she came back inside, she tossed her head and announced that if a woman really loved a man it wouldn't matter to her whether he had seven or twenty children by a previous marriage. Age was nothing compared with love, the twenty-four-year-old snapped when her mother pointed out—as if Julia wasn't aware of it—that her distinguished suitor was more than twice her age.

Four months after the death of her father, Julia met John in New York City and by prearrangement went with him to the fashionable Episcopal Church of the Ascension. The first president to be married while in office enjoyed a wedding breakfast at the Gardiner mansion, then took his bride to the capital. Anti-administration newspapers soon published numerous jokes featuring Tyler and "his lovely twenty-four-year-old daughter."

The marriage had taken place so suddenly and secretly that only a handful of intimates knew the purpose of the president's announced visit to New York. The *Madisonian*, a newspaper that habitually praised Tyler, had mistakenly informed its readers that the trip was being made so that the weary chief executive could have a brief respite from his arduous duties. After news of the wedding became public, the *New York Herald* reprinted the Washington story with commentary. An editor quipped that whether or not the fifty-four-year-old chief executive knew it, "his arduous duties will now tax his strength during many a night."

The second Mrs. John Tyler was mistress of the White House for only nine months, but she made the most of her time in it. Drawing heavily upon the fortune left by her father, she brought elegant French furniture to the mansion and began strolling around the grounds with an Italian grey-hound on a leash. Having boasted to her mother that she intended "to entertain with grace but elegance," the reception she held on New Year's Day in 1845 was for a time the talk of the capital. The youthful first lady wore plumes in her hair while greeting guests, and she was attended by maids of honor attired in pure white.

That event faded into the background six weeks later when a "vale-dictory celebration for the president" kept White House candles glowing until the wee hours. Three thousand celebrities attended and toasted the outgoing chief executive and his bride with fine French wine she had pur-chased. Many of them were so taken by surprise when the U.S. Marine Band played "Hail to the Chief!" in a precedent-setting gesture planned by Julia that they had to struggle to get on their feet to join in an ovation. That night, the first lady introduced Washington to the polka by dancing with four or five European ambassadors familiar with it.

Seasoned Washington insiders shrugged aside "the shenanigans at the White House" as unimportant. These analysts credited Julia with an achievement far more significant than giving the biggest party in years. Rightly or wrongly, she was widely believed to have been the determining influence in her husband's eleventh-hour solution to "the Texas question."

Previous chief executives and members of both houses of Congress had agonized over whether to accept the former Republic of Texas as a full-fledged member of the Union. With the slavery question central to the issue, seemingly endless debate over Texas had produced no results. Many veteran lawmakers expressed certainty that even if a treaty of annexation should be framed, the Senate would not ratify it. This verdict was based upon the fact that an April 1844 treaty by which Texas would have been annexed as a territory had been turned down by the Senate.

Democrat James K. Polk won the election of 1844, and soon after the votes cast in November had been counted, Tyler bypassed the Senate. Relying on a joint resolution of Congress that required no ratification, on March 1, 1845, he announced that Texas would become a state before the year ended. Although the formal admission of Texas did not take place until after Polk had assumed office, for all practical purposes the deed was done when Julia's husband signed the joint resolution.

The beautiful first lady didn't have the political savvy necessary to devise this stratagem, but she strongly encouraged John to move heaven and earth in an attempt to enlarge the United States by means of the Lone Star State. Each of her lavish entertainments had political motives, for at them she gave her time and attention to lawmakers who needed persuasion in order to support her husband's measures. She paid absolutely no attention to innuendos according to which she influenced legislation by means of sessions "in the bedrooms of men other than her husband."

SINCE LATE ADOLESCENCE, JULIA had been accustomed to publicity and had learned very early that some of it would likely be negative. At age nineteen the former debutante had been the central figure in the first-ever commercial endorsement by a person of high social standing. Wearing a sunbonnet topped with ostrich feathers and—significantly as time proved—hanging on the arm of a decidedly older man, she was depicted as lauding the merchandise sold at Bogert and Macamly's. Since the advertisement was labeled "Rose of Long Island," that name quickly and permanently attached to her.

Humiliated beyond measure, David Gardiner and his wife packed their beautiful daughter off to Europe for a year-long grand tour with fervent hope that both negative and positive reactions to her publicity stunt would cease. Soon after her return from abroad, the Rose of Long Island set out on her first visit to the nation's capital.

On the train she met John Tyler Jr., his father's secretary. Barely a year older than Julia, he took considerable interest in her and invited her to

John Tyler, our nation's tenth president.

bring along relatives and visit the White House. On January 20, 1842, at the time she and her father acted upon John's invitation, the son of the president may have sensed that she was more interested in John Tyler Sr., than in John Jr.

Critics of "the mating of April with November" liked to point out that Julia had always said she would find a husband who was very rich or very powerful. Before her momentous first visit to Washington, she had spent days poring over a volume made up of vignettes about New Yorkers worth $100,000 or more. John Tyler was poor by her standards—but when it comes to power, the president of the United States was at the apex of the pyramid.

Tyler didn't get there by accident, despite the fact that he was not elected by voters. After the 1840 presidential campaign, which touted "Tippecanoe and Tyler, too," he retired to his Virginia estate. Late in the afternoon of April 5, 1841, a stranger whose looks shouted that he had been riding hell-for-leather for hours pulled up at Tyler's home. He breathlessly informed him, the plantation owner who hadn't bothered to attend the inauguration, that William Henry Harrison had died less than twelve hours earlier.

Lawmakers had not yet given any attention to the matter of succession to the presidency. In the power vacuum that had been created by Harrison's sudden death, John Tyler boldly labeled himself as the successor to his running mate and took over as many reins of government as possible. Some political opponents scornfully sent letters to him that were addressed to "the Honorable Vice-president of the United States." Tyler didn't even open such communications, and clung so tenaciously to his claim that he won acceptance as Harrison's successor and set a lasting precedent.

His inflexible views upon states' rights and slavery came to be held by his second wife even more forcefully, if possible, than his own. In her post–White House years, Julia became "more southern" than many persons actually born and reared in the Cotton Belt.

Turning her back on her New York upbringing, she became an ardent defender of slavery and of secession. Nearly a decade before the second Mrs. Tyler became a widow, she created an uproar at least as great as that stirred up by her teenage publicity stunt. England's Duchess of Southerland had written "an open letter to southern women" in which she urged that they should take an active role in bringing slavery to an end.

Julia Tyler, no longer calling a New York mansion home, now depended heavily on her husband's sixty or seventy slaves. John said the statement of an English duchess wasn't worth the time it would take to frame a reply. His wife, who reputedly said no not once but three times when he first proposed marriage, ignored his opinion and took her pen in hand. She drafted a statement and sent it to numerous newspapers. She had the satisfaction of learning that it was reprinted in some of the countries she had visited as a very young woman.

Julia Tyler. (Anelli painting, Library of Congress)

Urging the English duchess to spare her sympathy for "the well-fed negroes," the Rose of Long Island dealt at length with the financial problems of Ireland and with England's refusal to advance the rights of women. Small wonder that two sons of the former New York debutante fought for the Confederacy during the Civil War. A pair of the first Mrs. John Tyler's sons filled important civilian posts during the administration of Jefferson Davis. Robert and John Jr. always said that they became Rebels out of deference to their mother, who was the daughter of a prosperous Virginia planter.

The former Letitia Christian, first wife of the fellow Virginian who literally seized the presidency in the lack of a formal succession policy, was already an invalid by the time she reached the White House. After having presented her husband with seven children during fifteen years of marriage, she suffered a crippling stroke of paralysis. Letitia eventually regained some of her life's functions, but she remained an invalid. Confined to upstairs living quarters in the White House, her only public appearance as first lady was at the 1842 wedding of her daughter, Elizabeth.

Elizabeth, wife of the versatile and talented singer who later saved the life of her father, did not try to conceal her resentment of her stepmother, who was not quite three years her senior. All seven of Letitia's sons and daughters were disdainful of the former Julia Gardiner and had as little to do with her as possible.

Their attitude suited Julia just fine; she never relished the notion of being a stepmother—but embraced motherhood with enthusiasm. John's first child by Julia, a fine-looking boy who was baptized as David Gardiner but grew up as Gardie, was born when Tyler was fifty-six years old. Fourteen more years passed before the ex-president's last child—a girl named Pearl—came along.

Inevitably, old political foes and brash young newspaper editors had a field day wondering publicly whether "some of the Tyler brood should be known by the names of their real fathers." John and his Julia gave no signs that they were annoyed by these allegations.

All available evidence indicates that the woman who gained fame—or notoriety—as the Rose of Long Island was strongly attracted to older men in general and that she adored her aging husband. Stories about her prowess in bedrooms of lawmakers and other public officials abounded but are not to be taken seriously. No one who knew her and her husband intimately gave the slightest credence to tales according to which John was too old to have sired the twelfth, thirteenth, and fourteenth child who bore his name.

11
James and Sarah Polk

S lightly more than three months after vacating the White House, our eleventh president died at his Tennessee home. Accounts about last words of dying persons are notoriously unreliable, but in the case of James K. Polk, half a dozen witnesses agreed about his final sentence. "I love you, Sarah, for all eternity, I love you," he managed to gasp before closing his eyes and slipping away.

Although she never gave so dramatic a profession of love, the former Sarah Childress had a cameo of her husband made into a pin and wore it every day for more than forty years. Long before he died, it was well known in Washington that she would go nowhere without her spouse. Invited to a dinner during his absence from the capital, Sarah declined instantly and emphatically. "I wouldn't have a good time without my Jim," she said, "so there's no use for me to go."

During the quarter century that the two lived together, the Polks had no children. Some biographers have speculated that this void in their family life—uncommon at the time—drew them closer and closer together. Whether that view is accurate or not, there's no doubt that they were virtually inseparable while in the White House, except during those hours he was forced to devote to official duties.

Thirty-one administrations later, Hillary Clinton came in for a torrent of criticism and downright abuse when it became known that she expected to serve as an unelected advisor to her husband. She would have been wiser to follow the example of the woman from Tennessee and keep her mouth shut—staying at her husband's side but maintaining a low public profile.

Members of the general public didn't know it at the time, but Sarah Polk was up to her chin in top-level business of the nation throughout her husband's 1845–49 term as chief executive. Only Washington insiders were aware that she served as his confidential secretary, often sitting up late with him and advising him as he considered decisions.

Until after the Polks left the White House, however, no one except household slaves and a handful of intimates knew how influential she was.

Sarah habitually scanned all important newspapers and periodicals, and from them she selected virtually everything her husband read about current affairs and the state of the country in general. She decided what letters should be seen personally by him and which should go to clerks for routine replies.

Their intimate working relationship began during Polk's fourteen years as a member of the House of Representatives. When James temporarily left Capitol Hill in order to run for the governorship of Tennessee, Sarah added the arrangement of his schedule to her responsibilities and never afterward relinquished this to her Jim or anyone else.

THEIR CHILDHOOD YEARS WERE spent far apart. James lived for ten years not far from Charlotte, North Carolina. Sarah was reared near Murfreesboro, Tennessee, in her father's plantation manor. Even when Ezekiel Polk persuaded his Tar Heel son that middle Tennessee was the land of opportunity, paths of the two families didn't cross. Worn to a frazzle, the Polk family reached Duck River, southwest of Nashville, at the end of a three-month wagon trip during which they skirted one mountain after another. Meanwhile, members of the Childress family were comfortably situated some distance away.

Joel Childress wanted nothing but the best for his daughter, and she eventually went to North Carolina to study at a female academy operated by Moravians. Her earliest formal education was received, however, from Murfreesboro teacher Samuel P. Black—who also taught Polk. Their paths crossed in his little schoolhouse, but nineteen-year-old Jim didn't give twelve-year old Sarah a second glance. Soon both of them were in North Carolina, but although the university Jim attended at Chapel Hill was close to Winston by today's standards, in 1818 they were separated by a full day's journey. It is unlikely that they ever saw each other in North Carolina.

When both of them returned to the region where Murfreesboro was the trading center, Jim and Sarah became acquainted and soon developed a strong friendship that ripened gradually and took them to the altar in 1824. In and around Columbia, Tennessee, a county seat that Jim's father helped establish, the story goes that Sarah agreed to become Jim's wife on condition that he throw his hat into the political ring. It is possible that she laid down such a condition, for he became a member of the legislature at age twenty-eight—not long before their wedding.

Much of Tennessee was still wide-open frontier country in which pockets of Native Americans were trying to cling to their land. Sam Houston, born the same year as Polk, went into Cherokee sections very early and later claimed that as an adolescent he had "tasted the charms of many a dusky maiden." When he abruptly quit as governor of Tennessee in 1827, Houston spent another interval with the Cherokees before going to Texas and winning lasting fame.

Houston was far from alone in taking advantage of young Cherokee females, but Jim Polk was not among those who spent evenings with them. Some of his political foes later speculated that he must have been impotent, since he was conspicuously unlike John Tyler and never sired a child. There is no evidence to support this conjecture, however. A few modern commentators speculate that Jim and Sarah may have practiced a crude form of birth control after having reached a deliberate conclusion to remain childless.

To those who didn't like him, Polk's black neckband stood out in sharp contrast to his long hair that was combed straight back.

SARAH FORMED AN EARLY friendship with Andrew Jackson of such nature that it weathered every storm. Old Hickory became furious with some of his top advisors after their wives ostracized the former Peggy O'Neale on the heels of her husband's suicide and her quick remarriage. Sarah Polk was among those who followed the lead of Mrs. John C. Calhoun and refused to call on the new Mrs. Eaton or to invite her to parties. Her close ties with Jackson may have persuaded the president to ignore her treatment of Peggy Eaton.

Instead of becoming angry at the Tennessean by adoption during the Eaton "petticoat affair," Jackson began grooming Polk for the White House. Part of Old Hickory's motivation stemmed from the fact that Polk had repeatedly gone on record as favoring the admission of Texas to the Union. Sarah's husband had additional leverage that grew out of the fact that he invariably supported the policies of the seventh president.

Even after having gained the nomination because of Jackson's influence, few persons except Sarah Polk thought her husband had a chance against the great Henry Clay. She helped organize a national campaign at least as large, as if not larger than, any previously conducted. As the first dark horse to win the White House, Polk scored one of the monumental upsets in American political history. His vice president, George M. Dallas of Pennsylvania, later cast a tiebreaking vote in a tariff measure of importance to Texas and was rewarded by having what was then a small settlement in the Lone Star State named for him.

Sarah Polk, who wisely kept mum about her role in national policymaking, had been reared as a strict Calvinist. As a result, she announced before becoming mistress of the White House that the "unseemly social events" hosted by Julia Tyler would come to an abrupt halt. Soon she was derided as Sahara Sarah because she banned strong drink, dancing, and card playing. Remembered by the public at large chiefly for this negative stance rather than for her positive achievements, the woman from Tennessee now gets from historians mostly high ratings for her stint as first lady.

Sarah Polk during her highly productive years as constant companion and advisor to her husband. (Library of Congress)

Sarah clearly helped influence her husband into take an unbending stand on what was then known as "the Oregon question," a dispute with Great Britain over land. Even more significantly, she encouraged him to seek and to find a flimsy excuse to lead the United States into war with Mexico. Annexation of Texas caused the long-simmering dispute over national boundaries to come to a boil. Mexico held that the Neuces River was the dividing point, while the United States claimed it to be the Rio Grande. Encouraged by his wife, the president dispatched troops into the disputed region and urged Congress to prepare for war. When Mexican and American forces clashed briefly in the region claimed by both nations, Polk requested a declaration of war and got it by an overwhelming majority in both houses of Congress.

Washington insiders who said little and wrote nothing about it at the time, later admitted that Sarah was often at her husband's side for twelve or fourteen hours during many business days. Some of them grudgingly admitted that she was highly influential in policy decisions by which only Jefferson

topped Polk in the amount of land added to the nation during his administration. She never claimed any public credit, but must have quietly calculated
that if her advice to her Jim affected his actions by a mere 10 percent, she
enlarged her nation by at least 7.2 million acres or fifty thousand square miles.

Widely regarded as having worked harder than any other White
House husband-wife pair, James and Sarah never took a vacation and spent
only about three days out of the mansion during four years. Numerous commentators cite that quadrennium of ceaseless toil as being responsible for
Polk's death a trifle more than three months after he retired from office.
These persons overlook the fact that he was never robust—and that he
may have contracted cholera when he and Sarah visited Louisiana soon
after leaving the nation's capital.

Sarah displayed her usual quiet dignity when she was suddenly made a
widow at age forty-six. She declared Polk Place in Nashville to be neutral
ground during the Civil War—so as to receive Confederate and Union
generals impartially. By the time distinguished military leaders on both
sides came calling, she had erected a splendid marble tomb in front of the
mansion and had turned it into a museum plus a library for preservation of
Polk's artifacts and papers. During forty-two years in which she always wore
mourning dress, Sarah devoted most of her time and energy to preservation
of her Jim's memory.

12

Zach and Peggy Taylor

This White House pair racked up a surprising number of first achievements despite the short time they spent in the mansion. They made up the first presidential couple known only by abbreviated names until they began to be listed in formal documents.

Neither of them knew for weeks after the nomination that they were involved in the 1848 race for the nation's highest office. A notice was mailed from Philadelphia, with postage to be paid by the recipient. Tired of paying for letters asking questions or offering compliments, they had notified their postmaster to send postage-due letters to the dead-letter office. A visit by a distant relative finally brought the news that although they didn't know it, the horse that represented Tyler had already gone around the first turn in the racetrack.

Zachariah was the only chief executive who never signed a letter or document with his full name—so he's the only president whose full autograph does not rest in a few or in many collections. He was the first career soldier to win the highest office and the nation's first soldier to be given a brevet—or honorary—promotion. This unsought honor made the U.S. Army captain an honorary major as a reward for his defense of Fort Harrison during the War of 1812. That was only an interlude in this man's colorful career, since he was the only president who fought in four wars.

Peggy, who probably wouldn't have responded had anyone been formal enough to call her Margaret, was believed to be the first mistress of the White House who had earlier prayed for her husband's defeat. She was the only first lady who played no role whatsoever in official White House doings. As though these two factors didn't put her into a class all by herself, she was the first presidential wife not to have had an artist's portrait of her rendered.

Zach—who didn't mind that abbreviated use of his name, although he really preferred to be called Old Rough and Ready—was the first chief executive with absolutely no interest in politics. He not only never voted before party hopefuls persuaded him to run; he is believed to have been the only president who didn't bother to vote for himself. He was the only man put in charge of the ship of state as an aftereffect of having disobeyed orders.

Zach and Peggy were the only White House pair to have both a son and a grandson who played major roles in the Civil War—as Rebels against the government. C. S. Gen. Richard Taylor followed in his father's footsteps, after a fashion. His commanding officer, Gen. E. Kirby Smith, accused him of having disobeyed orders and tried to have him cashiered. Taylor sidestepped a court-martial by asking to be relieved of his post—but instead was promoted to the rank of lieutenant general.

Second Lieutenant John Taylor Wood of the Confederate Navy would have made his grandpa proud—except for the fact that he was fighting on the wrong side as far as his grandfather would have been concerned. Aboard the first ironclad American vessel to go into combat, the CSS *Virginia* aka the *Merrimac*, Wood helped sink U.S. Navy wooden battleships at Hampton Roads, Virginia, on March 8, 1861. He later commanded a crew of gunners on a bluff above the James River, thwarting U.S. Gen. George B. McClellan's 1862 drive to take Richmond.

Unlike William Henry Harrison, Zach really was born in a log cabin—and a log cabin was the edifice in which he and Peggy said, "I do." A final "first" was jointly scored by Zach and his Peggy. He became the first ex-president and she the first former first lady to be buried in Kentucky. When their bodies were put into the Taylor plot of a cemetery near Louisville, their relatives and admirers had no idea that he would be the first former chief executive to be exhumed in order to solve a forensic mystery.

BOTH OF THESE REMARKABLE persons had more-than-prosperous parents, but neither received more than a rudimentary education. He was born in Virginia, and she first saw the light of day in Maryland. They wound up in that Taylor graveyard of the Bluegrass State because Zach's father had taken him there as a small boy.

Besides disliking his long baptismal name, Old Rough and Ready signed his documents as "Z. Taylor" probably because he despised the chore of writing anything. His spelling was so abominable that documents originating with him are extremely hard to read. There is no evidence that either of them yearned to be skilled in either reading or writing. Zach never really longed for anything except a chance to bury a musket ball inside a foe. Peggy's one great desire was for peace, quiet, and tranquillity as a retired military hero's wife, one who would have preferred to live almost anywhere except in the White House.

If Zach had earlier hankered for any other young woman, he kept very quiet about it. Without talking a lot, he persuaded Margaret "Peggy" Mackall Smith to say she'd go anywhere with him Uncle Sam wanted him to go. The only story of their courtship has been widely circulated but is not very believable. According to it, Zach got word late in 1810 that a good-looking young woman from Maryland was visiting her sister near Louisville, so he decided to drop in and get acquainted.

Peggy was riding a fast-stepping pony, headed for a quilting party, when a stranger in uniform came loping toward her. That spooked her animal, who bolted, and would soon have thrown his rider had gallant Zach not lifted her from the saddle with his strong right arm while at a full gallop. Naturally the grateful Marylander invited her good-looking rescuer to stay for supper. After the meal both went to the front porch and took a rocking chair. Zach tried to get up a conversation, but Peggy acted as though she didn't hear anything he said and kept her mouth shut.

Finally, in desperation, the young officer pulled the pillow from beneath his bottom. Then he reached into the little sewing kit that soldiers called a *housewife*, opened it, and removed a needle and thread. Peggy, who tried to turn her head but was burning up with curiosity, watched as he stitched one letter at a time:

This portrait in profile helped reinforce "Old Rough and Ready" as the popular nickname for Taylor. (Library of Congress)

HAs tHE CAT GOT yer tONGU

Zach never stitched the last letter of that question, because Peggy started laughing so hard she lost her breath. After he pounded her on the back a few times to get her breathing recalibrated, he popped the question and she giggled just one word: "Yes!"

That was all he wanted her to say, so they soon exchanged April vows in her sister's double log house. Then they both climbed onto his horse and rode off to his post of duty. Eight months later, he was promoted to captain, and off they went to Fort Knox in the Indiana Territory. Not long afterward he was put in command of Fort Harrison, named after territorial governor William Henry Harrison. When Indians and a few Redcoats showed up to take over the fort, the young officer managed to send them packing in the other direction.

That's when he was made a brevet major—holding the title but not the commission of an officer who was usually close to fifty years old before he got to pin stars on his shoulder straps. When Peggy found out that her Zach had been given a brevet, she asked him to let her polish it for him. He laughed sort of foolishly when he explained that it was just a piece of paper. After helping to push the British back across the Atlantic Ocean in a hurry at the end of the War of 1812, Zach quit the army and took to raising tobacco and corn.

It didn't take but a few years for life on the plantation to get mighty dull, so he became Major Taylor again—this time, for real. He and Peggy didn't spend very long anywhere. Uncle Sam sent them way up north to Fort Snelling in the part of the Northwest Territory that became Minnesota. Then they went to Florida, before ending up in Louisiana, where they bought a sugar plantation that turned out to be the only real home they ever had as adults. Zach was one of three future chief executives who participated in the Black Hawk War, which broke out in 1832: the other two were Abe Lincoln of Illinois and Jefferson Davis of Mississippi.

Zach never met the long and lanky Illinois militia officer, who would become known as "Honest Abe." He saw a lot more than he wished to see of Davis, whose angular face was a lot like Lincoln's and who was given the honor and responsibility of escorting captured Black Hawk to St. Louis. Lieutenant Davis aroused Taylor's ire when he spent so much time with the colonel's daughter, Sarah, that wedding bells could be heard from a distance when the wind was blowing in the right direction.

Old Rough and Ready blasted off to Peggy. "I'll be damned if another daughter of mine will marry into the military!" he fumed. Having forbade Sarah to see Davis again, he thought he had the situation under control. The young folks kept meeting in secret, however, then arranged a wedding in Kentucky that Zach and Peggy did not attend. Soon both of the newlyweds contracted malaria, and Sarah's case proved to be fatal.

TAYLOR MYTHS AREN'T AS numerous as Taylor "firsts," but they abound. One of them has it that Peggy shook her fist at the sky when she learned that her prayer that Zach wouldn't win had not been answered. According to this tale, she remained in Louisiana in a dudgeon and refused to be present at her husband's inauguration.

That isn't so; she was there but barely noticed. A newspaper artist who depicted her smoking a corncob pipe was pipe dreaming. She hated tobacco and persuaded Zach to smoke only outdoors—in an era when no one knew what secondhand smoke can do to lungs.

The tale that she secluded herself in an upstairs bedroom of the White House because she didn't want to be seen is as bogus as the cartoonist's sketch. Truth is, malaria had made her a semi-invalid, and she had the good sense to delegate the role of hostess to a daughter-in-law. By this time she had become acquainted with Varina, the second wife of Jefferson Davis, who often paid lengthy visits to her in her bedroom.

Varina, second wife of Jefferson Davis, became one of Peggy Taylor's most intimate and trusted friends.

Even his opponents avoided smearing Zach with tales of army post sex or cowardice in combat. If they had, the president probably would have sent them a steel-cold invitation to a dueling ground across the Potomac River. But his pistol-dueling bravado couldn't insulate him from the biggest financial scandal up to that time. The wealthy Galphin family of Georgia made a claim against the government and collected nearly $200,000 before it became known in the capital that their attorney was Zach's secretary of war, George W. Crawford. He was due to pocket half of anything paid to the Galphins and took office before anyone thought of making background checks. Lawmakers talked of impeaching Taylor for having failed to investigate properly, but in those days they didn't have the benefit of a special prosecutor to dig up dirt, so they took no action.

On July 4, 1850, our twelfth president attended a long ceremony at the Washington Monument. Hot and thirsty on his return to the White House, he reportedly drank a full pitcher of ice-cold milk and then finished off a bowl of cherries. In spite of the calomel and opium given to him by a

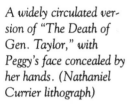
A widely circulated version of "The Death of Gen. Taylor," with Peggy's face concealed by her hands. (Nathaniel Currier lithograph)

doctor when he developed severe stomach cramps, he soon had a full-fledged case of diarrhea. Use of leeches plus application of mustard plasters that raised blisters on his skin only worsened his condition. Soon the tough professional soldier who had survived Indian arrows and Mexican bullets lay dying. Peggy came to sit beside his bed, and artists who sketched the scene had to show her with her head in her hands because no one knew what she looked like.

Decades later, a story circulated in which it was said that Peggy was so desperate to get out of the White House that she persuaded servants to slip tiny doses of arsenic into Zach's food. They said she put her head in her hands by his bedside so she wouldn't reveal how happy she was to finally be getting out of the White House. Those rumors led to his body's being dug up and samples of fingernail and hair tissues taken so they could be sent to Oak Ridge National Laboratory for investigation. Before members of the forensic team had started their work, they knew they were likely to find minute traces of arsenic; most bodies contain some of it. When they reported that remains of the twelfth president's held arsenic far, far below the lethal level, the name of the first first lady to be a murder suspect was cleared. She really was desperate to get back to Louisiana, but neither Peggy nor anyone else put enough arsenic in Zach's pine bark stew to kill him. If cold milk and cherries on a hot July 4 didn't do him in, it must have been his medical treatment that made Millard Fillmore our thirteenth chief executive.

13

Millard and Abigail Fillmore

A *nd this is liberty and Massachusetts!* The cry resounded through the tense courtroom packed with spectators. Thomas Sims, age seventeen, had nodded submissively when a police officer gestured for him to rise in preparation for returning to his place of detention. The runaway slave suddenly lifted his manacled hands as high as he could, began sobbing, and begged almost incoherently for a knife so he could thrust it into his heart in front of 125 witnesses.

In some respects, that was the emotional high point of "the Sims Case" that rocked Boston and the entire northeastern portion of the United States in April 1851. Tracked down after having fled to the city famous for its leading abolitionists, Thomas Sims had appealed to the courts. Anything was better than returning to Georgia and the overseer's whip, he urged.

While the runaway waited to be heard by commissioners, Wendell Phillips and his colleagues harangued the city into a frenzy. An angry crowd around the courthouse where the fugitive was held grew so large that the area was cordoned off. Under orders of the mayor, companies of militia took turns at guard duty. From Sims's improvised cell—a room in the courthouse that had been leased by Washington—the youth who was at the eye of the human hurricane heard snippets of phrases being spoken by street-corner orators.

"Millard Fillmore, by chance the president of the United States, should come here in person and issue a pardon!" one of Sims's defenders shouted. Some listeners yelled approval, but others silently hefted the sticks and clubs they carried. Only the awareness that a fraction of the crowd would soon be admitted to the courtroom prevented the outbreak of a major riot.

A formal order that Sims must be returned to his owner forthwith triggered the fugitive's mournful plea for something with which to commit suicide. Since no knife or gun was offered to him, he shuffled back to his room for his last night in Boston. Before dawn, squadrons of armed constables assembled in order to escort him to the ship on which he had to return to slavery. Surrounded by an estimated three hundred guardians of law and order, hearing the tolling of the city's church bells and an occasional snatch of "John Brown's Body," Thomas Sims proceeded to the dock. Before his ship had cleared the port, angry abolitionists were busy tacking warning posters wherever they could find places to put them.

In the White House, our thirteenth president grimaced as he read an account of the Boston incident in the capital's *Intelligencer*. Earlier he had been scornfully characterized as having been "Elevated to the nation's highest post by a pitcher of iced milk and a bowl of cherries." Now the outspoken advocate of sectional compromise who had put his political future at stake for that principle, realized that his quiet-spoken wife had been right.

Abigail Fillmore, the first mistress of the White House who had arrived there as a career woman, habitually discussed political issues with her husband, but she seldom tried to influence his decisions. The Fugitive Slave Law, the fourth of five separate bills that constituted the Compromise of 1850, was different and special according to Abigail.

She had spent only a few days in the capital during the long period when her husband presided over debate in the U.S. Senate. He didn't say a word to newspaper correspondents or to lawmakers who begged him for his opinion on the measure largely framed by Henry Clay of Kentucky. To Zachary Taylor he had confided that if the measure should result in a tie vote, which seemed likely, he would vote for it and send it to the president for his signature or his veto.

Although federal revenue measures and the rights of states often set the North against the South, hardly anyone denied that "the stone that could sink the ship of state" was slavery. Many in the North wanted it abolished immediately, while others took a more moderate stand and merely opposed its westward extension. A vocal majority of persons living in the South not only felt that slavery was divinely ordained; they wanted it extended into Texas as well as other new territories out west.

Clay framed a bill that included some measures sure to delight the North, along with others likely to please the South. His first proposal would have admitted California into the Union under its constitution that barred slavery. New Mexico and Utah, he urged, should immediately be organized as territories—with the question of whether or not slavery would be permitted in them reserved for later resolution.

Clay also wanted the vexatious issue of the boundary between Texas and the United States settled. That matter wasn't likely to arouse a great deal of emotion in the South or in the North. But to compensate the South for admission of California without slavery, Clay proposed that federal legislation concerning runaway slaves should be made much more strict. Giving a symbolic tip of his hat to the North, the Kentuckian added to his bill a provision aimed at bringing the slave trade—but not slavery—in the District of Columbia to an end.

Zach Taylor was all for the admission of California, but he balked at doing anything about New Mexico and Utah until they were ready for statehood. His stance stalled the Clay proposal, although his July 4 death and Fillmore's rise to power brought a surge of fresh interest. With Douglas at the helm instead of Clay, five measures that weren't totally acceptable to anyone were passed and the thirteenth president signed them into law on September 20, 1850.

Abigail was right; Millard's acceptance of the revised and toughened Fugitive Slave Law started a bonfire in the North. Simultaneously, the admission of California and the creation of the Territory of New Mexico were widely denounced in the South. The man who longed for national unity had tried to straddle the North-South gulf and had succeeded only in alienating followers in both sections.

MILLARD HAD BEEN REARED in western New York when the region was still raw frontier country. Today his name would be unknown had he not become a protégé of Thurlow Weed's. Although Weed listed his occupation as editor, he worked almost full-time to put chosen men—not himself—into political offices. He played a major role in sending John Adams, William Henry Harrison, and Zachary Taylor to the White House. He did not know it at the time, but his choice of Fillmore as Taylor's running mate was destined to put him into the role of "president maker."

No one who ever held that office had a more humble and inauspicious start in life. Millard grew up in a wilderness, literally, where his nearest neighbor lived four miles away. His father, a tenant farmer, bound him out at age fourteen as an apprentice to a fuller, who spent his days shrinking and beating cloth to increase its weight. Since the boy was under an indenture, or binding contract, in 1814 he was just one level above Thomas Sims when he became a victim of slave-catchers in Boston.

Millard might have spent his life on the bottom level of America's social and economic structure had he not decided to hit the books. At age nineteen his quest for an education took him to a newly established little academy, whose teacher was nearly two years his junior. Abigail Powers was a pert redhead with a knack for inspiring students, and she soon took a liking to the big new arrival who had decided to study under her.

They soon became interested in one another in ways that had nothing to do with reading, writing, or 'rithmetic. Yet if Millard's seven-year courtship included even a tiny smidgen of romance, neither of them ever revealed it. During much of this time he spent every waking hour as a would-be attorney, often practicing 150 miles away from Abigail. She once wrote him that "Your society is all I have thought of," and after her early death he told mutual friends that "I was always greeted with a happy smile during our entire married life." That was as close as either of them came to expressing undying devotion to one another.

Even though they must have been passionately in love, they managed to curb their animal instincts and waited for Millard to begin building his practice before going to the altar. Inevitably, that made Abigail a mother who seemed to her contemporaries to be uncommonly old when her son was born in 1828. Four years later at age thirty-four—old enough in those days to be a grandmother—her second and final child arrived.

Abigail spent little time in Washington, while her husband largely sat on the sidelines, believing like everyone else that Old Rough and Ready was likely to live another twenty years or so. When the veteran of the classroom became mistress of the White House, she was astonished and dismayed to find that the mansion didn't include books. Always yearning for just a little more knowledge, she managed to extract $250 or $300 from Congress to start a White House library. That is often cited as her sole achievement as first lady, although Abigail raised many eyebrows on other fronts. Although such a thing was unheard of, she went, without Millard at her side, to a concert by singer Jenny Lind, billed as "the Swedish Nightingale." Soon afterward, her hair arranged in tight curls, Abigail attended a banquet in honor of Hungarian revolutionist Louis Kossuth—not accompanied by her husband, but by her daughter.

Millard, whose chief longing was for tranquillity, occupied the White House for twenty days shy of three years. During that time he stirred up a hornet's nest by supporting a patchwork "compromise" whose flaws are very visible today. During his brief tenure, one little-heralded event soon had international impact. Surprisingly, during the same thirty-five months the president managed to achieve some things that to his contemporaries seemed insignificant but which loomed large a few decades later.

Some analysts say that our thirteenth chief executive had nothing whatsoever to do with the writing of *Uncle Tom's Cabin*, or *Life Among the Lowly*. These analysts were both right and wrong. Fillmore did not go to Cincinnati and enlist Harriet Beecher Stowe to begin a dramatic and highly fictionalized account of slavery. Yet he gave the push that is essential to starting a mammoth undertaking. His signature on the bill that legalized the Fugitive Slave Act of 1850 persuaded the Connecticut-born woman to offer to the antislavery *National Era* of the capital her serialized novel.

Abigail Fillmore, whose tightly knit curls set a short-lived fashion trend. (Henry B. Hall engraving)

Uncle Tom's Cabin is widely viewed as having been a major catalyst in the reaction by which fast-hardening abolitionist views helped to make the Civil War inevitable.

Clearly, Fillmore had no idea that the yearning for peace and harmony that persuaded him to sign the quintet of Douglas bills would help launch the most deadly conflict in which Americans have ever been the combatants.

Fillmore seems to have been quite aware of what he was doing in other instances, however. In an era when Japan was about as far away from the District of Columbia as the moon is from the Earth today, he put Capt. Matthew C. Perry in command of a squadron and sent it to the Orient. A personal letter from the president to the Japanese emperor informed him:

[The brand-new state of California] annually produces sixty millions of dollars in gold, besides silver, quick-silver, precious stones, and many other valuable articles.

Perry sighted the coast of Japan a year and four days after Zach Taylor had partaken of his fatal feast. A subsequent treaty granted the United States trading rights at Hakodate and Shimoda, and the Land of the Rising Sun began to be taken into account as a wee factor in world commerce. Fillmore

Fillmore, dressed for a formal occasion.
(Nicolay & Hay, Lincoln)

wanted Japan opened for the sake of coal needed for steam-powered vessels. American tars soon secured plenty of coal, and their descendants have acquired untold numbers of automobiles, cameras, VCRs, and other high-tech items from the land that was opened to trade by Abigail's husband.

Although Jefferson has been lauded for sending Lewis and Clark off into the uncharted wilderness west of the Mississippi River, Fillmore's interest in the far away has been virtually forgotten. He sent U.S. Army expeditions into the Amazon Valley, the China Sea, and the interior of Africa. Their achievements were not spectacular—but they might have been. Abigail's husband arrived at so many treaties with Native Americans that a series of Millard Fillmore Indian Peace Medals—now rare collector's items—was issued in 1850.

With Abigail's White House library and her flouting of convention by appearing in public without a male escort taken into account, the pair from upstate New York had much greater impact than is normally realized. Had tabloids been published in the 1850s, editors of these publications would have found little if anything in the lives of Millard and Abigail that they would have deemed worthy of putting on their front pages. Yet Fillmore's contributions to the nation, low key except for the Compromise of 1850, did a lot more than most historians recognize to shape the future of the United States and the world.

14

Franklin and Jane Pierce

Y ou sure didn't have to take it."

Franklin Pierce, president-elect of the United States, flushed pink and turned away from thirteen-year-old Bennie's scowling face. He started to try to explain why he had permitted Democrats gathered in Baltimore to put his name into nomination. After a long pause he decided that anything he might say would probably antagonize the boy, so he kept quiet and tried to look absorbed in the fast-passing countryside.

Bennie had never seen his two brothers, and he made the most of being the only surviving child. Had he lived, his brother Franklin would have been looking forward to graduation from college. His death in infancy caused his parents to pin their hopes on Frank Robert, who seemed sturdy but never made it to his fifth birthday. Naturally, Franklin and Jane Pierce were overly protective of Bennie, who arrived in 1841 and then had only vague and fuzzy memories of seeing a little white casket lowered into a grave when he was two years old.

Bennie's parents debated at length about whether to risk sending him off to school in Andover, Massachusetts, but they finally decided that they owed him the best education he could get. Almost certainly echoing what he had heard his mother say, he wrote to her from school as 1852 drew to a close. He didn't want his father going off to Washington to be president of the United States. Otherwise his father would be breaking a solemn promise, for he had said he was out of politics for good and would never hold another office. "I should not like to be in Washington," the boy wrote, and added that, "I know you would not either."

Franklin had not seen Bennie's letter, but he had learned about it from his wife Jane—who had dropped to the floor in a dead faint when she heard that Franklin was a nominee for the White House. As the family boarded a train bound for Concord, New Hampshire, the president-elect assured himself that he'd find a way to make amends to Bennie and his mother.

They had spent a brief Christmas holiday together at home. Franklin was so busy answering telegrams that he saw Bennie only briefly until the three of them took a train to attend a funeral in Andover, Massachusetts. On the way there, while Franklin and Jane talked soberly about the sudden death of her uncle, Bennie didn't try to enter into the conversation. On the return trip, a lull in his parents' conversation gave him the opportunity he'd been seeking to blurt out his hurt indignation over seeing his father leave home again.

About twenty miles north of Boston, while Pierce was still pondering what he could do to make his wife and son smile, suddenly there was a loud cracking noise, and the car in which they were riding plunged off the tracks. It lurched wildly down an embankment, before stopping at the bottom with a crash. One or two passengers had managed to hold to their seats, but most of the others were lying in a tangled mass on the floor. By the time some of them had begun to regain their feet, a conductor had already reached the car, where he was trying to count heads.

Everyone who had boarded the train car was still in it. A few had escaped injury, and most of the others had suffered minor bruises and sprains. There was only one fatality—passenger Benjamin Pierce. In the aftermath of the tragedy, one of Jane's relatives penned an account of it. She wrote:

> Franklin's last act before the car left the tracks was to seize Jane with one arm and helplessly reach the other toward Bennie, who was seated too far away. When the car came to a halt, Franklin found Bennie lying on the floor and thought he was all right. He looked closer and saw that something sharp and heavy had hit him, taking off the back of his head. Jane he had kept in his arm, but I believe she saw that dreadful sight for one moment. Franklin quickly threw her shawl over the precious little form and drew her away. Jane has shed few tears; she lies on her bed with her eyes closed and moans over and over, "Why, oh why, was my little boy killed?"

So devoutly religious as to be widely ridiculed as a fanatic, Jane soon found an answer to her own question. Bennie had died, she decided, because Almighty God in his infinite wisdom did not want Franklin to be troubled with family affairs when he took over the helm of the nation. Despite that view, she never recovered from the watershed event that took place when she was forty-six years old.

Bennie's father virtually wallowed in feelings of guilt that briefly dominated his grief. Upon arriving at Washington without his wife and son, he evaded a welcoming party headed by the mayor and slipped into Willard's Hotel. He remained in his room, which was soon littered with empty whiskey bottles, until March 4. When he went through the ceremony by which he became the president of the United States, by pre-arrangement he omitted the customary oath and simply affirmed his loyalty to the Constitution.

There is no evidence that he was unfaithful to Jane during their long engagement or after their marriage. Compared to his interest in alcohol, Franklin's interest in the opposite sex was always subdued. No hint of scandal was ever attached to Jane, although her morbid grief over Bennie led her to spend many of her White House months scribbling penciled letters to him. Desperate to get a message from the boy she knew was in heaven, his

mother consulted the most noted mediums of the day. At her request, the Fox sisters held the first recorded White House seance—but they adamantly refused to reveal what Bennie had transmitted to his mother through them.

ACCORDING TO HARRY S TRUMAN and numerous other analysts, Franklin was the most handsome of the presidents. His dark curly hair, very thick until late in life, may have been the physical feature that first attracted the attention of Jane Appleton, youngest daughter of a Congregational minister. Barely a year junior to the nineteen-year-old, would-be attorney,

Bennie, age nine, with his adoring mother.

she parted her own chestnut hair in the middle and wore two corkscrew curls on each side of her head.

Like several other early White House couples, Franklin and Jane were considered by mutual acquaintances to be an unlikely pair. She was so fiercely devout that some commentators called her "a religious neurotic," so zealous that she cared little for the company of others. From adolescence she was described as being sickly, a condition that seems to have pre-disposed her to become a victim of then-prevalent tuberculosis.

Franklin was just under six feet in height, and he was hale, hearty, and convivial. He made friends quickly, and some of these early bonds—such as those with Nathaniel Hawthorne and Henry Wadsworth Longfellow—lasted for decades. Although his father fought in the American Revolution as a general before becoming governor of New Hampshire, he was in real life a dirt farmer with few social graces. Jane's father was the second president of Bowdoin College in Maine, and her mother had been a Means. That meant she belonged to one of the wealthiest and most aristocratic families of New Hampshire.

No relative from either side of the married couple's families had a clear recollection either of when they met or how they became attracted to one another. An Amherst member of the Means family quipped that since no one else seemed strongly attracted to either of them, the pair must have simply drifted together. They seem to have entered into an engagement agreement of sorts about the time he launched his career as an attorney. If that was the case, they waited six years to marry and by that time knew that if they were to have children they must come along soon. Only Bennie, born when his mother was thirty-seven, lived past early childhood.

Franklin's wife was never thrilled by his winning one high office after another. Successively a member of the state legislature, the House of Representatives, and the U.S. Senate, he resigned from Congress in 1842 at Jane's insistence. He vowed he would never again run for office. When James K. Polk urged him to join his cabinet as attorney general, he turned the office down in order to stay in Hillsborough, New Hampshire, and tend to his law practice. One of his clerks there happened to be Albert Baker, brother of the Mary Baker Eddy who led the movement that produced the Church of Christ, Scientist.

Even though Democratic party leaders didn't believe he had a chance for the 1852 nomination, they persuaded him to let them enter his name "in the event of a deadlock." After forty-six ballots the convention seemed to be stalled, so the name of the New Englander, a professed friend of the South, was tossed into the fray. Just three ballots later, delegates turned to the man noted as a conciliator and chose to pit him against the Whig candidate.

Almost immediately, Pierce confided to intimates that he regretted getting into "the mud bath" that was the campaign of 1852. Whigs properly touted their candidate, Winfield Scott, as the man chiefly responsible for a quick and easy victory in the Mexican War. They derided his Democratic opponent as a political general whose most notable feat had been to lead his troops on foot after falling from his horse. Derided as "Handsome Frank," he was charged with having fathered illegitimate children by several women. There was no substance to this accusation, but cartoons that

Pierce, highly idealized and depicted as a major hero of the Mexican War.

showed him fondling whiskey bottles publicized his greatest weaknesses.

American voters, perennially enamored with war heroes, turned down the victor over Mexicans in favor of a man who had virtually no impact on the Mexican War. His known eagerness to conciliate the South entered into the upset victory by the second dark-horse nominee for the presidency. His political foes neglected to capitalize on his young age, even knowing that he would become the youngest president ever if he managed to defeat Scott. To no one's great surprise, Jane Pierce was not with her husband when he took over the mansion on Pennsylvania Avenue.

As White House hostess, Jane never even attempted to cut the mustard. She demanded that each stateroom should display mourning bunting indefinitely. Furthermore, she held no dinners or balls, and she put an end to Saturday night concerts by the U.S. Marine Band. Loud music, she explained, made it impossible for her to prepare suitably for Sunday worship—the only public function in which she participated for many months.

One of her aunts took charge of presiding over White House social events until Jane became extremely fond of the wife of her husband's secretary of war, Jefferson Davis. Widely regarded as one of the most competent men who ever held that office, Davis cheerfully agreed for his Varina to substitute for the woman who by then was widely derided as "the Shadow in the White House."

Although international activity was at a high level during the Pierce administration, only one endeavor brought a positive result. A final-draft treaty with Japan, considered by Washington to be highly advantageous, was drawn up and ratified. Attempts to purchase Alaska from Russia and to annex Hawaii failed. Far worse, Pierce yielded to southern pressure, reversed positions reached earlier, and went about trying to annex Cuba.

Franklin fared little better in dealing with major domestic issues. Only the purchase from Mexico of about forty-five thousand square miles that were subsequently assigned to Arizona and New Mexico met with general approval. Even then, because the treaty was negotiated by U.S. Minister to Mexico James Gadsden, the move was credited to him rather than to the chief executive who had authorized the purchase.

More than eager to placate expansionists in the Cotton Belt, Franklin made the worst mistake of his presidency. Against his better judgment, he yielded to pressure and agreed to support measures designed to render the Missouri Compromise null and void. This change of stance led to the creation of a major legislative bill designed to deal with problems related to vast expanses of land in the West. Under terms of the Kansas-Nebraska Bill, which Pierce signed, both regions became territories, and their citizens were authorized to settle the slavery question at the ballot box themselves.

Nebraska's climate was not conducive to the spread of slavery into that region, but Kansas was mistakenly considered to be suitable for the cotton-slavery complex. As a result, the territory became a battleground between abolitionists and pro-slavery forces. Both groups sent armed and determined settlers into Kansas, and both established a skeleton government—one at Lecompton and the other at Topeka. Soon "Bleeding Kansas" became a literal description of the war-torn territory, and Pierce was subsequently widely blamed for brutal murders and wholesale arson.

Tempers flared in Congress, and debate raged in both houses over the decision made by Franklin and its consequences. Massachusetts senator Charles Sumner delivered a blistering speech in which he castigated a pro-slavery colleague and earned the hearty congratulations of fellow abolitionists. Shortly afterward, however, Representative Preston Brooks of South Carolina came on the Senate floor and, literally, clubbed Sumner into unconsciousness. Brooks was forced to give up his seat, but voters of the Palmetto State presented him with a gold-headed cane and delightedly sent him back to Congress.

As a result of these and other developments stemming from the New Englander's genuine yearning for conciliation, his administration is remembered chiefly for civil violence and increasing sectional tension. He did not seek and was not given renomination, but he left the capital at the end of his term with "a strange mixture of profound relief and lasting bitterness."

His successor, James Buchanan, magnanimously provided the USS *Powhatan* as a cruise ship, so Franklin and Jane set out on a vacation voyage that stretched into nearly three years. Back home in New England, the ex-president became a bitter critic of Abraham Lincoln and the Civil War that was launched in order to bring seceded states by force of arms back into the Union. Jane, who had never been strong, died of tuberculosis during the year in which Bennie would have celebrated his twentieth birthday.

Bennie's father somehow clung to life until 1869, despite irreparable damage done to his body by years of heavy drinking. Doctors agreed that an inflammation of the stomach plus a serious case of dropsy did him in. A handful of relatives and friends briefly mourned his passing, but the nation did not.

Today the man who went to the White House after promising his wife that he wouldn't be a candidate is close to the top of the list of nearly forgotten chief executives. It's doubtful that Franklin ever realized that his longing for conciliation persuaded him to make decisions that created civil violence on an unparalleled scale. American fury in Bleeding Kansas reached a level not equaled until the Vietnam era.

15

Old Buck and Rufus

Old Buck and his "better half," according to Congressman Aaron V. Brown, "might be lookin' for a divorce." Sarah Polk, the former president's widow, didn't need any explanation. Like everyone else who had spent years in the capital, she knew that hostesses routinely invited W. Rufus King of Alabama and James Buchanan of Pennsylvania as a couple.

Decades before persons whose sexual preferences run to members of their own sex came to be called "gay," at least one newspaper account described Old Buck and Rufus as "a gay [that is, openly happy] and scintillating pair." Although the two national leaders were all but inseparable for a period of about fifteen years, no openly snide comments about them entered public record. When the fifth decade of the nineteenth century was winding down, no one—absolutely no one—put into print any reference to homosexuality.

People talked about it, of course, in the safety of all-male or all-female groups. Yet in an era that can be viewed only through a high-powered mental telescope, a man or woman of breeding wouldn't have thought of uttering such a word as "homosexual" in the presence of a member of the opposite sex. Andrew Jackson, however, termed the senator from Alabama a "Miss Nancy." Chang and Eng Bunker, the original Siamese twins, had catapulted to world fame in 1829. At least as early as 1836 Buchanan had unabashedly referred to himself and King as "the Siamese twins" in his personal correspondence.

It apparently didn't bother Buchanan at all that Rufus was often identified as "Old Buck's old wife." This usage stemmed from the fact that the Alabama senator was the senior member of the pair by five years. Congressman Brown's letter to James K. Polk's widow, Sarah, didn't surface until fairly recent times. Marked "Confidential," it warned against angering "Col. K[ing]," but included a reference to "Mrs. B[uchanan]." Writing during the heat of the 1844 presidential campaign, the congressman knew that James Buchanan badly wanted the office. He didn't dream, however, that in just a dozen years "K[ing]'s husband" would become our nation's only bachelor president.

Rufus never had the special privilege of presiding over White House balls and banquets. Old Buck turned these matters over to his beautiful young niece, who became the first woman to be referred to in print as first lady. As a tribute to her, the treasury department named its only steam-powered revenue cutter the *Harriet Lane*.

BORN IN NORTH CAROLINA, William Rufus DeVane King went to the House of Representatives from the Tar Heel State. After five years he resigned in order to go to Italy and Russia as secretary to the legations there. After he returned to the United States, he settled in Alabama and became one of the new state's first two senators. During thirty years in the Senate he became its president when Fillmore went to the White House. Hence, he presided over much of the debate about the Fugitive Slave Law, whose expansion enraged abolitionists everywhere.

In 1852 Rufus vigorously supported Buchanan for the presidency. Probably as a result of a gesture of conciliation, King became the vice-presidential nominee when Franklin Pierce snared the brass ring. By the time voters went to the polls, doctors had informed Rufus that he was a victim of tuberculosis and might have only a short time to live.

Illness took King to Cuba in search of invigorating air that would restore him to health, but he became steadily worse instead of better. An Act of Congress framed and passed on his behalf gave him permission to stay on the island during inaugural ceremonies. As a result, he became the only nationally elected official to take his oath of office on foreign soil. He managed to return to Alabama, but he was too weak to assume his duties and died within a month. No provision having been made for selection of a successor, the nation was without a vice president for forty-seven months.

Again seeking the nomination and the White House in 1856, Buchanan led the pack on the first ballot and scored victory on the seventeenth. Unhappy backers of Lewis Cass and Stephen A. Douglas swapped among themselves—but did not put into print—misgivings about "a widower taking over the helm of the nation." Some of them publicly charged that the bachelor nominee "never showed the slightest interest in even the most enticing of females."

That accusation was false; in a period when he was termed a young buck instead of Old Buck, the man from Pennsylvania was formally engaged to Anne Coleman of Lancaster. Five years his junior, the young woman was described as being lovely but quite shy. Mutual acquaintances speculated that James was far more interested in her father's fortune than in Anne.

Harriet Lane, mistress of the White House. (J. C. Buttre engraving)

They quarreled before setting a wedding date, and Anne changed her mind. She informed her relatives that she had made a grievous mistake, so she could not go through with the wedding. After that confession she hurried to Philadelphia for a visit and soon died under circumstances that virtually prove she took her own life. A modern conjecture that she may have experienced a fatal "hysterical fit" is difficult to accept. Since James quickly destroyed all correspondence, conjecture has to substitute for certainty concerning life-shaping events that took place.

In the *Overland Monthly*, a writer characterized Anne as having been "somewhat domineering" and confided to readers that the engagement was broken off as a result of "a foolish misunderstanding" that was of no consequence. Viewed from the perspective of distance, it's hard to avoid wondering whether Anne discovered the sexual proclivities of her betrothed. If she did, that may have led her to dismiss him and go far from home in order to end her life in despair. If this explanation of the sudden death of an apparently healthy woman of twenty-three is accepted, it suggests that today's political leaders are more like those of yesterday than we had ever thought. Whatever happened in Lancaster, Buchanan was deeply involved in the death of a young woman. Unlike Ted Kennedy's 1969 role in the death of a young woman at Chappaquiddick, the scandal that was not publicized in 1819 did not nail the door of the White House shut just as Buchanan began hoping to enter it.

In conversation and in some letters, William Rufus DeVane King was mocked as "Mrs. Buchanan." (Dictionary of American Portraits)

As a candidate for the presidency in 1856, Old Buck received slam-bang blows from rivals concerning his pro-southern stance but not about the long-ago suicide of his fiancée. Surviving campaign literature is conspicuously silent in this respect. Rallies held by members of rival political parties often featured a chant: Who - ever - heard - in - all - his -life - of - a - presi - dent - without - a *wife?*" Some Republicans favored a positive rather than a negative approach; these persons chanted: "Free Speech - Free Press - Free Soil - Free Men - FREMONT!"

At least in print, no one seems to have speculated that Buchanan's long and intimate association with a male from Alabama may have helped to account for the openly pro-southern views of a Pennsylvania native. Since he constantly boasted about his ceaseless efforts to conciliate the South, it was natural for the convention to choose John C. Breckinridge of Kentucky as his running mate.

At age thirty-six the youngest of vice presidents up to that time, Breckinridge opposed the extension of slavery into the territories. The handsome young leader from the Bluegrass State served his full term, then became an outspoken leader in Kentucky's announced goal of remaining neutral in the North-South quarrel. He accepted a Confederate commission early in the Lincoln administration, and as a result became the only former vice president to be expelled from the U.S. Senate. Fellow lawmakers from New England in particular and the North in general branded him a traitor. He was never formally charged and put on trial, but everyone concerned knew that conviction as a traitor carried an automatic death sentence.

Old Buck's use of a candle in reading inspired this cartoon showing him as a candle that gave out very little light.

BUCHANAN WAS CLOSE TO the tail end of a long string of executives who, unlike William Henry Harrison, had actually been born in log cabins. James did not grow up in poverty, however; he went to Old Stone Academy in Mercersburg in preparation for Dickinson College in Carlisle. Having barely completed his formal education and not yet qualified for admission to the bar, for a time he served as a soldier in the War of 1812. He was probably within sight of Fort Henry when "the rocket's red glare" helped to inspire Francis Scott Key to write "The Star-Spangled Banner."

After 1812 all of Buchanan's wars were political. Some of them were as fierce if not as deadly as the Mexican War in which he did not participate. When he threw his hat into the ring in a race for a seat in the House of Representatives, some opponents jeered that "So odd-looking a fellow will never persuade voters." They were wrong; he won the race and spent a decade as a Congressman.

Opponents and foes were right about the appearance of Old Buck, though. Even the most flattering of his portraits reveals that the six-footer practically always cocked his head to the left. Old Buck's left eye was far-sighted, while his right eye was nearsighted. In conversation, he habitually closed his left eye and rotated his head a bit in order to see at close hand with his nearsighted eye. Many a male or female would have treated Buchanan's visual anomaly as a handicap serious enough to bar a try for public office. But he not only learned to cope with it; he was an omnivorous reader who put a candle in front of a book in order to better focus his mismatched eyes.

John C. Fremont, the first Republican nominee for the presidency, was a formidable opponent in 1856. Yet Fremont's father-in-law, noted senator Thomas Hart Benton, went on public record as backing Buck. A major factor contributing to his victory was lack of public knowledge about his stance on the Kansas-Nebraska issue. Fortunately for him, Buchanan had seldom made a public statement concerning it. Hence, his views had not alienated a large bloc of voters. Later it was found that he favored territorial status for both, plus "self-determination"—or choice by voters involved. His split position concerning slavery, made public at least as early as 1826 and never significantly modified, was well known. Early in his Washington career, he said:

> I believe [slavery] to be a great moral and political evil. I thank God that my lot in life has been cast in a State where it is not permitted. But while I hold to this view, I realize that this evil cannot now be escaped without introducing infinitely greater evils. There are portions of the Union in which slaves will become masters if they are emancipated.

Pulled out and stressed during the campaign of 1856, this statement led Thaddeus Stevens of his own state to describe the Democrat's position as "a bloated mass of political putridity." Montgomery Blair of Missouri, destined to become an advisor to Abraham Lincoln, charged that Buchanan's views made sectional collision inevitable.

Yet Ulysses S. Grant, seldom greatly interested in politics, voted for Buchanan because he was seen as more likely to prevent or postpone secession than his opponents. He may have been influenced by knowledge that, although Buchanan favored leaving slavery alone where it existed, he was adamantly opposed to disruption of the Union.

One after another, a series of smashing blows demonstrated the frailty of the human breakwater Buchanan tried to be. With both the North and

President James Buchanan, rarely seen without having his head cocked to the left. (Library of Congress)

the South "surging with all their force against him," he lost support in both sections and wisely decided not to run for a second term.

The 1857 Dred Scott decision of the U.S. Supreme Court delighted the South but permanently alienated much of the North. Dred Scott and John Brown, executed after leading a raid on Harper's Ferry, Virginia, were monumentally significant in bringing long-simmering North-South antagonism to a boil. Although the Panic of 1857 turned many voters against the man in the White House, its long-range impact upon the nation was insignificant by comparison with events in which a slave and a zealous abolitionist were central figures.

Many seasoned observers predicted that the election of a Republican president—regardless of who he might be—would trigger the secession of South Carolina and perhaps of other Cotton Belt states. Lincoln won less than 40 percent of the popular votes cast as Old Buck's term of office neared its close. Yet it was generally and correctly predicted that he would gain a smashing victory in the electoral college.

That was all South Carolina needed to act on its long-suppressed yearning for separation from the Union. An ordinance of secession received enthusiastic support, and leaders of the Palmetto State immediately began seizing federal installations. Under the constitution of the independent Republic of South Carolina—which made plans to send emissaries to Britain and Europe—U.S. fortresses, armories, and custom houses were viewed as situated on foreign soil. Several were seized, and state leaders demanded that the rest be sold to South Carolina under terms that were to be negotiated.

Old Buck was put in an agonizing position when Maj. Robert Anderson and his men took over formerly unoccupied Fort Sumter at Charleston. If he remained true to his long-standing alliance with the South as symbolized by Rufus King, he would have to be a spectator to a splintering of the Union. If he took action to force South Carolina back into the Union, he would be seen in the South as a weakling and a traitor to ideals he had expressed for decades.

In this dilemma, the man from Pennsylvania decided to re-supply Fort Sumter and retain it as a Union installation but to do nothing else. Having pondered the Constitution plus congressional actions that he considered pertinent, he concluded that he could do no more—and no less. As a result, he dispatched to Charleston a relief expedition whose purpose was to provide the Sumter garrison with necessities plus about two hundred more fighting men.

Cadets at Charleston's military academy, the Citadel, fired the first shots by which the relief ship *Star of the West* was forced to turn back without reaching its objectives. Northern warmongers screamed for retaliation, but the president did nothing. Soon castigated by his successor in office as having helplessly wrung his hands, he became widely viewed as too chicken-hearted to deal with the secession crisis.

Much evidence supports the conclusion that he honestly believed it was beyond the power of the chief executive to initiate a military move. He seems firmly to have felt that the matter should be settled by Congress and the courts rather than on fields of battle.

As a result of his hands-off policy during the last few weeks of his administration, our only bachelor president is ranked by historians as close to the bottom. In 1861 he simply retired to his sixteen-room brick mansion called Wheatland and devoted much of his time and energy to criticism of Lincoln and the war that was waged for preservation of the Union.

16

Abraham and Mary Todd Lincoln

Springfield, March 27, 1842
Dear Speed:
On that other subject [marriage], to me of the most intense interest, whether in joy or in sorrow, I never had the power to withhold my sympathy from you. I can not be told, how it now thrills me with joy, to hear you say [in your recent letter] you are *"far happier than you ever expected to be."* That much I know is enough. I know you too well to suppose your expectations were not, at least sometimes, extravagant; and if the reality exceeds them all, I say, enough dear Lord, I am not going beyond the truth, when I tell you, that the short space it took me to read your last letter, gave me more pleasure, than the sum total of all I have enjoyed since that fatal first of Jany. '41.
As ever LINCOLN

Most of the second paragraph of a long letter, quoted verbatim above, is at the heart of a controversy that is more than a century old. In his next sentence, the Springfield attorney confided to Joshua F. Speed, "that there is *one* still unhappy whom I have contributed to make so."

Traditional Lincoln scholarship has interpreted this letter to mean that the man born in Kentucky broke off his engagement with Kentucky native Mary Ann Todd on January 1, 1841. There is convincing evidence that the two had been engaged to be married prior to that time and that Lincoln subsequently broke the engagement. No existing document, however, provides sure clues that this particular traumatic event in the life of a deeply troubled man subject to bouts of severe depression actually took place on the date indicated. So, just exactly what significant event or events made January 1, 1841, one of the most memorable days in the life of the unmarried attorney who was then thirty-three years old?

That was the day on which Kentucky native Speed shook the dust of Springfield off his feet and returned to his native state. In doing so, he gave up a partnership in a general store in order to become a farmer—a vocation that had long interested him. His departure from the new capital of Illinois meant that Lincoln's bedmate of more than forty-four months had gone so far away that their long and intimate relationship could never be resumed. It was Speed's departure—not an interruption in the off-again-on-again relationship of Lincoln and Mary Ann Todd—that made January 1, 1841, a day that the attorney dubbed "fatal."

Pulitzer Prize winner James M. McPherson, consulted about this specific matter, concurs in the unproved and unprovable assumption that Lincoln was emotionally devastated over the loss of his bedmate rather than a rupture with his betrothed (Mary Todd). Other matters about which McPherson has expressed no opinion give pause for thought concerning the sexual orientation of our sixteenth president.

THE TWO MEN HAD met on April 15, 1837, when Lincoln arrived from New Salem and let it be known that he was seeking lodging. Speed offered a place in his bed in the loft over his store, and it was quickly accepted. In itself that was not unusual on the frontier at the time. Beds were scarce, so letters and diaries sometimes speak of three or four males sharing a bed for a night. Such an arrangement was usually adopted as an emergency measure for a short period, however.

Speed, who has been characterized as the only intimate friend Lincoln ever had, may be presumed to have spontaneously offered a haven to a stranger. Had they remained bedmates for a week or a month, the matter would be unimportant and incidental. They slept together, however, until Speed's departure for Kentucky on "the fatal first" dissolved their physical bonds.

This decidedly unusual relationship is by no means all that is known about the pair of unmarried males of whom Lincoln was older by five years. Both men were interested in marriage—at least as an abstract idea—but both were inordinately and abnormally fearful of entering into such a bond with a woman. This aspect of their mutual thought emerges over and over in Lincoln's letters that followed his former bedmate to Kentucky.

An appraisal of a stray mare, dated December 16, 1830, is one of the earliest documents from the hand of the man revered today worldwide as the Great Emancipator. It runs to eight printed lines and is signed by A Lincoln and John W. Reed. That early signature of the future attorney seems already to have become standard; nearly all later documents and letters from his hand bear same signature with a period usually added to form "A. Lincoln." Glaring exceptions to this general pattern occur, however, in the case of letters directed to Speed. At least seven of them bear the signature "Lincoln."

Joshua Speed and his wife after the marriage over which both he and Lincoln agonized for weeks. (Nicolay & Hay, Lincoln)

Although striking, this departure from a custom established as early as 1830 proves nothing. Letters of the attorney to the farmer-in-the-making that end "Yours forever" are highly suggestive, however. That formula hints that the letter to which it was appended might easily be mistaken for a missive to a sweetheart of the opposite sex.

The Lincoln-Speed correspondence didn't start in the wake of their separation; during an interval of more than six months they did not communicate. Once they began exchanging letters, Lincoln began chomping at the bit to be with Speed again. Hence, he spent about six weeks beginning in early August on Farmington—the Jefferson County, Kentucky, plantation of his former bedmate.

This out-of-the-ordinary relationship between the two male natives of Kentucky is enough to raise questions during an investigation into *Love, Lust, and Longing in the White House*. Other factors, typically ignored by biographers of the man whose Good Friday martyrdom led clergymen of the North to place him at the right hand of Jesus Christ on Easter, strengthen the unprovable guess that our sixteenth president might have been bisexual.

IN AUGUST 1860 A native of New York arrived at Lincoln's Springfield office with plans to read law. Barely twenty-three years old, Elmer Ellsworth cut a dashing figure—especially when wearing his uniform as a major in the Illinois National Guard. According to some accounts, the young would-be attorney spent the fall of 1860 working in Lincoln's campaign for the White House. If that is correct, he was not in Springfield during this period. Lincoln gave no interviews, delivered no speeches, and did not wage a campaign in his own behalf. Elmer was definitely in the Illinois capital in February 1861, for he was among the party who accompanied the president-elect to Washington for his inauguration.

Lincoln became the chief executive of the United States on March 4, 1861. Less than twenty-four hours later he penned a letter, addressed to the secretary of war, that may be telltale in character:

> If the public service admits of a change, without injury, in the office of chief clerk of the War Department, I shall be pleased if my friend, E. Elmer Ellsworth, who presents you this, shall be appointed. Of course, if you see good reason to the contrary, this is not intended to be arbitrary.
> Yours truly, A. LINCOLN

The context suggests that this memorandum from the brand-new president was hand-delivered by the man he wished to place in a key position.

Nothing came of the proposal to shift the chief clerk of the War Department into a new spot in order to put a twenty-three-year-old with no background of experience behind his desk. Consequently, another letter addressed to the same cabinet member was drafted six weeks later. In it, the veteran attorney, now the head of the nation, requested that Lieutenant Ellsworth be detailed for special duty "as Adjutant and Inspector General of Militia for the United States."

In order to act upon his request, Lincoln realized it would be necessary to create a new and separate militia bureau—of which Ellsworth would be chief. No longer indicating that his proposal was "not intended to be arbitrary," the president wrote: "You will please assign him [Ellsworth] suitable office rooms, furniture &c. and provide him with a clerk and messenger, and furnish him with such facilities in the way of printing, stationery, access to public records, &c. as he may desire for the successful prosecution of his duties." Creation of this new post and assignment of Ellsworth to it, wrote the chief executive, would entitle the New Yorker to receive "pay equal to that of a Major of Cavalry"—a rank for which West Point graduates waited for decades.

There is no certainty that this thinly veiled order was ever seen by Simon Cameron. The president seems to have submitted it to his attorney general for approval. He received an unfavorable opinion from Edward Bates concerning legality of his urge to create a new post of national importance and to put Ellsworth into it. Hence, the proposal was probably withdrawn without going to the War Department.

At a bare minimum, this series of post-inaugural events strongly suggests that the fifty-two-year-old president took inordinate interest in a twenty-three-year-old youth whom he met for the first time only a few months earlier. That didn't end the matter, however. When Ellsworth did not get the cushy job Lincoln planned to create for him, he took command of a company of colorful Fire Zouaves from his native state. As their head, he led the first federal invasion of Confederate soil and was killed at Alexandria, Virginia, two months after the attorney general said no to the president's plan to put him in charge of the seventy-five thousand militia he intended soon to raise.

Elmer Ellsworth was young and ambitious. (J. C. Buttre engraving)

The body of the youth who had abandoned the reading of law a few months earlier was brought to the Executive Mansion, where it lay in state. The mansion was draped in black in order to let the capital and the nation know how deeply the president—described as having shed copious tears—grieved over a youngster of whom he was inordinately fond.

Extensive literature concerning the Ellsworth case no more provides proof beyond question than do the long and emotional letters sent from Springfield to Joshua Speed in Kentucky. Ellsworth's sudden death, however, did not end the future Great Emancipator's interest in young males. John G. Nicolay, with whom Lincoln became acquainted when he was about forty-eight years old and Nicolay twenty-five, became his private secretary. At the same time John G. Hay was made Nicolay's chief assistant. Lincoln was about forty-nine years old and Hay was about twenty-four years old when they became acquainted.

None of these male-male relationships prove anything. Yet collectively, they suggest an explanation for the fact that an attorney well past the usual age of marriage did not pursue Mary Ann Todd or any other female with ardor. It is possible—barely possible—that although he did not

follow in the footsteps of James
Buchanan and take a male partner who was derided as his wife,
our sixteenth president apparently was as interested in males
as he was in females.

Thomas Huxley observed
long ago that "It is the customary
fate of new truths to begin as
heresies." To multitudes of persons who joined in denouncing
the unbridled lust of Bill Clinton, it may seem heretical to suggest that Abraham Lincoln
hankered in some fashion for
men. Proof of such longing on
the part of Old Buck's successor
in office is not likely to be found.
Proof that he never cast an
amorous eye upon another male

*Abraham Lincoln in 1857. (Alschuler
ambrotype, Nicolay & Hay, Lincoln)*

is equally elusive, however. Each male or female who is genuinely interested
in the broad topic explored in this volume must come to his or her own conclusion.

This much is certain: Mary Ann Todd came to Springfield in order to
live with her sister and brother-in-law because she couldn't get along with
her stepmother. In the Illinois capital she soon met attorney Lincoln, who
was nine years her senior. Although he was a spell-binding orator, he was
self-educated and never learned to spell. He spoke in a high-pitched nasal
whine that irritated many persons who heard it. She had the cultured voice
of a genuine southern belle who spent years in an academy where students
were permitted to converse only in the French language outside class.

Whatever else may be said about the woman generally regarded as
having had an ungovernable temper plus ambition that wouldn't quit,
Mary Ann Todd was truly beautiful. His most ardent admirers have never
claimed that Lincoln was handsome. Mary Ann was a walking fashion
plate; Abe's feet and arms protruded from his clothing in such fashion that
persons who saw him for the first time were prone to dismiss him as a country bumpkin who had outgrown his coats and pants. Mary Ann was an
accomplished ballroom dancer who dearly loved to show off her skill. Abe
couldn't dance a lick. Unwilling to venture onto the dance floor, he had to

watch other men cavort with the lovely young woman from Lexington, Kentucky.

No one knows what brought such an unlikely pair together. Conjecture on this matter can no more be proved beyond doubt than can the notion that Mary Ann's off-and-on friend was reluctant to fully commit himself to any female. Numerous biographers assert that she was inordinately ambitious and was determined to become the wife of a future president. This analysis of their friendship that ended in marriage represents pure speculation based upon second guesses rendered in hindsight.

Mary Todd Lincoln. (Godey's Ladies' Book)

They went to the altar in November 1842, and their first child was born three days shy of nine months later. Robert Todd Lincoln's birth so close in conjunction to the nine-month pregnancy period proves little about his father's sexual orientation. Still, a person inclined to ponder about the latter might wonder whether the bridegroom, in being late in going to the altar, deliberately proved his virility in a hurry.

William H. Herndon, Lincoln's long-time law partner, was convinced that the bride who dropped "Ann" from her name upon marriage but insisted upon putting "Todd" into it was a household tyrant. If Herndon is to be believed—and some of his evidence cannot be lightly dismissed—Abe bit off a lot more than he could chew when he said, "I do." Despite the fact that Mary Todd Lincoln spent money her husband did not have on shoes and clothing she did not need, there is no concrete evidence that she really ruled the roost.

There is no convincing evidence proving that either had premarital romances of any consequence. They came together because of factors and forces that are beyond analysis; they remained together through thick and thin.

17

Andrew and Eliza Johnson

A ndrew, age eighteen, showed no visible sign of being a wee bit nervous. Sixteen-year-old Eliza had wiped away a tear but was now smiling radiantly. They held hands and did not relax their grip of one another until after they had exchanged vows in the front room of Sarah McCardle's house. Passing up the traditional kiss in front of kinfolk, the newlyweds walked on air through tiny Greeneville, Tennessee, to the unpainted shanty that Andrew had rented a few days earlier. It was newly adorned with a crude sign that read: "A. JOHNSON TAILOR."

They hadn't even mentioned the word *honeymoon* while they made last-minute plans. To both of them, the crude little shack with a sign over the door was so grand looking that they had no desire to go to Chuckey or even to Bull's Gap. Eliza couldn't keep her eyes off Andrew's sign as they pushed open the door before passing through the tailor shop and into the room that was to be their living quarters. To both of the newlyweds, their two-room place was about as close to heaven as one could get in 1827.

Andrew—who hated being called Andy, even by his best customers—had everything ready so he could begin work on an elegant black suit the next morning. Eliza had taken special care to hone his shears until they were razor-sharp; that was her wedding present to him. Andrew had shyly presented her with a pair of pillows just right for their tumble-down double bed with two broken slats. "They've got feathers inside them—the real thing," he had confided proudly.

Before sundown on the first day of their married life, the tailor who looked too young to have nearly five years of experience behind him called loudly: "I'm quittin'! Ready or not, here I come!"

"Take your hands off me this very minute," Eliza protested as he gave her a hug. "You know perfectly well we've got to have a lesson before you dig into some of the ham that Ma gave us." Pulling a slate and a piece of chalk from off their bed, she challenged: "What does this mean?" as she put one letter at a time on the slate until it read: "C L O T H."

"Don't rightly know," he grunted. "Don't have to tell you that, either. You know I never spent a single day in a blab school. But I bet I'll know what it means, and maybe another word or two, by suppertime tomorrow."

Smiling while trying to pretend to frown, the bride shook her head vigorously. "Not tomorrow, Andrew, today—right now!"

THE FORMER ELIZA MCCARDLE had come to Greeneville from Leesburg as a small child. Her mother, a shoemaker's widow, figured she stood a good chance in a place as big as Greeneville to sell the shawls and quilts she had made after being afraid she'd starve to death in Leesburg.

Sarah McCardle had guessed right; she hardly ever had completed more than three or four finished pieces before somebody would come along in a buying mood. Some of her customers were headed for Knoxville, thinking they'd find work in a big city. Others planned to stay in Greeneville but wanted to dress up their houses or themselves with something fancy from the newly arrived whiz with knitting needles. She made enough pieces to keep plenty of corn meal on hand, and neighbors didn't have to be asked to come by at hog-killin' time. They just showed up, opened the gate to the hog pen, and asked whether she thought one of 'em would carry her through the winter or had they better kill and dress two for her?

Eliza, who first learned to sew when she was four years old, was doing fancy embroidery by the time she was ten. Somehow her tattin' never turned out to suit her mother, though, so she'd sit in front of the fire on winter nights knitting and repeating to herself what she had learned at the Rhea Academy that day. Had her manual dexterity been tested, she would have scored high. On top of that, she was as bright as she was pert.

Neighbors said they thought she was coming home from the academy when a creaky old one-horse cart pulled into town piled high with belongings of the two males and one female who walked beside it. Eliza was sure she hadn't told her friends that there was no tailor in town, so Greeneville residents must have found out from somebody else. Anyway, the Johnson family from North Carolina decided to stay awhile. Andrew, who had run off before finishing his term as a tailor's apprentice, was the wage earner for his mother and ne'er-do-well stepfather, Turner Dougherty.

Andrew got a good look at Eliza even before he'd been in Greeneville forty-eight hours, and he liked what he saw. She hadn't had a sweetheart before, and she soon fell for the new fellow in town. They waited only a few months to say their vows, not dreaming that the bride would go into record books as marrying younger than any other first lady of the United States.

Eliza Johnson, who called herself "only a plain country woman," looked the part.

Eliza didn't mind cooking on their little wood stove. This was something she had done all her life, and she knew how to bake corn bread that was lip-smacking good. There wasn't much to do in the way of keeping house, at least not in a room of about 150 square feet. She continued doing piece work for her mother to sell, but that still left her plenty of time every day to decide what to teach her husband about reading and writing when he put his shears and needles aside.

Andrew was hungry to learn. He knew he didn't have a chance to get ahead in life unless he could read and write. An eager student and a willing teacher made them an ideal pair for fast learning. They hadn't been at it much more than a couple of years when he pulled a yellowed piece of newspaper out of the Bible his mother had given him as a wedding present. Waving the paper at Eliza, Andrew sometimes stumbled, but he managed to read to her a notice that had run in the *Raleigh Gazette* four or five years earlier:

TEN DOLLARS REWARD
Ran away from the subscriber on the night of the 15th instant two apprentice boys, legally bound, named WILLIAM and ANDREW JOHNSON. I will pay the above reward to any person who will deliver said apprentices to me in Raleigh, or I will give the above Reward for Andrew Johnson alone. JAMES J. SELBY, *Tailor*.

Eliza got a good laugh when her student showed off how much he had learned, even though she had heard about the ad a long time ago.

Andrew's mother, who had been a widow for eight or nine years, had become destitute and desperate. Her earnings as a spinner and weaver sometimes weren't enough to keep even coarse food on the table. Believing that she had no other choice, she did what Millard Fillmore's folks had done earlier. She sold the services of her two boys to a tailor for whom they worked in return for something to eat and a place to sleep.

By the time he had learned how to cut and sew garments, Andrew wanted to strike out on his own. So he persuaded his brother to go with him and they lit out for Carthage, nearly eighty miles away from Raleigh. It wasn't a good move. Hardly anybody in Carthage would trust a good piece of cloth to a sixteen-year-old who had just arrived in town claiming to be an expert tailor. Andrew soon drifted southward and landed in Laurens, South Carolina, where his luck was a lot better. When he had squirreled away a few dollars the boy heard that Selby had gone out of business, so he returned to Raleigh.

The news he had heard was correct: Selby's tailor shop had been closed. That didn't cancel the apprenticeship arrangement, though, and Selby was mean enough to go to court and try to have Andrew locked up. Learning that he was in danger, the youngster persuaded his folks to put what little they owned on a cart and head west. They traveled very slowly, with no destination in mind, and they decided to give Greeneville a try when they found it had no tailor shop. Had a tailor been doing a thriving business there, they would have pushed on and Andrew would never have met a good-looking girl who was also a patient teacher.

Nothing is known about their teenage romance except that they said their vows before Mordecai Lincoln in the home of the bride's mother, who later claimed to be kin to the sixteenth president of the United States. Within fifteen years Andrew and Eliza had three sons and two daughters, but nothing else is known about their early married life. Not long after he and Eliza celebrated their thirtieth wedding anniversary, he was elected to the U.S. Senate by the state legislature. Almost incredulous when he received word that he would soon sit in the most august body of lawmakers in the nation, he exulted, "I have reached the summit of my ambition!"

Although Andrew and Eliza were slave owners, both of them were so strong for the Union that ideas of nullification and secession horrified them. And, like self-taught Abraham Lincoln, Johnson was a gifted orator who could hold listeners spellbound even if they didn't agree with what he was saying.

By February 1, 1861, seven states had pulled out of the Union: South Carolina, Mississippi, Florida, Alabama, Georgia, Louisiana, and Texas. Johnson's vigorous stumping across the state didn't prevent Tennessee from seceding in June. It may have influenced Abraham Lincoln, though, for the president a year later appointed Andrew military governor of occupied Tennessee and presented him with a commission.

Johnson, with headquarters in Nashville, never commanded in battle, but he got permission from Lincoln to take Tennesseans he labeled "seventy vile secessionists" as hostages for the safety of seventy Unionists imprisoned at Mobile. He shut down Rebel newspapers, jailed clergymen who preached secession, and commandeered railroads in federally held sections of the state. Eliza rejoiced with him when their two older sons put on

Andrew Johnson was on record as favoring quick reconciliation with the former Confederate states.

blue uniforms, and she aided and abetted their son-in-law, who became a guerrilla and fought against Confederates of the region.

Greeneville was located slightly north and well to the east of Knoxville—in the heart of fervently Unionist east Tennessee. Rebels made things so hot for folks there that many of them packed up and left voluntarily. Eliza Johnson chose to stick it out, so she was included in a Confederate order issued one month after Andrew became military governor that gave "alien enemies" just thirty-six hours to leave. By this time she was sick—unbeknownst to her, she was in the earliest stage of tuberculosis—so managed to get permission to remain at home for a while. Her youngest child, Andrew, was barely nine years old when she took him through Confederate lines to Nashville in September 1862.

Senator Johnson was the only man from the Cotton Belt not expelled or resigned from the lawmaking body by the time armed conflict began. Yet he was taken by surprise when the president picked him as his running mate in 1864. Facing a desperate fight for re-election, and for several months afraid that he would not win, the man from Springfield knew that a southerner on the ticket would give him at least a tiny boost.

During the campaign of 1864 Lincoln and his followers were galvanized by Gen. William T. Sherman's capture of Atlanta. That didn't stop political foes from deriding Andrew as a drunkard and as a friend of secession, however, even though both charges were absurd. He served as vice president for only forty-two days before events over which he had no control sent him to the White House.

Eliza, in Nashville at the time, didn't know until April 16, 1865, that her former pupil had a day earlier taken the oath of office as president in the lobby of his hotel. She was keenly conscious that he had spent many a sleepless night over sectional rivalry dividing the nation and had persuaded Lincoln to exempt Tennessee from provisions of the Emancipation Proclamation. Despite never thinking of herself as politically knowledgeable, Eliza knew beyond a doubt that Andrew yearned for North-South healing and would strive to achieve it.

He did precisely as she expected—he tried to implement Lincoln's nonpunitive plans for "Reconstruction" of the defeated Confederacy. Numerous powerful congressional leaders, widely known as Radical Republicans, had other ideas. They passed measures designed both to humiliate and to oppress white citizens in states that had belonged to the Confederacy. Johnson vetoed these bills, one after another. In turn, Congress overrode his vetoes one after another. One of these Reconstruction measures would have had the effect of disenfranchising most or all whites; hence, the Radical Republicans are blamed by some analysts for the surge in racial tension that produced the Ku Klux Klan plus southern legislation aimed at barring blacks from the polls.

Johnson had for some time suspected that the secretary of war inherited from the Lincoln administration, Edwin M. Stanton, was an ally of the Radical Republicans. Concrete evidence about this clandestine relationship surfaced about six months after Congress passed legislation forbidding the removal of civil officers without the consent of the Senate. Fully aware that he was defying his foes on Capitol Hill, but believing that the congressional mandate was unconstitutional, he asked for Stanton's resignation on August 5, 1867.

Many newspapers mocked Johnson as a would-be king, and Stanton refused to give up his office. Johnson suspended him by executive decree, and U. S. Grant briefly held the post that had been forcefully vacated. Four days after Congress reconvened on November 21, a judiciary committee report recommended impeachment of the president. During a period of ninety days, eleven articles were agreed upon, and on March 5 the Senate convened with Chief Justice Salmon P. Chase presiding. Everyone in Washington knew that the body would function as a court in order to weigh evidence against the first president to be impeached and that it would reach a verdict as to his guilt or innocence.

*A session of the Senate during impeachment hearings, with Chief Justice Chase standing at right. (*Frank Leslie's Illustrated)

The struggle, far more political than legal, did not end until Senator Edmund G. Ross of Kansas cast the vote that cleared Eliza's husband of all charges. Andrew remained in office, but was powerless to prevent Congress from continuing to enact statutes that were destructive of the social and economic fabric of the South.

Although Eliza was in Washington for most of her husband's administration, she spent her days in a small second-floor room. Ten members of the family had moved into the White House, so she spent much of her time conversing with adults and playing with children. Crocheting, reading, and sewing took up the rest of her time, and she made an appearance at only two public functions. The traditional duties of the first lady were performed by one of her daughters-in-law.

Andrew did not stand for re-election, and he returned to Greeneville before the inauguration of his successor, U. S. Grant. Six years later he became the only former chief executive to be elected to the U.S. Senate. Upon taking his Senate seat, he undoubtedly had vivid memories of his reaction upon entering that same body when civil war merely loomed on the horizon. A stroke took him to the grave on July 31, 1875, and Eliza succumbed to tuberculosis the following January.

18

Ulys and Julia Grant

U lys, there's a doctor right here in the capital who can look after my eyes, and I've just about made up my mind to let him do it."

Taken by surprise, the eighteenth president of the United States chewed on his cigar for a moment. "Didn't know you were thinking about having something done," he responded.

"The doctor says a minor operation will do the job," Julia Grant explained. "He says it's been done in Europe for a long time and that it won't hinder me from anything that I do—won't even keep me away from a state dinner if I plan ahead a little."

"I hope we can go to Europe some day, but Europe is a long way from the District of Columbia."

"Maybe I didn't explain it right. I wouldn't have to go Europe. I can get it done right here, and then nobody can make fun of you behind your back because you have a cross-eyed wife."

Ulysses S. Grant, normally mild in speech, nearly exploded. "*Whadda ya mean, cross-eyed?*" he demanded. "Don't you remember I talked to the surgeon general right after Appomattox, and he said you've got *strabismus*. That's a great big name for a little ailment—nothin' more than a muscle or two that makes your right eye move around sometimes."

"I know; I know; if I didn't, I'd be mighty dumb. But I can't control it when my eye starts to move. Ulys, you're makin' like you never noticed it. But you'd be the very first one to holler if I sat for one of Matthew Brady's men without turning my head to the side so my eyes don't show."

"Sure. That's the natural thing to do when you sit for a photographer; I understand that much."

"Then you don't mind if I make a date to get my crossed eye—I mean my *strabismus*—straightened out?"

"You bet your bottom dollar that I sure do mind!" he grunted so softly that she could hardly hear him—a sure sign that he was beginning to become angry. "What got you started on such a tangent, anyway?"

"I'm mighty sorry, Ulys, I didn't mean to get your goat. I just wanted to let you know that you can have a wife whose eyes focus like other people's. You know I've always had dreams that wake me up. A couple of weeks ago, I dreamed both of my eyes were straight and I was walkin' down the stairs holdin' to your arm and lookin' a whole bunch of foreign diplomats straight in the eye."

Visibly calming down, the chief executive tossed his wife what, for the self-restrained man who had forced Robert E. Lee to surrender, was a great big smile. "Julia," he explained, speaking deliberately and very distinctly and punctuating every word with his outstretched right hand, "you had those same two eyes when I first laid eyes on you close to St. Louis with Fred standin' by.

"An operation might make you look better to other folks, but not to me. I love you exactly the way you are. I always have, and I always will!"

Julia Grant did not pursue her tentative plan to have corrective surgery. For the rest of Julia's life, her right eye often moved up or down in a fashion she could not control and yet it was so familiar that she was barely conscious of it. During her eight years in the White House, she sat for numerous portraits—always turning her head away from the camera, or looking straight ahead and insisting that the camera had to sit well to one side.

A few Washington hostesses, with whom she had little in common, went out of their way to explain to newcomers that the president's wife had a cast in one eye. This lame and inaccurate description would have infuriated Ulysses S. Grant had he known about it. He rarely used the technical name given to him by the surgeon general of the United States but casually thought of Julia's eyes as being crossed.

The condition with which she had been born didn't matter to him at all. He meant every word he said to her on the night he persuaded her to forget the surgery. Everyone who knew the couple intimately agreed that their marriage was "one in ten thousand." They never quarreled, even in private, and the New York newspaper correspondent who wrote that they exhibited "true love of the very rarest kind" was reporting facts, not indulging in puffery.

The newsman confided to readers, "The Grants always sit next to one another in restaurants and hold hands when they think no one is looking." He probably never knew that Julia of the wandering eye could and often did rave about her husband's eyes, describing them as "beautiful windows to his great soul."

HAD IT NOT BEEN for Julia's younger brother, Fred, they might never have had a chance to look each other over. During the 1842–43 term at West

Point, the sloppy-looking fellow known to other cadets as Sam Grant had Fred Dent as his roommate. No degrees were conferred at the Point in those days, but Sam managed to finish his studies as number twenty-one in a class of thirty-nine. That wasn't good enough to get him into the artillery or cavalry, but he was glad to be starting on the road toward becoming a second lieutenant in the infantry.

When Grant got word that he had been assigned to Jefferson Barracks in Saint Louis, his roommate jumped up and down with delight. He'd been telling Sam a lot about his sister, who lived only ten miles from the city, and Fred had often said he'd sure like for the two of them to get acquainted. Sam's assignment meant that he'd be living practically in the Dents' front yard for at least a few months, and Fred lost no time in taking his friend home with him as soon as both of them reached Saint Louis.

A powerful "electrical current" flowed the instant Sam and Julia met. Still, in their highly individual ways, they both let it be known that they were interested. To the brand-new infantry officer, it didn't matter a bit that most persons would have described Fred's sister as decidedly plain in appearance. She was jolly and kind, even to the family slaves, and to her new acquaintance that "meant a whole lot more than looks." To her, Fred's roommate was positively handsome in his glistening uniform, and she sat up and took notice as soon as she found out he loved horses with a passion.

He and Julia probably came to some kind of an understanding within sixty days of the time Fred had introduced them to each other. They couldn't do anything but hope and plan, however, because Sam's salary of $779 per year wasn't nearly big enough to support a young woman who had grown up without ever really wanting anything her father's money didn't buy for her. To make matters worse for the two, neither of their fathers would listen to even the slightest hint that they might some day become man and wife.

Julia's father, sufficiently well off to assume the honorary title of colonel, made it clear that he didn't want his daughter shackled to "a poor boy who'll never make anything but a bare living." Jesse Grant, father of the fledgling army officer whose relatives and close friends called him Ulys, had already piled up at least half as much money as farmer and merchant Frederick Dent—and was destined to make and accumulate a lot more. Rough looking and rough in his speech, the harness maker, who ran a string of shops in three or four states and who had moved from Ohio to Illinois, was tenderhearted about slaves. Since the Missouri planter owned at least a dozen of them, Jesse didn't want Ulys to get tangled up with Julia Dent—no matter how much his son might think of her.

Paternal objections, alone, would have made it impossible for the two young adults to make firm plans short of an elopement and a ceremony by a justice of the peace. Even if everything had been going smoothly with both of their families, they would have been torn apart by the Mexican War. Ulys was transferred to Louisiana less than nine months after he and Julia first got acquainted. Barely two years after Grant first saw Saint Louis on the heels of leaving the Point, his regiment was sent to join the force commanded by Gen. Zachary Taylor.

Julia Grant's strabismus was not shown in her portraits. (Samuel Sartain engraving)

Lieutenant Grant fought at Palo Alto and Resaca de la Palma before war was declared. He soon took part in the capture of Monterey. Then he fought at Cerro Gordo, Churubusco, and Molino del Rey well enough that he was given a brevet as a first lieutenant. After Chapultepec and Mexico City, he became a brevet, or honorary and temporary, captain—and soon afterward was promoted to permanent rank as a first lieutenant.

Grant left Mexico five years after he and Julia became deeply interested in one another. Returning to Saint Louis on leave, he lost no time. He and Julia were married on August 22, 1848. The rest of his leave was spent on an Ohio honeymoon, after which he was ordered to Sackets Harbor, New York.

It was the first of numerous assignments to places far from the plantation owned by Julia's father and the giddy whirl of Saint Louis social life. She went along when she could, but both of them knew she'd have to stay behind when he was ordered to California. After a few weeks in San Francisco, he had to go to a fort located on the Columbia River in the Oregon Territory. A few weeks shy of his fifth wedding anniversary, Grant, who now had two sons, became a captain and was stationed at Humboldt Bay, California.

It was in Humboldt Bay that the bottle probably got the better of him. Having previously tried to drive away loneliness by drinking, he seems to have quit trying to be sober for even a few days at a time during his second stay in California. Records about the period are muddled, and men

Lt. Gen. U. S. Grant usually dressed casually, but portraits depicted him as being both dapper and handsome. (H. Wright Smith engraving)

who served under an officer who would later became president of the United States didn't like to talk about what they knew, if anything. Some accounts say that Captain Grant was on the verge of becoming a chronic alcoholic. Whether that assessment is right or not, he turned in his commission on July 31, 1854, and headed back to Julia and their two boys, who were now strangers to him.

THE FORMER JULIA DENT spent the next six years as a patient, supportive, and uncomplaining wife. But she had plenty to complain about. Because her father had given Julia a sixty-acre farm, Ulys cleared as much of the land as he could and built a rough house. Its name, Hardscrabble, points to one failure after another on the part of Julia's husband.

He tried his hand at selling real estate and got nowhere. Then he worked hard to win appointment as county engineer, but didn't get the job. In desperation Ulys started selling cordwood on the streets of Saint Louis, but he didn't make enough to stay out of debt. He figured there would be good money in collecting overdue accounts, but he soon found out that he was mistaken. When he hit absolute bottom and stayed there, he appealed to his father in desperation. Jesse put Ulys to work under his younger brother as a clerk in his Galena, Illinois, leather goods store at twenty-one dollars a year more than he had been paid fresh out of West Point.

Even when civil war broke out and the Union was in desperate need of experienced officers, bad luck dogged Julia's beloved. He wrote to Gen. George B. McClellan, offering his services, but he never received a reply. Largely through the influence of the congressman in whose district Galena was located, the former U.S. Army captain was put in charge of a regiment of volunteers. Just sixty days later he was a brigadier general—on the road to the first significant Union victory at Fort Donelson and then on to leadership of Union forces as the first lieutenant general since George Washington.

Julia's support, which never wavered during the bleak and nearly hopeless years in which her husband was out of uniform, went to his headquarters over and over during the four years of the Civil War. She became one of the few females to be mentioned repeatedly in the *Official Records* of the war—not because she was a general's wife, but because she was with him so much of the time.

In a gesture that very few wives of commanders in blue or in gray would have made, she encouraged her husband to take their eleven-year-old son Fred with him to war. When Ulys ventured to suggest that it might not be the right thing to do, she reminded him that in ancient times Philip of Macedon took his juvenile son with him on his military expeditions. She didn't have to tell her husband that the boy became Alexander the Great. Properly persuaded, Gen. U. S. Grant was the only commander on either side of the Civil War who habitually and consistently kept his adolescent son with him during his campaigns.

SENT TO THE WHITE HOUSE as the man whose battlefield victories had preserved the Union, Grant depended heavily on Julia for advice. She, in turn, consulted wealthy Mrs. Hamilton Fish of New York about what clothes to wear and how to preside over a banquet at which all of the guests were national or international figures. Despite the fact that Julia did her best to help him reach crucial decisions, the man whose war of attrition brought the South to its knees failed to detect graft and corruption on the part of some of his appointees. Until the Teapot Dome Affair under Warren G. Harding eclipsed in size any of the scandals of 1869–77, the Grant administration was the most corrupt on record.

Guided by Mrs. Fish, Julia dressed and entertained on a scale so lavish that Washington society said her eight years in the White House were "at the top of the top." She and her husband were happy to leave the capital, however, and settled in New York after a long foreign tour. No better at managing money than he had been earlier, Grant invested heavily in a brokerage firm that soon went under and left him hopelessly in debt.

Admirers had showered an estimated ten thousand cigars upon him after his victory at Fort Donelson. Tobacco undoubtedly triggered continuous hoarseness that soon became diagnosed as cancer of the mouth and throat. That set the man who had conquered Vicksburg, Mississippi, on a quest far more daring than any military expedition he ever led. Hoping desperately to be able to leave enough to make Julia comfortable, he set about dictating his memoirs. When his voice became too weak for him to be heard, he scribbled page after page in pencil. Racing against what he knew to be a fatal condition, he somehow managed to complete his two-volume *Memoirs* shortly before his death.

Julia Grant saw to it that the wedding of their daughter, Nellie, was a memorable event in the social life of the capital.

Mark Twain published the epic work, first of its kind produced by any chief executive, and sent salesmen to hawk it door-to-door. Veteran publishers who didn't believe that Twain—or Samuel L. Clemens—knew how to produce and merchandise a book got the surprise of their lives. The lengthy autobiography that for Ulys was literally the fruit of love eventually brought Julia at least three hundred thousand dollars—far more than she needed in order to be comfortable until her own worn-out body joined that of her beloved in a lavish burial place in New York City.

19

Rutherford and Lucy Hayes

F ighting battles is like courting girls: those who make the most preten-
sions and are boldest usually win."

This summary by a mature Rutherford Hayes had special meaning for
him. At age twenty-four, fresh out of law school, he had fallen in love, or at
least with the idea of being in love, with Fanny Griswold Perkins. Quite
taken with her, he found himself unable to express his feelings to her or
fully to commit himself to the pursuit of her as his wife. He was obsessed
with her even though he had known her for only a short time while she
was visiting friends in Ohio. Fanny was of a distinguished family in New
London, Connecticut. Her father was a wealthy judge, and relatives
included Edward Everett Hale, Peter Lorillard, and Harriet Beecher Stowe.

Hayes's emotional state as he thought about Fanny after she returned
home deteriorated. He wanted to marry her but was afraid of rejection if he
told her his true feelings. His body responded by taking on symptoms similar to tuberculosis—including coughing up blood. Doctors could find no
cause for the symptoms. He was in emotional agony, but he could not
muster the courage to try to win her. Rutherford's family called in doctors,
who recommended that he make a change in his lifestyle to get more fresh
air and exercise.

After several months of poor emotional and physical health, he
decided to face his fear. With a burst of courage, Hayes went to visit Fanny
in Connecticut. Instead of rejecting his advances, she agreed to marry
him—with only one stipulation: He would have to move to New London
because she would not leave her mother. They reached an impasse. Hayes
had too many ties in Ohio to consider a drastic move, even though Fanny's
father would have guaranteed his professional success. He returned home a
healed man whose emotional anguish was gone. Since Fanny had agreed to
marry him he had won a victory, even though they were not to wed. He
again was a winner.

His diary—which he considered to be "sacred"—may be the most
intimate and revealing of all such records penned by a president. Because it

is both compelling and unique, it reveals a chief executive who was unlike any other. The beginnings of his journey through Hell are reflected in his diary on his twenty-fourth birthday:

> I hardly know what to write today. A year ago I expected to be married before this time. I wish I were now a married man. I have had no loves as yet. Before another birthday I am resolved at least to make a choice. I've said enough on this topic to show what is now uppermost in my thoughts. I know of two fine girls, either of whom I might love. F.G.P—, who is engaged already to another, I fear, and Car'l W—, whose acquaintance I made last winter.
>
> I still have the same or similar feelings, desires, hopes, and views in looking forward into the future that I have had for several years. I still feel young, cheerful, and boyish. Still make good resolutions in regard to study, habits, etc., etc., and still break them as of old . . .
>
> What of the past? I have succeeded, in all the senses of that word, as well as I could desire in my professional career; but I have not by labor, application, and energy deserved success as I ought. I've studied less, trifled more, been changeable, fickleminded, and heedless in many things. This is partly in consequence of certain incipient courtships; smitten, but not in love; fancy pleased and tickled and heart untouched. Reflection and observation prevented anything serious, at the same time that there was enough to unhinge the fixed habits of the mind, etc.

After he had recovered from Fanny Perkins, Rutherford was introduced by his sister, Fanny Hayes Platt, to Helen Kelly. Helen was an exciting and sexually attractive young woman. She may have intimidated Hayes because of her beauty and charm. With additional paragraph breaks added, his relationship is revealed by his diary entry of March 17, 1850:

> As Byron says, "It is awful work this love and prevents all a man's projects of good and glory." I have not dared put on paper, even in my sacred diary, much of my love. I have been afraid of profane eyes, and, with shame be it said, that one day I might myself blush to see it; not the love, but the repulse.
>
> Success, success even in affairs of the heart, is the thing which crowns and ennobles. For almost two years I have been in love with———. She has been at times "coy and hard to please" and again yielding and kind, smiling sweetly upon my protestations of affection. "Woman nature is, indeed, a mystery past all finding out." I now fear she is thinking of another. She asks for her letters but wishes to keep mine! To take from my hands all proofs of her former feelings and to keep the evidence which is good against me. To free herself and to keep me in chains. As long as there is a hope, my love is so blindly strong I must cling to it, though my pride prompts decision. When a straw indicating a favorable "air from heaven"

is seen, I am happy as the angels; could strive and labor and learn, be good, and if in me lies such power, great . . .

This giving up letters severs a few more of the frail strands which seem to hold us together; but that must be and shall be—this night, if possible. She loves and don't love.

Rutherford broke off their relationship the following January.

WHEN HE WAS BORN in 1822, his father, a merchant, had been dead for ten weeks. His mother, Sophia Birchard Hayes, and her bachelor brother, Sardis Birchard, raised him in Delaware, Ohio. His older sister, Fanny, was his best friend and companion. From an early age he felt special; Fanny encouraged him in the belief that some day he would accomplish great things. He was an excellent student and popular with girls, although he gave academics priority over personal relationships until he was finished with law school. This might help explain Rutherford's inept behavior with Fanny Perkins and Helen Kelly.

When Hayes was twenty-three he was introduced to fourteen-year-old Lucy Ware Webb, chosen by his mother as his future wife. He was not impressed. Two years later he saw her again. At sixteen she was more mature but still seemed a child to him. In a letter to his mother in October 1847, a few months after he had seen Lucy for the second time Rutherford wrote:

I wish I had a wife to take charge of my correspondence with friends and relatives. Women of education and sense can always write good letters, but men are generally unable to fish up enough entertaining matters to fill half a sheet. By the by, I hope you and Mother Lamb will see to it that Lucy Webb is properly instructed in this particular. I am not a-going to take a wife on recommendation unless her sponsors will fulfill to the utmost what they assume.

Don't forget now.

It would be another three years before he saw Lucy again and four years before he would ask her to be his wife.

IN DECEMBER 1849, HAYES moved to Cincinnati to establish his law practice. It was there that his relationship with Lucy Webb began to blossom. She was a student at Ohio Wesleyan Female College, also in Cincinnati. The youngest of three children and the only daughter of Dr. James Webb and Maria Cook Webb, Lucy was the only female in Ohio Wesleyan's prep

Fun-loving Hayes turned serious when posing for the camera.

school for her last six years there before she went on to attend Ohio Wesleyan Female College. She graduated from college with high honors.

After their engagement in the summer of 1851 Rutherford confided in a letter to her:

> The first mention I find of you in my diary is Vol. 1, p. 109: "July 8, 1847. - Visited Delaware with Mother and Laura. Attended a Sons of Temperance celebration; saw Miss L. Webb and left for home next morning."
>
> Nothing very much like love in that. Still it wouldn't have been written if I hadn't heard a good deal about you from Mrs. Lamb, Hatty Solis, etc. I remember I thought you a bright, sunny-hearted little girl, not quite old enough to fall in love with, and so I didn't.

Later in the same letter he revealed how he analyzed things:

> I have noticed a number of heresies as to matters of love which I propose to discuss with you. I think between us we can get at the true orthodox doctrines on this subject. Emerson says: "The accepted lover has lost the wildest charm of his maiden in her acceptance of him. She was heaven whilst he pursued her as a star: she cannot be heaven if she stoops to such a one as he."
>
> This it seems to me to be rank heresy. Instead of losing, the "accepted" lover gains the wildest charm. Before, the star was distant, cold, its heaven

unappreciated and not understood—distance lends no enchantment but coldness rather. Mr. Emerson didn't know anything. Talk about stars in heaven when your sweetheart is leaning on your arm and her hand clasped lovingly in yours!

RUTHERFORD AND LUCY WERE married in 1852, a year and a half after his marriage proposal. They were a handsome couple. He was five-foot-nine with blue eyes; she, five-foot-four with very dark eyes. This marked the true beginning of confidence for Hayes. His law practice began to flourish.

In 1853 Hayes appealed the case of Nancy Farrar who had been convicted in 1852 of murdering ten people. He won her a new trial, but the trial never took place. Arguments by Hayes persuaded authorities that she was insane, so she was sent to an asylum instead of being executed. This was a landmark case for the defense plea of insanity, and it launched him into prominence.

His passion for winning bought him the respect of the judicial community in Cincinnati. In 1858 Rutherford was appointed to the post of city solicitor. In 1859 he was elected city solicitor. In 1861, after being defeated in the city solicitor election, Hayes joined the Union Army as a major. He served under Gen. John Charles Fremont in the Shenandoah Valley, was wounded and promoted at South Mountain. After the battles of Winchester and Cedar Creek, for which he was made a brevet brigadier, he served in garrison until the conflict ended.

While still in uniform, Rutherford was nominated as the Republican candidate for the House of Representatives. Supporters urged him to take a leave from the military so that he could campaign. His response was, "An officer fit for duty, who at this crisis would abandon his post to electioneer for a seat in Congress, ought to be scalped." He was elected without campaigning.

Re-elected in 1866, he became governor of Ohio the following year. By 1872 Hayes was ready to retire from public life. He retired in 1873 but was pressed out of retirement in 1875 to be elected governor again. While filling that term he was nominated for the presidency at the Republican National Convention in June 1876.

The November 1876 election gave Hayes 165 electoral votes. His Democratic opponent, Samuel J. Tilden, received 184; an additional 20 votes were in dispute. The conflict centered in the returns from Florida, Louisiana, Oregon, and South Carolina. A commission was appointed by a joint Senate-House committee to decide the disputed votes. It consisted of equal numbers of Democrats and Republicans from the Senate, the House, and the Supreme Court. Justice David Davis, an independent, was to be

Though derided as "Lemonade Lucy," the first White House mistress to hold a college degree was gregarious and outgoing, loved by her own and other children. (Hayes Memorial Library)

the tiebreaker. At the last minute Davis resigned to take a seat in the U.S. Senate, and Justice Joseph P. Bradley took his place. Now the tiebreaker was a Republican rather than an independent. Tilden won the popular vote, but Hayes became our nineteenth president.

BOTH RUTHERFORD AND LUCY were committed to temperance. He neither smoked nor drank. Alcohol was forbidden in the White House during his term with only one exception—a dinner for Grand Dukes Alexis and Constantin of Russia. For these members of royalty, rum flavoring was added to the punch. Although the first lady was ridiculed as "Lemonade Lucy," one result of her stance was a major reduction in household expenses—for which Congress had not yet provided an allowance. During their White

House years, Lucy initiated the annual Easter Egg Roll on the lawn of the mansion and supported homes for veterans and the handicapped.

Lucy suffered a stroke and died at age fifty-eight. An excerpt from Rutherford's diary of June 24-25, 1889, gives an inkling of his feelings for her after thirty-seven years of marriage:

> It is past midnight, almost one o'clock. We do not expect Lucy to see the light of another day. All of our children, Birchard, Webb, Rutherford, Fanny, and Scott, are waiting for the inevitable close. With us are our dear young friends—our darling daughter Mary, wife of Birchard [and] our cousin and much loved adopted niece has come from Mississippi to be with us, Adda Cook Huntington. Lucy Elliot Keeler, so near and dear to both of us, and, more fortunate than could be hoped, the eldest child—the representative of my never to be forgotten sister Fanny—Laura Platt Mitchell, so beloved by both Lucy and myself that no sacred circle could be complete in my home without her . . .
>
> And Lucy herself is so sweet and lovely, as she lies unconsciously breathing away her precious life, that I feel a strange gratitude and happiness as I meditate on all the circumstances of this solemn transition we are waiting for.
>
> Would I change it? Oh, yes, how gladly would we all welcome the least indication of the restoration of the darling head of the home circle. But we cannot, we must not, repine. Lucy Hayes is approaching the beautiful and happy ending of a beautiful, honored, and happy life. She has been wonderfully fortunate and wonderfully honored. Without pain, without the usual suffering, she has been permitted to come to the gates of the great change which leads to the life where pain and suffering are unknown . . .
>
> If ever a man or woman found exquisite happiness in imparting happiness to others, the dear companion of my life, my Lucy, is that woman. Should I not be full of joy and gratitude for the good fortune which gave me her? Few men in this most important relation of life have been so blessed as I have been. From early mature manhood to the threshold of old age I have enjoyed her society in the most intimate of all relations.

20

James and Crete Garfield

"James, I should not blame my own heart if it lost all faith in you," Lucretia Garfield—universally known simply as Crete—wrote her husband after five years of marriage. She had somehow found out about a fling he had enjoyed with a much younger woman while in New York City. "I shall not be forever telling you I love you, when there is evidently no more desire for it on your part than present manifestations indicate," she continued.

Guilty of adultery and having no defense to offer, the Civil War general, whose first legitimate offspring was due to arrive shortly, put the future of their union on the line and begged for forgiveness. Then he added insult to injury; after having commented that if his wife really felt as she said, he suggested that "I should consider it wrong for us to continue any other than a business correspondence."

The diary of the man born in Orange, Ohio, was given a grandiose title: *Journal of Daily Events and Private Cogitations; or Confidential Friend to Whom the Secret Thoughts of the Heart are Entrusted.* This voluminous record is much less poignant than that of Rutherford B. Hayes and includes vernacular Latin plus cryptic notations that are difficult to decipher. Yet scattered passages clearly indicate that he meant what he said in 1863. If Crete couldn't forgive and forget, he was willing and ready to call their relationship quits—although he would not agree to a divorce because that wouldn't be respectable and could damage his career.

James had the upper hand, and both of them knew it. He was a devout member of the Disciples of Christ and was the only future president who regularly filled pulpits as a lay preacher. His faith, which seems really to have been deep, had already led him to one of the most satisfactory states in which a human can find himself or herself. "The hand of the Lord has been with me," he observed not once but repeatedly. That divine hand, he was positive, guided his everyday actions in so profound a fashion that God—not James—was responsible for much that he did. God had some great purpose in mind for him, he confided to intimates, although he had no idea what that purpose might be.

His plea for forgiveness that closed with what amounted to a repri-
mand and a threat had the effect he anticipated. Crete wilted, then turned
around and asked his forgiveness for having been unduly blunt with her husband whom she knew to have indulged in "passions of the flesh" with a
woman she had never seen. Her switch from anger to meek contrition led to
a reconciliation that they both regarded as no more than "a truce to sad-
ness." For the rest of her life, Mrs. James A. Garfield often thought about
one of the half-dozen rivals for her husband's affection and perhaps his body.

BORN AND REARED IN Hiram, Ohio, Crete became acquainted with James
during a period when both of them were students. Working on Ohio canal
boats was his only job experience, but he was bright, eager, and extremely
self-assured, and he soon won a place as an instructor in ancient languages.
Crete, who became one of his pupils, developed with her teacher a relationship that was genderwise reversed of the teacher-student attachment of
Abigail and Millard Fillmore.

James didn't lose much time in indicating that he was deeply interested; but, in much the same fashion as Fillmore, he let it be known that
his career took precedence over marriage. After their relationship had
progressed to a formal engagement that dragged on for five years, Crete
offered to release him from the promises he had made to her. "No," he told
her in response, "I can't afford to lose you—but you'll have to give me
time." Time dragged on until nine years after they became interested in
each other.

Although documentary evidence is lacking, it is all but certain that
Crete had found out much earlier that her beloved had a roving eye. Mary
Hubbell, another Eclectic student, had caught his interested attention
when she enrolled in one of his classes. Despite the fact that he knew Crete
was expecting to wait for him, James expressed his passion for Mary in language that soared to the sky. His heart throbbed violently, he told her,
when he realized that a girl of her intelligence and beauty could "bestow
her warm love upon a poor, penniless, orphan like me."

Late in 1852 his relationship with Mary threatened to spin out of
control. Hence, the self-styled "instrument of Providence," who was by
no means ready to go to the altar, decided to break his tie with her. She
and members of her family were both humiliated and angry, so she threatened to make his love letters public. Her attitude later softened, and she
returned the letters. Some of them were preserved and were found years
later tied in a neat bundle and identified only by an enigmatic Latin
memorandum.

Garfield at age sixteen. (Ohio State Historical Society)

Despite having avoided public exposure, James was plunged into the depths of self-pity and despair. When he rebounded from having wallowed in the bottom of the pit, he did penance by recording his conviction that:

> Of all characters in society, none is more despicable, heartless, and truly deserving of the frowns and contempt of every good man and woman, than is the man who wantonly trifles with the heart of a woman.

Garfield could have saved his paper and ink; he could no more resist a female he found attractive than a moth can resist the flame that nearly always burns it.

While Crete continued to wait patiently for him, James had a torrid affair with Rebecca Sellick—one of Crete's acquaintances. Rebecca ("Rancie," or "Ranca"), who had gone so far as to suggest that she and Crete should become "sisters in spirit," may have been the only female taken into what Garfield dubbed his "chamber of the prophet." This upstairs room almost certainly was the scene of sexual encounters that made his relationship with Mary Hubbell seem mild and commonplace. Although she didn't realize that she was revealing a great deal by her reaction, Crete laid all of the blame upon Rebecca and had none left over for James. She married him in November 1858, which was after he had been elevated to the presidency of Hiram Eclectic Institute.

James made numerous derogatory comments about marriage in general as well as about their union, described by him to her as "a great mistake." Before and after they became man and wife, he decried "the narrow exclusiveness of marriage." He was pained, he said, by the realization that nuptial vows brought with them "necessities and hateful finalities."

Four years after going to the altar with Crete, he encountered a provocative female who told him she was a reporter for the *New York Times*. Although Mrs. Lucia Gilbert Calhoun was only eighteen years old, she explained to her new friend that an unfortunate accident had made her a widow. Garfield's relationship with Lucia has been characterized as making him "the first future president who cheated on his wife." Discovery of their trysts prompted Crete's letter about her own love for her husband that behaved like India rubber and bounced back upon her.

After having spent a term in the House of Representatives and having been a Civil War general, Garfield decided it was in his best interests to make another trip to New York. Crete, knowing that he planned to retrieve a bundle of unidentified papers from Lucia, was less than happy at the prospect that the pair would again be in close physical proximity. To her, it seemed wise for James to stay away from Lucia so that "the fire of lawless passion" that had made their blood run hot could "burn itself out unfed."

Disregarding this pointed warning, James pursued his plan and apparently managed to retrieve everything he had written to Lucia. If she withheld anything, it never surfaced. Nothing would be known about their relationship were it not for the fact that it is repeatedly mentioned in correspondence between Crete and her husband, as well as his hard-to-decipher diary.

His fear that word of their affair might get out and damage his career apparently had taught him little or nothing. Soon after leaving Lucia behind in order to return to Washington, General Garfield was temporarily without a military assignment. During this interval he was a house guest of Salmon P. Chase, U.S. secretary of the treasury.

Kate Chase, daughter of the cabinet member, was one of the most talked-about women in Washington. Described as beautiful, vivacious, and absolutely crazy about males, she spent so much time with James that word about them got back to Crete, back in Ohio. Having learned the hard way that accusations by her would backfire on her, she chose her words cautiously and asked whether or not "Miss Kate is a very charming, interesting young lady." If so, wrote his pregnant wife, "I may be jealous, since you have a fashion of becoming enamored with young ladies."

Garfield's casually worded response called Kate Chase a woman with "a good form but not a pretty face." He said nothing to his wife about having made a trip to see one of his old flames, Rebecca Selleck. Weeks later Crete learned of that visit and labeled it as having been harmless— but it was while he was in New York to see Rebecca that her husband became deeply involved with Lucia Calhoun.

An early friend of James—male instead of female—wrote poetry and one of his efforts in blank verse so impressed Garfield that he committed it to memory and on occasion recited it. The eight lines entitled "Ambition's Dream" put into words the deepest yearnings of the man who was positive that Almighty God had made plans for him. Although it was poetry of mediocre quality at best, the composition spoke for the future president by saying:

> But oh! To die and be forgotten! This
> Is tenfold death! To pass away and leave
> No mark to tell the world that I have lived!
> I could not sleep in peace even in the grave,
> Were I to know that none remembered me.
> Then grant, O Ruler in the heavens above,
> That I may live till I have done some deed
> To clothe my name with immortality.

Standing an even six feet in height, after sixteen years in the House of Representatives Crete's husband had not abandoned his conviction that he was "marked out from above for some special purpose" whose nature he didn't dimly comprehend.

His eye-opener came during the seventh national convention of the Republican party. Delegates who gathered in Chicago's Exposition Hall listened attentively as Garfield delivered the nominating speech on behalf of John Sherman of Ohio. Yet on the first ballot, U. S. Grant led the pack and James G. Blaine of Maine was not far behind. Sherman received only 93 of the 755 votes that were cast. With 378 votes required for nomination, no man seemed able to reach that magic number. Weary delegates began looking around for an attractive dark horse, and some of their eyes lighted up when they caught sight of the chairman of the Rules Committee. When the thirty-eighth ballot was tabulated, James A. Garfield of Ohio had snared the brass ring with 399 votes.

Although he met with delegates who sought him out at his two-and-one-half-story home at Mentor, Ohio, Garfield played his cards very close to his vest and managed to antagonize only a few men of national influence. With Chester A. Arthur as his running mate, Crete's husband managed to snare a crucial ten-thousand-vote edge on November 2, 1880. When electoral votes were cast, however, he came within a hair of receiving 60 percent of them.

THERE IS NO WAY to know whether our twentieth president would have continued in the White House his pursuit of women as he had done for so many of his earlier years. That's because he and Crete occupied the mansion at 1600 Pennsylvania Avenue less than four months before tragedy struck.

Venerable Williams College in Maine, his alma mater, invited him to deliver the 1881 commencement address. As he started to board a train at Washington's Baltimore and Potomac railroad station, he was approached by a man who appeared to be a fervent supporter. Charles J. Guiteau, who had favored a third term for U. S. Grant, fired two shots that hit Garfield in his back and his arm. Soon tried for murder, Guiteau through his attorneys entered a plea of insanity that failed to keep his neck from the hangman's noose.

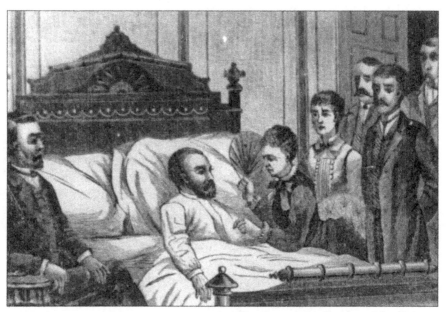

While physicians and surgeons conferred, Crete Garfield fanned.

Rushed back to the White House, Crete's seriously wounded husband managed to gasp that he was tough and would soon be back at his desk. Somehow, though, providence seemed to be occupied with other matters and did not intervene in his behalf. Washington was experiencing one of the most torrid summers on record, and the temperature in the sick room worsened the wounded chief executive's condition.

No one had yet conceived a way by which to lower air temperature. After consulting several experts who insisted that nothing of that sort could be done, Crete took matters into her own hands. She secured huge buckets, had them filled with ice, then used fans to circulate the air. Her pioneer attempt to achieve air conditioning lowered the temperature in her husband's room only a few degrees, but it was enough to make him more comfortable and cheerful despite the fact that he showed no signs of recovering from his wounds.

Weeks spent by the two Ohio natives in the artificially cooled White House brought them closer together than they had been in twenty-three years of marriage. For the first time in his life, Garfield lauded what he called "feminine ingenuity and refusal to take no for an answer." Crete reveled in her suddenly elevated status and managed to keep blocks of ice sitting in their containers around the clock.

Garfield persuaded his physicians that sea air would hasten his recovery. Hence, a special train took him and his ever-forgiving Crete to Elberon, New Jersey, early in September. His wife was overjoyed when he seemed to gain strength slowly for a few days. She collapsed, however, when informed that he had taken a sudden turn for the worse and was not expected to live.

The first chief executive positively known to have permitted lust to strain marriage bonds almost to the point of bursting probably gained a week or two of life as a result of Crete's primitive air conditioning. When he died, she was inconsolable for days and never encouraged any of the males who offered to comfort her and share her grief. She outlived her husband by thirty-three years, during which her dreams were punctuated at intervals by what she identified as visions of women with whom James had affairs.

21

Chester and Nell Arthur

Nell, I know you are thinking of me because I feel the pulses of your love answering to mine. If I were with you now, you would go and sing for me 'Robin Adair.' Then you would come and sit by me—you would put your arms around my neck and press your soft sweet lips over my eyes. I can feel them now."

That brief passage from a letter by "Ever Loving Chester" is one of the few scraps of written material that escaped destruction when ex-President Chester A. Arthur knew he faced death. Suffering from Bright's disease, his condition deteriorated rapidly after he left the White House and returned to New York City.

For reasons unknown Arthur directed servants to thoroughly search the brownstone mansion in which he lived. As soon as a batch of personal papers was in hand, he directed it to be burned. After being repeated several times, this process was believed to have stripped the place of written records and memorabilia. Somehow, an undated fragment of a letter directed to his sweetheart was overlooked. Ellen Lewis Herndon Arthur, known as Nell to her intimates, may have kept this outpouring of love in a Bible. There its size would have made it almost impossible to find unless one knew exactly where to look for it.

The young woman, a Culpeper, Virginia, native, made a trip to New York at age nineteen. She went there in order to visit a cousin, Dabney Herndon, who roomed with a twenty-six-year-old attorney. Dabney found special delight in introducing his relative to his roomie—Chester Arthur. Years later he confided that he had been positive that "they would hit it off as soon as they became acquainted with one another."

Herndon was right; friendship soon blossomed into love, but the pair were separated by many miles and a colossal cultural gap. It is possible that after having exchanged love letters for a few months, one or both of them would have found another interest—had it not been for tragedy on the high seas.

William L. Herndon, Nell's father, was a career officer of the U.S. Navy. In those days Washington routinely released naval officers for temporary duty on commercial vessels. This was done to persuade gifted leaders to stay in the navy, where salaries were low compared to those paid to masters of merchant and passenger vessels. In 1857 Herndon accepted an offer to serve briefly as master of the *Central America.*

Exceptionally large for the period, this commercial vessel carried more than four hundred passengers, a crew of about one hundred, and a full cargo of freight. Cape Hatteras, North Carolina, was already notorious as "the graveyard of the Atlantic" because so many ships went down in its vicinity.

Winds of destructive force hit the *Central America* sometime on September 10, 1857. Nell's father and his crew rode out the storm for hours before losing most of their sails. When the vessel began tossing helplessly, he directed passengers toward lifeboats and sent them through extremely choppy seas to a desolate beach. One of the boats returned to rescue Commander Herndon, alone on deck in the long-standing tradition of the sea. He was dimly seen, standing on the bridge in full uniform, as the *Central America* made an especially violent lurch that capsized and sank her.

Spontaneous offers of help came to his widow from ports along the Atlantic and Gulf coasts. Congress ordered a medal struck in honor of Herndon. A monument was erected in his memory at Annapolis. Enough gifts were received by a special committee to fund the purchase of a townhouse on West Twenty-first Street. Although they were reluctant to leave Virginia, Nell and her mother moved into their new home early in 1858.

Chester Arthur was among the first to call on them after their relocation, and a romance that might have died a natural death took on new life. He and Nell were married in Calvary Episcopal Church at a time when his career as an attorney was beginning to take off.

IRISH-BORN WILLIAM ARTHUR, an itinerant Baptist preacher, seldom stayed very long in any of the churches he served in Vermont and New York. It is known that his son, Chester, was born in 1830 in North Fairfield, Vermont. This void concerning him led some political foes to charge in 1881 that he was born in Canada, which would have made him ineligible to succeed James A. Garfield upon the death of the twentieth president.

His father was in Schenectady by the time Chester was old enough to think of higher education, so it was natural for him to attend Union College. He became a part-time school teacher in order to pay his way. He studied late into the night and became a member of Phi Beta Kappa prior to his 1848 graduation. During five years in which he read law, he continued to teach and later joked that he did so because he had "developed a habit of eating three meals a day." Soon after he moved to New York City, he won a case involving racial discrimination and became better known than most struggling young attorneys.

Chester was relatively affluent by the time he and Nell became man and wife. After a little more than a decade of married life, they bought an elegant home of their own, and in 1867 they moved into it with their two sons. Located on Lexington Avenue in Grammercy Park, the brownstone was just right for entertainment. Nell, who had already won acceptance into the top social circles of the city, was an early member of the Mendelssohn Glee Club and became a featured soprano soloist.

The Arthurs enjoyed what was then called "a picture-book marriage"— except for periods of tension during the Civil War. Chester did not don a uniform and march off to fight Rebels, but as a top officer in the state militia he was responsible for feeding and housing regiments en route to the South. Although she never took part in secret meetings of pro-southern New Yorkers known as Copperheads, Nell openly sympathized with the Confederacy.

Her cousin, who had introduced her to Chester, was far more belligerent. Soon after completing his medical training, Dabney Herndon made his way south and became an assistant surgeon in gray. Captured when Rebel-held Island No. 10 in the Mississippi River fell to Union forces, Dabney became a prisoner of war. It took weeks of inquiry to locate him before Chester's influential political allies won his release.

NELL EXPERIENCED ONE DREARY month after another in 1878. First came news that her mother, who was in France, had become seriously ill. While Nell was preparing to go to her side, word came that her mother had died. Although never robust, Chester's wife went to France and claimed the body of her mother. Two six-week voyages on the stormy North Atlantic Ocean during a period of deep grief were too much even for the daughter of a naval hero. Nell became violently ill on the return voyage, and although she seemed briefly to be gaining strength after returning home, the forty-two-year-old contracted pneumonia from which she never recovered.

A widower at age fifty, Chester's friends plied him with offers to introduce him to eligible women. He invariably shook his head, insisting that since no one could ever take Nell's place it would be useless for anyone to make the effort. Six months after having been left desolate, he went to the Republican National Convention in Chicago as a delegate who was committed to nominating Grant for a third term.

Although Grant was widely regarded as the Republican most likely to win in November, the corruption of his administration prevented him from becoming the nominee. James A. Garfield, whose surprising surge after

*Ellen Lewis Herndon "Nell" Arthur,
whose widower said her eyes twinkled
at him from a stainedglass window.
(Library of Congress)*

many ballots put him in the running for the White House, felt that it was essential to placate the wing of the party that had supported Grant. He therefore offered the vice-presidential nomination to Levi P. Morton of New York. Morton hemmed and hawed, saying he could not make a decision without consulting party leaders in his own state. As a result Garfield offered the place to Arthur, who had never been elected to office. To the surprise of some of his friends, Arthur accepted instantly.

He confided to his children that the nomination was a far greater honor than he had ever expected to receive. "Your mother would have been as proud as a peacock," he said, "and my willingness to become a candidate for office is a tribute to her." News that Garfield had been shot and might not pull through sent the entire nation into shock. Urged by key leaders of his political party to hurry to Washington in order to be instantly available if needed, Chester was adamant in his refusal.

"Nell wouldn't want me to stand in the wings, waiting for the president to die," he said.

That's why the fourth man to become president of the United States without having been elected by the people took his oath of office in his own residence. Although his earlier career had been spent as a diligent worker in the "machine politics" for which New York was notorious, Arthur became a surprisingly effective chief executive.

Upon learning that Garfield was dead, Arthur consented to take the oath of office in a rare ceremony that was held in his New York residence.

Always pondering what his "feisty little Virginian" would have advised him to do, our twenty-first president vetoed an enormous "rivers and harbors bill" because he saw it as the product of special interest groups. Although the measure was passed over his veto, he won a long, drawn-out fight for reform of the U.S. civil service, and the first steps toward reform became law when he signed the Congressional act early in 1883. Yet he confided to his intimates that his most notable achievement during his White House years had nothing to do with politics. As a memorial to Nell, he paid for a stained glass window in Saint John's Episcopal Church.

"It's a beauty," he triumphantly told his children. "Luck was with me, or your grandfather Up Yonder has more influence that I thought. I didn't ask for it, but they placed the window in the south side of the building. When the sun hits it just right, from the White House I can see it shining and imagine that your mother's bright eyes are twinkling at me!"

22, 24

Grover and Frances Cleveland

You're all set for Thursday night, and, boy, is she a knockout!"

"You're not kidding?"

"Not for a second, my boy," responded Buffalo, New York, attorney Oscar Folsom. "I was there Monday night, and believe me, I'll be back next week."

"I hear she's a widow; are there children around the house?"

"Nary a one; says she left two behind in Jersey City. Why do you ask?"

"Because I'm trying to be a half-decent fellow," Grover Cleveland snapped, "and I wouldn't patronize her if there were children on hand."

"Don't you worry your big head for even a minute, my boy. She's a real pro. Been around a lot and knows how to take care of herself."

Having dismissed his doubts, the thirty-seven-year-old attorney, already showing a bit of a paunch, knocked on the door of Mrs. Maria Halpin's rented house promptly at eight o'clock Thursday night. She had tea and scones ready for him, and as he munched she told him a bit about herself.

Work had petered out in Jersey City, she explained, and everyone there said that Buffalo was a good place to make a new start. An experienced collar maker, she had already found a job and was at work. It paid so little, though, that "in order to send some money back to Mamma and the children" she had decided to take on a select list of clients. "Never more than one in a night," she emphasized.

Half a dozen prominent business and professional men of the thriving city availed themselves of Maria's services, and they paid her generously. All of them were puzzled one day when summoned to a hasty council of war in Oscar Folsom's office. When the room was full and the door was closed, the attorney said simply, "Maria's pregnant. She's just found out, and the baby is due in less than six months."

Except for Cleveland, every man on Maria's list was married and had a family. No member of the group wanted to risk losing his wife and children over a high-class call girl who claimed to be a widow. They looked at one another wordlessly for an instant, and some of their faces began to

A cartoon that depicted Cleveland as thunderstruck by the revelation of his indiscretion was not strictly accurate; it was never a secret. (Punch)

flush. Grover patted one of his comrades on the shoulder. "Don't worry," he assured him. "I'll take care of everything."

According to some accounts, when Maria's bouncing baby boy arrived at the end of the summer of 1874, she named him Oscar Folsom Cleveland. She said she picked that name because she wanted him to have his daddy's surname. Because no reliable paternity test was available in those days, there was no earthly way for Maria to pinpoint the man who had sired her little boy. Other versions of this saga, considerably more believable, insist that Grover manfully said that since he was the only bachelor in the bunch, he would take the responsibility for claiming the child and giving it his name.

He didn't have the remotest intention of marrying Maria, but he regularly paid child support for little Oscar. With her chief source of income having dried up at least temporarily, "Mrs. Halpin" took to the bottle and became a confirmed alcoholic. Judge Roswell L. Burrows, who possibly might have been one of her clients, ordered Maria into an insane asylum for a lengthy stay and put Oscar into an orphanage that charged five dollars a week to keep him.

Cleveland grumbled that "the freight at that orphanage is mighty high," but he paid it regularly. After Maria was released, he tried to get her started in a little business located at Niagara Falls. This venture failed, so the man who had been sheriff of Erie County for three years decided he had to get the woman off his hands. To do so, he paid her off—an even five hundred dollars—and directed her to get herself to New Rochelle, find a job, and stay there.

Nearly every man of any importance in Buffalo kept up with these developments, and some of them said Grover had lost his mind to give so much money to "that woman." He shook his head to signal that he didn't agree with that verdict and let it be known that he'd try to see that the boy got a decent education.

When delegates to the Democratic National Convention of 1884 convened in Chicago—the fast-growing "windy city" where many a future president had been chosen—they knew that their candidate would face the formidable James G. Blaine of Maine. To the surprise of many, the former sheriff of Erie County garnered about 80 percent of the votes he needed to win on the first ballot. His momentum was too great to be stopped; on the second ballot he swept far over the top with 683 votes.

Blaine's campaign managers, who had chosen Civil War hero John A. Logan as their nominee for the vice presidency, knew that Democrats had picked up some key cities and were on a roll. As a result, they pulled out all the stops in an effort to persuade the general public that Cleveland was "morally unfit to serve as chief executive."

DESPITE HIS VICTORY AND a constant round of official dinners, Cleveland found himself desperately lonely in the White House. Earlier, he had made up his mind not to spend the rest of his life alone in bed, but he had told only one person of his decision.

Once he made up his mind to take a wife, he had no difficulty in choosing the woman he wanted to make his own. Following the sudden death of his long-time friend and booster, Oscar Folsom, he had voluntarily assumed responsibility for little Frances Folsom. Without going through the process that would have been necessary legally to become her guardian, he had assumed that role.

His interest in the child began during her infancy and ran very deep. Well before Oscar Folsom's premature death, Cleveland had selected and purchased for Baby Frances the first little carriage in which she rode. As executor of Folsom's estate, he later poured substantial amounts of his own money into support of his friend's widow and his unofficial ward.

He probably had a decisive voice in choosing Wells College for Frances, and before she had been there very long began regularly sending flowers to her. Any veteran reader of light romantic novels would have predicted that the godfather's interest was likely to become intensely personal, and it did. He corresponded frequently with the college student he had known her entire life and decided to thumb his nose at established conventions in order to make her his wife.

When he first broached the subject rather gingerly on the heels of her graduation from college, Frances threw her arms around the neck of the man she had always called Uncle Cleve and squeezed very hard. Marriage couldn't come too soon for her, she insisted with stars in her eyes. He reluctantly explained that he thought it best to keep their romance a secret for the time being. "Just you wait, Little One," he then promised, "When the time is ripe, you'll have a wedding that will make folk sit up and take notice."

That was the understatement of the decade. Word that something very big was about to take place in the capital leaked out late in May 1886. Veteran White House correspondents thought the news would focus on a proposal to back U.S. currency with silver instead of gold or with the acquisition of the Hawaiian Islands. Even when Frances came under the same roof as her Uncle Cleve, it was taken for granted that she was making a family visit. The president confided to a few special friends on May 28 that he did not plan to remain a bachelor much longer.

At 7:00 P.M. on June 2, 1886, a handful of relatives, intimate friends, and cabinet members and their wives converged upon the Blue Room. There the first White House wedding took place without a public announcement. The forty-nine-year-old president beamed at his twenty-one-year-old bride in a fashion that no one could construe as being avuncular. As soon as Mrs. Frances Folsom Cleveland became the mistress of the White House, John Philip Sousa and the U.S. Marine Band struck up tunes that made conversation virtually impossible.

Most people could have been expected to be scandalized over the notion of a man taking as his wife a girl who was next thing to his daughter. Surprisingly, the public's reaction to news of the wedding was positive. Great numbers of citizens thought it was wonderful to have a first lady who was about a year younger than the second Mrs. Tyler.

At age twenty-one the youngest-ever mistress of the White House soon showed herself to be a competent and charming hostess. Many who had spent their lives in the capital agreed that Frances's receptions, balls, and banquets ranked among the best in memory. She showed absolutely no sign of haughtiness, and she received anonymous visitors as cordially as she did high-ranking officials or foreign diplomats.

SOME EXPERTS POSTULATE THAT the presidential succession act of 1886 was the most important legislation enacted during the tenure of the second bachelor ever elected to the presidency. Although it was modified sixty years later, the legislation had the virtue of spelling out for the first time

For an official photograph, Mrs. Cleveland donned formal evening wear. (Charles M. Bell photo, Library of Congress)

what would happen when a chief executive died in office. Had it been in effect earlier, John Tyler wouldn't have been able to seize the presidency and therefore set a precedent of profound importance. Instead, chief executives who were killed or who died a natural death before their terms ended would have been succeeded by secretaries of war.

Although popular among the rank and file of Americans and usually given a surprising high rank among presidents when historians are polled, Cleveland took a drubbing from Benjamin Harrison of Ohio in 1888. Oral tradition insists that when Frances learned that Grover had been defeated, she promised a few White House staffers that she and her husband would soon be back. He moved his legal practice to New York City and joined the high-profile firm of Bangs, Stetso, Tracy, and MacVeagh. After having attended Harrison's inauguration, he said he was through with politics and in the future couldn't be persuaded to run for dogcatcher.

DURING HARRISON'S FOUR YEARS in the White House, the nation grew by leaps and bounds. North Dakota, South Dakota, Montana, Washington, Idaho, and Wyoming were admitted to the Union. Yet this smashing success in terms of territorial expansion didn't prevent many who had voted for Harrison from becoming unhappy with him. He had no interest in foreign affairs, and the nation experienced financial instability. Popular opinion underwent so great a change that Democrats had a surprisingly easy time of it when they suggested to the former president, who "was through with politics," that he should run for an unprecedented nonconsecutive term.

With their national convention again being held in the city from which Lincoln took over the helm of the nation, delegates this time nominated Cleveland on the first ballot. Incumbent president Benjamin Harrison, also nominated on the first ballot, had run out of steam. His lackluster campaign never attracted wide and deep support in states that were crucial to his re-election. This time, the man who bought his way out of military service during the Civil War topped his opponent by nearly four hundred thousand popular votes. Having carried twenty-three states against Harrison's sixteen, there never was the slightest doubt that he would win overwhelmingly in the electoral college.

As a husband, Grover quickly made up for lost time. During a period of a dozen years he fathered three daughters and two sons. Frances gave birth to Ruth in New York City in the interval between her pair of Washington stays. One of Ruth's sisters was born in Washington and another at Buzzard's Bay, Massachusetts, while her brothers first saw the light of day at Buzzard's Bay and at Princeton, New Jersey.

When self-possessed, two-year-old Baby Ruth danced and bounced her way into the White House before a bevy of photographers, she captured the heart of the nation. There is no certainty that makers of candy asked parental permission before deciding to exploit the child. Whatever the case, Baby Ruth candy bars have perpetuated the little Cleveland's name far longer than did the song "Alice Blue Gown" that was dedicated to Alice Roosevelt. When Ruth died at age twelve, her father and mother said that they would never get over the tragedy.

Another tragedy was kept from the public at the insistence of Cleveland's very pregnant wife. She read newspapers and magazines avidly and from those learned that the nation faced new financial troubles. When her husband's physicians told him that his constant use of cigars had probably caused U. S. Grant's malady—cancer of the mouth and throat—it was Frances rather than Vice President Adlai Stevenson of Illinois or Secretary of War Daniel Lamont of New York who took charge and began making plans.

If news of her husband's condition were given to the press, she insisted, it would cause the stock market to plunge, and many investors might be wiped out. Should the tiny cancer in his mouth be made public, news of the danger he faced could throw business firms into bankruptcy. Hence, she made plans for a top-secret surgical operation and probably suggested that the yacht of wealthy investor Elias C. Benedict of New York could be had for the asking. In order to divert attention away from the fact that the president would temporarily disappear from sight, she announced that she and Baby Ruth would go to Cape Cod and take the entire press corps with them.

Her scheme worked precisely as she had hoped it would. Not a single photographer or reporter trailed her husband as he made his furtive way through Manhattan in order to board the yacht *Oneida*. Cleveland, who angrily refused to tell anyone his weight, is believed to have topped 250 pounds at that time. Physicians feared that he might not survive anesthesia if administered to him prone, so they propped him up in a chair and put him to sleep.

In order to keep Cleveland's face smooth, surgeons worked inside his mouth and took out sections of tissue and bone before inserting a French-made device of hard rubber that substituted for an upper jawbone. He was at his desk, waving away questions about where he had been, before Frances and Baby Ruth and the press corps returned to the White House.

Apparently fully recovered after about two months, the president wanted to bring an obstetrician to the White House. Frances demurred, pointing out that Dr. Joseph D. Bryant was ready to come at an instant's notice. As she knew he would, Bryant arrived in plenty of time to make all necessary preparations before delivering Esther—the first child born in the White House.

Words and actions of Frances always indicated that she positively adored her husband who was more than twice her age at the time of their marriage. To her it seemed only natural to help Grover use his stomach pump when in retirement he began experiencing agonizing bouts of indigestion. At Princeton during the spring of 1908 Cleveland's health deteriorated rapidly despite the constant attention of his wife.

She remained in Princeton after his death, and there the former Frances Folsom Cleveland again made news. Five years after Grover's death she became Mrs. Thomas J. Preston and headlines through the nation for the first time announced: *"Presidential Widow Has Remarried."*

23

Ben, Carrie, and Mame Harrison

A few political enemies guffawed, but most of official Washington reacted with surprise to the wholly unexpected news. Regarded as being cold and austere—the facade he presented to the public—the president was widely reported to have wept without restraint when a train rolled into the station early on September 21, 1892. Old-timers could remember no similar incident since Abraham Lincoln had shed copious tears over the body of his youthful protégé, Elmer Ellsworth.

The former Caroline Lavinia Scott, known to her husband and family simply as Carrie, had just reached the capital—reclining in a hospital bed installed in a railroad car. Exhausted from her five-hundred-mile journey from Loon Lake, the demeanor of the wife of the president was markedly different from that of her husband. Although too weak to speak in normal fashion, she was completely calm despite the fact that it was impossible to fail to notice that her husband's eyes were red from weeping.

Oral tradition in Indianapolis, the city that knew the couple far better than any other place they lived, has it that the mate she knew simply as Ben shut his eyes when he leaned over to embrace her. Carrie held him tight for a moment and then whispered, "It won't be long."

Their children indignantly denied the rest of the brief conversation that was supposed to have taken place in the railroad car. The children's emotional involvement, however, makes it doubtful that their views were impartial and unbiased. It was not necessary for the mistress of the White House to explain what she meant by her initial comment. Harrison already knew that an early medical diagnosis of grippe—later known as influenza—had been wrong. His wife was in an advanced stage of tuberculosis and had only days or weeks to live.

Most persons—except for their children—who knew the presidential couple well believed the story that a railroad employee standing near the head of Carrie's bed had seen her gesture for Ben to bend his ear toward her mouth. Almost stone deaf and highly skilled in lip reading, the railroader saw the president's wife mouth a few phrases between coughs.

"I will soon be gone," she managed to say. "Make me a promise. Find somebody to take care of you. You can't make it by yourself."

Too choked to speak, Harrison gave a tiny nod. Carrie, taking it for assent, used what little lung power she had left to urge him: "Don't wait too long. You'll be helpless." He nodded tearful understanding and the bedside interlude ended with a gasped exhortation: "Do it for my sake!"

Carrie clung to life for another six weeks, then slipped away. By then, her Ben had persuaded her that no one else could ever take her place in the White House. Grief-stricken, he refused in February 1896 to seek nomination for a second term. Three months after he had bowed out of the presidential sweepstakes, Harrison took widowed Mary Scott Lord Dimmick as his second wife.

MARY, KNOWN TO INTIMATES as Mame because so many relatives with the same name had crowded into the White House, was a niece of Carrie's. During the entire administration of the second Harrison to serve as U.S. chief executive, she worked faithfully as secretary to her aunt. Harrison's forty-two-year-old son, Russell, refused to attend the wedding ceremony held in New York. His unmarried sister, Mary Scott, followed his example. Both insisted that their cousin could never replace their mother, and they insinuated that no woman would marry a man twenty-three years older unless she had her eye on his pocketbook.

They were right in at least one respect; no other woman had precisely the same set of values, personality, and outlook as the woman who spent her first twenty-one years as Caroline Lavinia Scott. One year older than her lover, she became the bride of Benjamin Harrison, grandson of William Henry Harrison, in Oxford, Ohio. Like other men destined to head the nation, he hoped to find a career as an attorney. Still, he was so passionately in love with Carrie that he couldn't spend years separated from her while building up a practice.

Her father, a minister and an educator, spent two decades at Miami University before going to the faculty of Farmers' College—later Belmont College—at Oxford, not far from Cincinnati. The Reverend John W. Scott and his family had just reached the Oxford Institution when Harrison enrolled there. He and Carrie met on campus, developed a strong mutual interest in each other, and maintained it even after Ben transferred to Miami University. He began full-time reading of law immediately after graduating from "the Yale of the West," and waited only fifteen months to marry his sweetheart who had been waiting for him.

Caroline "Carrie" Harrison, wife
of the twenty-third president.
(Library of Congress)

After being admitted to the bar in relatively old and staid Cincinnati, he decided to move to young and brash Indianapolis. In the Hoosier capital, he formed a partnership with William Wallace, whose brother Lewis ("Lew") later wrote a brief account of Harrison's career. No one dreamed in 1855 that Lew Wallace would win international fame with his novel called *Ben Hur* or that staid and colorless Ben Harrison would go on to occupy the White House.

When he was at home, the attorney, who would soon turn his attention to politics, was not the same cold and formal person as known to outsiders. When his daughter was born, he was so affectionate to the child that his wife sometimes chided him mildly, saying, "You'll spoil her if you're not careful."

Carrie had already persuaded him to begin to share what she called her "passionate interest in all living things." An enthusiastic amateur painter, she dearly loved using watercolors to depict some of the flowers Ben cultivated. With his hearty approval, she soon went outside the home in order to teach Hoosier ladies the art of painting china. Far warmer than her husband in dealing with persons outside the family circle, she tried in vain to coach him in the art of relaxing with clients and strangers.

HARRISON SPENT MORE THAN two years as a Civil War officer, rising to the postwar rank of general despite the fact that his aides described him as being "distant." Fighting under Gen. William T. Sherman, he was present for much of the long and memorable federal march through Georgia and the Carolinas. Near Durham's Station in North Carolina, he was an observer when Gen. Joseph E. Johnston surrendered the last substantial Rebel body to Sherman.

Carrie, more openly ardent in patriotism than her husband, was unable to follow the example of Julia Grant and spend weeks with her husband in the field. She did, however, manage to visit him twice while he was stationed in the Cotton Belt.

Back home in Indianapolis, Julia's husband became an increasingly noted and financially successful attorney who devoted more and more time to the youthful Republican party, to include campaigning for Garfield in 1880. While stumping in Bloomington, Illinois, he came close to becoming the victim at the hands of a former Rebel who blamed him for the oppressive measures that Radical Republicans had imposed upon the South. A gun leveled at him failed to fire, and the would-be killer was dragged from the hall so Harrison could continue his bland and uninspiring campaign speech.

John Sherman, brother of Harrison's old commander, was one of the chief contenders for the 1888 presidential nomination. Sherman led the pack on the first ballot, but the 225 votes he received represented virtually all of his supporters. Harrison, who badly wanted the nomination but confided about his hopes in no one but Carrie, at first received only eighty-three votes. Seven ballots later, however, he became the nominee—and persuaded Lew Wallace to write his campaign biography.

Despite the influence of that document, in November he trailed Democrat Grover Cleveland by one hundred thousand votes. Normally Democratic New York, more than any other state, tilted the electoral college count toward Harrison. He and Carrie moved into the White House in March 1889, taking with them the largest entourage of relatives ever to occupy the mansion.

Carrie's ninety-year-old father found a nook that no one else wanted and made himself comfortable in it. Mame Dimmick, who had recently become a widow, was put on the payroll as her Aunt Carrie's personal secretary. Carrie's daughter Mary Scott—now thirty-one-year-old Mrs. McGee and known as Mamie—brought her husband with her to the executive mansion. Carrie's son Russell and his wife, Mary ("May"), never moved into 1600 Pennsylvania Avenue to stay, but spent a great deal of time there and brought their children when they came.

William Allen White, an editor in Kansas who was beginning to win some national recognition, informed readers that no previous administration had been anything like that of Harrison's. Through the influence of the wife adored by Ben but to whom he did not display public affection, four generations of Carrie's family were represented at 1600 Pennsylvania Avenue. Her two-year-old grandson, known to the family chiefly as Baby McKee, was described by White as "forever crawling over the first pages of newspapers."

Ostensibly developed for the sake of the grandchildren in residence, one of Carrie's ideas eventually grew into an annual White House tradition. On a brisk fall day she suggested to Ben that the little ones "really would enjoy having a Christmas tree of their own, right here in the mansion." As usual, he readily assented to her suggestion and seems later to have come close to intimating that it was his idea. The first Christmas tree to adorn the White House was a direct ancestor of today's huge and elaborately ornamented national Christmas tree.

Before bedtime on their first day in the mansion, Ben and Carrie had agreed that some drastic changes had to be made. There was plenty of office and entertainment space, but there were only five "sleeping apartments" in the White House, and four of them didn't have an adjoining bathroom. There were other problems: The coal-burning heating system and the kitchen were antiquated; many chandeliers were grimy with soot; a lot of the paint was damaged and dingy; and both the basement and attic were crammed with junk judged by previous occupants to be too good to throw away.

For several years foreign diplomats had been openly critical of the badly rundown White House. Ultimately, lawmakers who had been squabbling about what to do with a huge surplus in the Treasury allocated thirty-five thousand dollars for use in bringing the White House up to Gay Nineties standards.

Chandeliers were scrubbed, some walls were painted and others re-papered, and brand-new plumbing and four additional bathrooms were installed. When the latter were ready for use, the president, who seemed to be as cold as a fish to the outside world, positively glowed and said his wife's four new bathrooms "would tempt a duck to wash himself every single day."

Ben soon told Carrie he believed she should stop shaking hands. Having no idea that his wife was a victim of tuberculosis, the president noticed that her right hand would often suddenly go limp after she had greeted several hundred guests or sightseers. Without making a formal announcement, she began arranging things so that streams of persons could not get close enough to reach out and grasp her hand.

To the surprise of Washington society, ladies soon found themselves invited—twenty-five at a time—to learn china painting and needlework at the White House. The teacher of these informal classes was the first

President Benjamin Harrison, grandson of William Henry Harrison. (Brady Studio, Library of Congress)

lady herself, whose hands were seldom idle while she was awake. She decorated flowerpots, candlesticks, and even cracker boxes for use in the mansion. Hundreds of other examples of her work went to charities and to church bazaars. Materials were easy to come by. At first, while scrounging around for cast-off items that might be worth restoring, Carrie was aghast at the way previous occupants had trashed china. But she soon saw beyond the trash to produce small treasures. Many unbroken pieces were cleaned and placed on exhibition to provide a tiny glimpse of the way earlier presidents and their families had lived. This, in turn, launched the custom of preserving and exhibiting historical White House China.

Constantly encouraged by Ben to do things as she wished rather than as the world at large demanded, Carrie astonished the capital with her lavish use of the flowers that so often were subjects of her brush and paint. One newspaper correspondent, who probably made an exaggerated guess rather than the accurate count he claimed, told readers that he found nearly five thousand decorative plants in the East Room, alone. That total, he said, included hundreds each of roses, carnations, tulips, hyacinths, and asparagus ferns that made the White House seem to be "a greenhouse with formal floors and ceilings."

Long before he became the nation's chief executive, Harrison was profoundly affected by Carrie's enthusiasm for "all things beautiful and nearly everything that lives." Ben never exhibited the outward enthusiasm for which Carrie was noted, but he was far ahead of most of his contemporaries in his mature views about what later came to be called conservation.

With Carrie's behind-the-scenes encouragement (if not at her instigation), the twenty-third president issued a proclamation warning hunters of all nations to obey the letter of the law concerning fur-bearing animals of the Bering Sea. He followed up by pushing for and getting legislation designed to limit hunting in these waters to specific seasons of the year.

Industrialists who had helped pay for his campaign were surprised and some were angry when he secured legal sanction for a plan to limit the use of trees—one of the continent's greatest natural resources. Soon afterward, Carrie's husband issued a proclamation that established a forest reserve in New Mexico. That was followed by a similar edict under whose terms the Pike's Peak forest reserve was set apart in Colorado.

The behind-the-scenes impact of "a frail and consumptive woman" upon her husband, who would have been deeply embarrassed publicly to confess his love for her, had lasting impact upon the conservation movement in general and on our system of national forests and parks in particular.

25

William and Ida McKinley

"What will I see?"

"Not gonna tell you; you have to see for yourself."

"Will it be much longer?" demanded the new porter at the Neil House Hotel in Columbus, Ohio.

"Naw. Maybe a couple of minutes."

"My watch says three o'clock."

"You may be a little fast. Look out! Here he comes!" exclaimed a veteran doorman.

An immaculately dressed gentleman with a red carnation in his buttonhole stepped to an open window in a large building directly across from the hotel and leaned slightly forward. Pulling a handkerchief from his pocket, he waved it vigorously for what seemed like an eternity to the newcomer to the capital. Bowing a trifle, he pocketed the handkerchief and faded out of sight as he returned to his desk.

"What in the world is goin' on in this crazy place?"

"You just saw Governor William McKinley givin' a salute to his wife. She's right here in the hotel, third floor front, sittin' at her window. He always waves at three on the dot. People say she always waves back, but I've never seen her—can't leave this place to take a look from across the street."

Five years before the turn of the twentieth century, few of McKinley's colleagues and subordinates considered his behavior to border upon the eccentric. Throughout the Buckeye State, he was widely praised as "one of the most ever-loving husbands any woman could hope to have." It was universally known that the governor's wife was not well and that she cherished his afternoon greeting that had become a ritual. Only a handful of intimates knew that the 3:00 P.M. wave of his handkerchief and the response from the Neil House meant as much to the governor as it did to his wife, Ida.

Some hotel attendants knew that at age forty-eight Ida's face was unusually pale. Except for persons who had been at banquets attended by the governor and his wife, comparatively few voters of the state were aware that she suffered from a seemingly incurable malady that no one talked about.

YEARS EARLIER IDA SAXTON had been the belle of Canton, Ohio. Many female contemporaries openly envied her azure eyes whose color seemed to be enhanced by her delicately pale skin. Topped by masses of well-tended auburn hair, she was a real beauty—and she knew it.

Ida's father, a more than prosperous banker, wanted nothing but the best for her. That's why he insisted that she go to Pennsylvania in order to study at regionally noted Brook Hall Seminary in Media. As a graduation present, James Saxton sent his lovely daughter on the European Grand Tour. When she returned, bone tired but sparkling, she did not finish describing the trip before turning to her father and demanding: "Now that I'm back, I want a job!"

Women had entered industry in great numbers a full decade earlier. Manpower shortages during the Civil War had placed an intolerable strain on manufacturers. In desperation, hundreds of them had turned to the immense pool of young females in the Union. The example was set by Washington, where the War Department gave formal approval to the use of women as cartridge makers. A trifle reluctantly, because it would mean a break with tradition, Ida's father offered her a chance to work in his bank. She accepted instantly. It took bank patrons quite a while to become accustomed to seeing a vivacious redhead occupying a teller's cage—a spot not known to have been previously filled by a female anywhere in the nation.

There was considerable talk in Canton about the fact that "Jim Saxton's daughter will handle your money for you at his bank." One interested patron was a young lawyer who had not been in town very long. Civil War veteran William McKinley had been introduced to Ida before she went to Europe. There is no record that she made more than a fleeting impression when they met at a picnic. He saw her regularly in the bank, however, and soon began asking her to go out with him.

Four years Ida's senior, William soon stirred up a great deal more talk than had accompanied Ida's appearance in her father's bank. Working hard to make Rutherford B. Hayes governor of the state, William would usually end a campaign speech by taking questions from the audience. One night a fellow, acting like he was half drunk, tossed a bombshell by demanding how anybody got the notion that "some of them black fellers ought to have a say in who's governor of Ohio."

Knowing that the concept of Negro suffrage was highly unpopular throughout the state, the ex-soldier, who had fought under the command of Hayes, gave a capsule account of his war experiences. He put on a uniform as a buck private in the rear rank of Company E, Twenty-third Ohio volunteer regiment, he explained. He enlisted to fight for the Union and first saw the elephant—or experienced combat—at Carnifax Ferry, Virginia. He was at Antietam, Maryland, on the bloodiest day in American history, and he saw comrades mowed down like ripe wheat at Cedar Creek, Virginia.

"By then," he told his questioner and his audience, "the war had changed. President Lincoln had issued the Emancipation Proclamation. Lots of free blacks and ex-slaves were in blue uniforms, just like mine. They were fighting for the Union just like I was. Some of them settled right here in Ohio after the war. That's why I think they have as much right to vote for a governor as I do and you do."

That brief but impassioned message from a Hayes campaign worker won no votes for William's former commander and briefly made him conspicuous in and around Canton. Ida heard all

President William McKinley. (Library of Congress)

about the rally and the speech the next day, but she tossed her head and confided to fellow employees that she didn't give a fig what other people thought of Major McKinley. She said she liked him a lot, regardless of whether she agreed with every one of his opinions. By this time, old acquaintances of Canton's most sought-after young woman were saying to one another that they were sure they "heard wedding bells ringing from somewhere not far away."

That verdict was accurate; William and Ida exchanged vows on January 25, 1871, in Canton's unfinished Presbyterian church. Many of the estimated one thousand guests who attended the ceremony agreed that it was one of the prettiest and most expensive they had ever seen. Some guessed that the bride's satin gown, trimmed in pointe lace, must have come from a shop in Paris she discovered during her long European journey. John Saxton's wedding present was the deed to a nice home on North Market Street. It would still be big enough after two or three children came along, he confided to William.

The first little McKinley, a girl named Katherine and affectionately called Katie, made her debut eleven months to the day from her parents' wedding day. She looked a bit frail but healthy, yet she died during infancy. William and Ida tried again, got another girl, and named her for her mother. She, too, survived only a short time after a difficult pregnancy and an unusually painful delivery that neighbors thought greatly weakened her mother.

The death of little Ida triggered a long period of depression for the elder Ida. Although it was then common for children to die in infancy, William's wife seemingly blamed herself for her daughters' deaths. Many of her earlier interests vanished; she occupied herself by making crocheted bedroom slippers that she gave away by the dozens and by listening attentively to William's musings about their future.

UNLIKE NUMEROUS WIVES, IDA never discouraged her husband from seeking a political office. On the contrary, after listening to him talk about running for days or weeks, she would typically say that it was time to stop talking and start running. In 1876, William defeated Democrat Leslie L. Sanborn and became the U.S. Representative of Ohio's eighteenth district.

Ida reveled in the dozen years they spent in Washington prior to William's decision to give up his seat in order to run for governor of Ohio. Life in the capital had provided just the right amount of extra zest that she needed in order to boost her permanently weakened body. She took part in social activities, even when she did not feel well, and continued to crochet bedroom slippers by the score. Until her husband became a member of the ways and means committee, after having helped to create a vacancy by working hard for James Garfield's election as president, Ida did not rise above the lower level of political wives. When William became chairman of the august body, she encouraged him every time he talked at home about drafting a protective tariff measure.

Ida, whose voice was far from strong, clapped her hands with child-like delight when the McKinley Tariff Act was signed into law by Benjamin Harrison in 1890. She embraced her triumphant husband and congratulated him because industry-rich Ohio and most of the rest of the North could get along without imported goods, and now he had hit a home run in the national political game.

Ida McKinley, extraordinarily lovely. (Library of Congress)

Although documentary evidence is lacking, Ida clearly knew in 1890 that her handsome five-foot-six husband had his eye on the White House. Beginning with U. S. Grant, one Ohio-born Civil War veteran after another had won the highest office in the land. She remembered that William had enlisted at age eighteen. She calculated carefully and informed her husband that "Men who fought in blue are thinning out fast; that makes you stand out above the crowd."

William, who knew that she was right, decided—with Ida's strong approval—to yield his influential post in Congress in order to seek top leadership back home. He had long been advised and aided by wealthy Marcus Hanna of Cleveland—who pushed very hard for the North Bend native because he knew that McKinley was likely to follow his guidance any time he faced a difficult decision. Hanna's fortune combined with McKinley's Civil War and congressional record proved unbeatable; he won the governorship in a landslide and used his four years in office to strengthen his national position.

Hanna volunteered to manage McKinley's 1896 bid for the Republican nomination, and he spent so much money so well that McKinley went over the top on the first ballot. Ida worried a bit when she learned that the Democratic nominee was William Jennings Bryan. His Illinois roots would likely generate strong support for him in that key state, she correctly reasoned. Even though she didn't like to do so, she admitted to her husband that she was afraid that the man famous as "the Silver-tongued Orator" would campaign very hard and would persuade many voters.

Ida was right; Bryan traveled an estimated eighteen thousand miles— far more than any earlier candidate for the White House. He gained enough followers to garner about 6.5 million votes—but his 47 percent total in November left him well behind McKinley. Although admirers of the Democrat stuck with Bryan in the electoral college, the man from Ohio won the electoral vote by a margin of 3 to 2.

During their eight years in the White House, Ida's husband must sometimes have felt that the ship of state was in a hurricane off Cape Hatteras. He saw his tariff act of 1890 replaced by a somewhat less-severe measure. That didn't seem to give him or Ida any sleepless nights, but both of them tossed and turned as they pondered what to do about foreign affairs. With Ida's wholehearted support, her husband eventually signed a joint congressional resolution that called for annexation of the Hawaiian Islands. Far more important, in her judgment, events in Cuba triggered the brief but victorious Spanish-American War.

"When it is over, let's keep what we want," Ida proposed before the battleship *Maine* was sunk under unexplained circumstances. Her husband made no public promises or threats, but at war's end he followed her advice and saw to it that Guam, Puerto Rico, the Philippines, and Wake Island were attached to the United States. No administration before or since stretched so far and so permanently into places at great distances from the mainland.

Long before the many achievements of our twenty-fifth president came to an end, everyone in official Washington was privy to Ida's incurable physical condition. Absolutely no one, however, talked about it in public or labeled it a handicap to her husband's administration. When diplomats and high-ranking civil servants and their wives went to the White House for an evening, they knew that it might be marked by actions never before seen in the mansion.

Having suffered seizures of some form since the birth of her second daughter, Ida had gradually become worse. Feeling the onset of a public exhibition of her condition, she typically whispered softly to William or bent the fingers and thumb of her left hand into a tight little fist. He invariably responded by swiftly pulling a clean white handkerchief from a pocket and deftly placing it over her face so that contractions of her muscles wouldn't be seen by guests. When the spasm passed and she returned to normal, she lifted the thin covering off and resumed her conversation or her meal as though nothing had happened.

Virtually every scholar who has dug into the inner recesses of the joint life of William and Ida has lavished praise upon him for boundless love that enabled him to deal almost casually with what may have been epileptic episodes. There's no doubt that he loved her from the day he proposed until his death, for his last concern was about her.

Yet few analysts have paused to praise the ceaseless courage of a once-beautiful woman who time after time had to make an abrupt mental departure from a reception or a dinner. Many a man who had faced enemy bullets without flinching would have found himself incapable of "going on as usual" after two or three seizures in public. Ida managed to master her humiliation because she loved William too much to be separated from him if it was possible for them to be together.

With his weapon concealed by bandages, the killer (center) pumps bullets into the president. (Buffalo Express)

Having accepted an invitation to visit the Pan American Exposition in Albany, New York, they went to it as usual—together. More than normally fatigued by the journey, Ida went to their hotel and her husband was escorted to the exposition grounds. Self-styled anarchist Leon F. Czolgosz, a mentally unbalanced mill worker who was unemployed, managed to pump two bullets into William at close range.

A team of six doctors tried to extract the bullet lodged in his abdominal cavity but failed. He might have survived had not gangrene developed, possibly because surgeons who had inadequate lighting in the operating room failed properly to cleanse the path left behind by the bullet.

Close friends predicted that Ida would collapse as soon as William was buried, but they were wrong. "He always begged me to be strong for his sake," the widow said. "I've done the best I could for thirty years and My Precious wouldn't want me to quit now."

No one on the top side of Earth could take her husband's place in good times or in bad. Yet she lived six lonely years before giving death-bed instructions that the only spot where her spirit wouldn't be restless was beside William's grave in Canton.

26

Teddy, Alice, and Edith Roosevelt

The metamorphosis of Teedy, who became Teddy and then Theodore Roosevelt, has no close counterpart among chief executives. He was an asthmatic seventeen-year-old who for forty-three years dominated the body and mind of a mature man who had a bad heart, suffered from chronic nervous diarrhea, and had lost the hearing of one ear and the sight of one eye.

When the body he inhabited was fifty-five years old, he announced that he planned to spend seven months on a fifteen-hundred-mile journey exploring Brazil's little-known Rio Duvida, or River of Doubt. Relatives and friends tried to dissuade him, saying that such a stunt was far too dangerous for a person in his physical condition. The ex-president shook his head vigorously and in the falsetto voice for which he was noted explained that he had no choice. "I have to go," he said; "it's my last chance to be a boy."

Speaking at a conference devoted to attempts to understand our twenty-sixth president, biographer Edmund Morris mused that "No matter how large the confines of the study [devoted to him], he always requires extra space and added dimensions." Staffers of the *Chicago Tribune* shared their collective views of Theodore Roosevelt with readers by means of a six-panel cartoon that purported to depict him resting at his Oyster Bay, New York, home. Sketch captions read: "He first chops down a few trees . . . After which he takes a brisk stroll of twenty miles . . . And rests a moment or two . . . Before taking a little cross-country canter . . . He then gives the children a wheelbarrow ride . . . By which time he is about ready for breakfast."

Frenetic self-indulgence on the part of the chief executive who never grew up took the form of hunting in the West and in Africa; charging up Cuba's San Juan Hill—not on horseback as would be expected of a Rough Rider—on foot; delivering a political speech with a bullet in his chest; trying to ride faster, jump higher, and get to the quarry ahead of any other fox hunter; running from the past with such frenzy that he pretended never to have seen it; taking the punches of a sparring partner until he was too

170

Clad in buckskin and carrying both rifle and hunting knife, mighty hunter Roosevelt posed for the camera this time without his otherwise omnipresent spectacles. (Harvard University)

groggy to find his corner; and joyously demonstrating to boys and girls that he could outdo them in everything that youngsters do.

He convinced himself, his family, and his associates that he enjoyed each and every one of these activities, but put showing off before children at the head of the list. In his autobiography he mused:

> There are many kinds of success in life worth having. It is exceedingly interesting and attractive to become a success as a business man, a railroader, a farmer, a lawyer or doctor, a writer, a President, a ranchman, colonel of a fighting regiment or killer of grizzly bears and lions. But for unflagging interest and enjoyment, a household of children certainly makes all other forms of success and achievement lose their importance by comparison.

FROM FEBRUARY 14, 1884, until January 6, 1919, Teddy succeeded remarkably well in keeping a door that led into the past bolted and padlocked. The first of his children with whom he frolicked until he turned pale with exhaustion was born on that dreadful Valentine's Day of 1884. The love of his life, wife Alice, died then, after giving birth to a daughter and namesake whom her widower called Baby Lee in order to avoid having to speak the name Alice. Years later nationally renowned Alice Roosevelt Longworth confessed that she never understood why her father absolutely refused to ever speak of her dead mother.

The former Edith Carow, stepmother of Alice, bore Theodore four sons and one daughter. Born to wealth and prestige, she seldom tried to whittle her exuberant husband down to size and never succeeded when she made the attempt. In addition to being a prolific and a good mother, Edith was a wise counselor and a never-failing source of comfort. Although she seems never to have put the matter bluntly into words, she spent her thirty-three years with Roosevelt fully aware that she stood in the shadow of the former Alice Hathaway Lee, whose life ebbed away at the same time that of her daughter began.

Strangely in the light of subsequent events, Edith knew Teedy long before Alice made his acquaintance. He is believed to have been all of three years old when Baby Edith and he first played together in New York City. The children became acquainted because the Union Square home of Teedy's grandparents sat next to the residence of Edith's father and mother. Corinne, Teedy's younger sister, made her arrival less than two months after Edith, and the two girls formed an inseparable bond that in time had a profound and unplanned influence upon the life of the future president.

Already meticulous in recording events and thoughts in a diary, Teedy trailed around Europe with his mother and father. His lack of enthusiasm for the lengthy tour was revealed by a telltale diary entry scribbled in a small boy's handwriting: "Mama showed me a picture of Eidith [*spelling as in original*] Carow, and her face stirred up home sickness and longings for the past" wrote the eleven-year-old who sometimes thought and acted like an adult.

He and the girl who lived next door to his grandparents (and whom he had begun to call Her Little Ladyship) hit it off splendidly for years. As they matured and began to think of parting when he left home to go to college, they probably talked dreamily of someday getting married. That supposition is strengthened by the fact that Edith forcefully substituted Teddy for the Teedy of his childhood.

Teddy received Edith with open arms when she visited him during his freshman year at Harvard, but something soon happened to their fast-ripening relationship. Neither of them ever revealed what

Alice Hathaway Lee, shortly before her marriage to Teddy. (Harvard University)

led to a rift between them, but by the time he reached nineteen they had begun going their separate ways.

Whether Roosevelt casually shrugged off the loss of his long-time sweetheart or dropped into a pit of despair is unknown. If he experienced the latter reaction, the Harvard student was on the rebound when he met a vivacious seventeen-year-old from Boston. Described as "simply stunning" in appearance, Alice Lee shared her new friend's interest in sports and the outdoors. She was a lively conversationalist who had read nearly every book Teddy asked her about and seems to have been a veteran of many flirtations. After having been with the girl called Sunshine just twice, Roosevelt made up his mind to win her if possible, saying that he had never earlier cared a snap of his finger for any other.

Sunshine quickly made it clear that she was interested in Teddy, but she was not ready to commit herself to him or anyone else. "How I love her!" he exulted. "She is so high above other girls that she seems like a star of heaven." Probably without realizing that he was getting dangerously close to his earlier pet name for Edith, he habitually referred to Alice as his Little Queen. He played whist with her, taught her the five-step waltz, and had his favorite horse shipped to Cambridge so he could demonstrate to her his skill as a rider. Aboard Lightfoot, he towered above Alice and momentarily felt invulnerable.

In an instant of supreme confidence he confided to his diary during a Thanksgiving season his solemn pledge that he would soon make Alice his very own at the marriage altar. She had numerous other admirers, however, and most of their noses didn't have spectacles perched on them. When she made it clear that she had no intention of marrying him or anyone else soon, Teddy was so crushed that he ripped from his diary the entry about his determination to make her his bride.

Talking to his diary almost as though he were pouring out his feelings in conversation with a trusted comrade, he wrote:

> She is my sweet, pretty, pure queen, my laughing little love! How bewitching she is! I can not help petting her and caressing her all the time, for she is such a perfect little Sunshine. I do not believe that any man ever loved a woman more than I love her.

The Boston debut of Alice nearly drove him mad with doubts. Young males of the city were already hovering around her "like moths around a candle." What if one of them should persuade her to ditch her earlier admirers? Both tormented and angry at the thought, he placed a mail order for a set of dueling pistols so he'd have them at hand if they should be needed.

Having received one rebuff after another, he was almost as surprised as he was delighted when Alice finally said "Yes" and agreed to set a tentative date for their wedding. Teddy and Alice became man and wife in a ceremony held in the Unitarian church of Brookline, Massachusetts. He wanted their vows to be spoken on October 18, 1878, since that was the second anniversary of their first meeting in the home of neighbors of the Lees whose son was a classmate of Roosevelt. He greatly regretted that circumstances caused their union to take place on October 27, but exulted that it was the happiest day of his life and would appear in bold red letters on every subsequent calendar.

TEDDY TRIED HIS BEST to become enamored with law under the guidance of faculty members of New York City's Columbia Law School, but he never succeeded. His election to the state's assembly prompted him to shove his law books aside and never return to them; he would spend the rest of his life in public office, he told Alice. Probably thinking that it would advance his political career, he joined the New York national guard but did not attend regularly. With no other military training or experience, he seems really to have believed that with his Rough Riders behind him he could meet and master the best soldiers Spain could send to the New World in 1898.

With Alice decidedly less bewitching because she was very pregnant, Teddy deserted her during the fall of 1883 in order to hunt buffalo in the Dakota Territory. Entranced by anything and everything western, he invested fourteen thousand dollars during this expedition and returned to the East boasting that he was now part owner of a cattle ranch. They had decided in advance that if the baby should be a girl she'd be given her mother's name, and Alice Lee arrived on schedule forty-eight hours ahead of Valentine's Day.

With the legislature in session, Teddy was in Albany. A telegram brought him home to learn from his brother Elliott that both his wife and his mother were in a critical condition. Martha Bulloch Roosevelt died of typhoid fever about 3:00 A.M. on Valentine's Day. Eleven hours later, his bride, who was now the mother of their daughter, was felled by Bright's disease plus complications from childbirth.

Marked with a bold black cross, his diary entry for the fateful day consists of a single sentence: "The light has gone out of my life."

On February 16 a double funeral marked an end to one of the most vibrant chapters in the life of a man who took many of his adolescent traits to the White House. His actions show that he formed a resolution to wipe Alice from the slate of his memory and to live as though she had never existed. He made it an inflexible rule never to speak of Alice and discarded Teddy in favor of Theodore—although he could not prevent his political followers and the public at large from using the name that had sounded so warm when it came from the lips of Alice.

Having hardly thought of Edith since their parting of the ways in what seemed to him as eons ago, Theodore accidentally came face to face with her one day while she was visiting his sister. Harvard alumni who knew him well insisted that "his drooping tail feathers began to signal that he had new vitality within twenty-four hours of having encountered the girl friend of his youth."

Whether the transformation was that abrupt, he was soon paying court to Edith and was hinting of marriage. She did not discourage him, and he took a drastic change in Carow family plans in stride. Edith's father, who was affluent during her childhood and adolescence, had fallen upon

Colonel Roosevelt, who with a few of his men made it up San Juan Hill on foot, preferred horses to automobiles.

comparatively hard times just as his health began to give way. Following his sudden death, an appraisal of his estate convinced his widow that she and her two daughters should move to England where their money would go farther.

That's how a future president came to be married on foreign soil. Edith became Theodore's second wife in Saint George's Church at Hanover Square, London. As had been the case in the Brookline ceremony, the bride was three years younger than her mate. That's where the similarity between Alice and Edith ended, however. Edith was six years older than Alice had been at the time Teddy took her as his wife. Edith was less striking in appearance and was much more prone than Alice to rebuke her husband for what she regarded as adolescent exhibitionism.

Edith did not have the iron will and boundless ambition attributed to Mary Todd Lincoln, however. When Theodore was approached about becoming William McKinley's running mate in 1900, she scoffed at the idea. Her husband's political career would come to an end, she told friends, if he spent four years doing little but preside over sessions of the U.S. Senate.

Documentary evidence is lacking, but it appears likely that Senator Henry Cabot Lodge played a decisive role in persuading Roosevelt that after four years in the nation's second slot he might have a good chance at first place. To the open disappointment of Edith, Theodore tossed his hat into the ring and at the Republican National Convention in Philadelphia received 925 out of a possible 926 votes on the first ballot in 1895. Since he was a candidate, Theodore refrained from voting for himself—so garnered one vote less than had McKinley.

Theodore cut a wide swath through twenty-four states, and he was shot in Milwaukee as he prepared to deliver one of his more than six hundred campaign speeches. His folded thick manuscript plus a spectacle case deflected the bullet considerably, so with lead partly embedded in his fourth rib and his shirt spattered with blood he continued with the rally.

In Milwaukee and in Chicago, surgeons felt that it would be unwise to try to remove the bullet fired by John Schrank. Consequently, Roosevelt was carrying it when he went to have lunch with friends on September 6, 1901. Receiving word that McKinley, too, had been the target of a crazed assailant, he hurried to Buffalo to see his chief and received assurance that the president would soon be back on his feet.

Theodore then took Edith and their children on a vacation in the Adirondacks. A week after Theodore learned of the Czolgosz shooting, a messenger reached Lake Tear-of-the-Clouds with a telegram that informed him the president was dying. By the time he arrived at Buffalo, McKinley was gone; consequently, Theodore took his oath of office as president before a U.S. district judge in the home of Ansley Wilcox.

THEIR MARRIAGE, ALTHOUGH LACKING the emotional intensity of Theodore's brief time with Alice, was stable and mutually fulfilling. For the most part, Edith managed the household and finances and let her husband cavort as he pleased—which he would have done no matter how strenuously she might have objected to a pet project or a planned expedition.

Roosevelt was firmly rebuffed by Woodrow Wilson when he offered to raise two hundred thousand men and lead them to Europe in 1917. Staying out of the war, but not by choice, the former president mourned when he learned that his son Quentin had been killed in an airplane crash while fighting in France. He said with frankness and honesty that he would have rather died fighting the Germans than to lose his son. "It might have been me," he mused to his wife, "had it not been for that weak-kneed Democratic weasel who sits in the White House."

Edith's husband, who was beginning audibly to wheeze after slight exertion, was admitted to a New York hospital four months after the death of Quentin. He had known for years that childhood ills had weakened his heart, so he was gratified to learn that his symptoms seemed to result from inflammatory rheumatism.

Theodore, who continued to rebuke anyone who called him Teddy to his face, still had a lot of boyish Teedy inside him. He brushed objections of doctors aside, said he couldn't possibly remain in the hospital on Christmas, and returned to his Oyster Bay home. There the man who never ceased to glory in having been a Rough Rider suffered an embolism in a coronary artery on January 6, 1919. He slipped away from the home he had planned to occupy with Alice without saying good-bye to Edith.

27

Will and Nellie Taft

Nellie Taft encouraged her husband to spend every possible hour with his father, whose doctors said had only hours or days to live. Alphonso Taft clung to life longer than anyone expected, and his thirty-four-year-old bear of a son often turned his head when at the bedside in order to prevent his father from seeing his tears.

To his wife of five years, the six-foot-two attorney, who was already recognized as a powerhouse in the Republican party of Ohio, confided in a letter:

> You know I am not superstitious, yet I cannot escape knowing that Father has been a guardian angel to me. His wishes for my success have helped bring it to me. As his life ebbs away, I have a presentment that I shall cease to have the luck which has followed me so far. Maybe I will settle down to humdrum commonplace practice in Cincinnati, managing to eke out only enough to support us.

There is no record that Will's dire view of the future evoked a direct response. His wife, the former Helen Herron, may not have thought gloomy notions deserved to be pondered and answered. She had a great deal of respect for the dying man who had been U. S. Secretary of War, U.S. Attorney General, and ambassador to both Austria-Hungary and Russia. He clearly had done everything in his power to advance the career of his son, and the absence of his powerful backing would be sorely felt.

Yet his daughter-in-law never wavered in her conviction that her husband didn't need the influence of his family. A lackluster courtship dragged along for years before she made up her mind to take her sweetheart to the altar. By then Nellie had decided she'd push him as hard as necessary in order to get him into a place in which both would feel fulfilled and happy.

FRIENDS WHO HAD KNOWN the Cincinnati resident all of her life knew that only one spot would meet Nellie's specifications. By far the most memorable experience of her early years took place when she was about seventeen. Her father, John W. Herron, had been a law partner of Rutherford B. Hayes's. Their intimate friendship continued after Hayes went to the White House in the aftermath of what many historians term "the stolen election."

Before the end of 1877, President Hayes began urging his old partner and close friend to bring his family to Washington for a visit. They notified Hayes in 1878 that they were taking him up on his invitation and that they would be staying at a downtown hotel within a short distance of the White House. When Herron stepped up to the desk to register, the clerk informed him that the reservation had been canceled because he and his family would be guests at 1600 Pennsylvania Avenue.

Their Washington vacation proved delightful to both John and Harriet Herron. They hoped that their upcoming baby would be a girl so they could name her Lucy in honor of Mrs. Hayes. They talked about their stay in the White House for years and treasured souvenirs that reminded them of pleasant days there.

Nellie's parents realized that their daughter, whose friends had virtually scrapped "Helen" in favor of "Nellie," was far more impressed than they were. "It will soon fade away," her mother believed; "she's at a very impressionable age." Whatever the tangible and intangible factors that contributed to Nellie's reaction to her White House visit, her feelings about it did anything but fade away—they became stronger and stronger. Within a few months after having returned to Cincinnati, all of her friends—male as well as female—knew that Nellie intended some day to live in that Washington mansion.

All she needed in order to achieve her life goal was a male who seemed to be a logical and likely candidate for the presidency. Nellie quickly did her homework by poring over biographies of chief executives. Beginning with U. S. Grant, she learned, one Ohio native after another had gained the presidency: the friend of her parents, Hayes; James A. Garfield, whose birthplace of Orange was virtually unknown outside the Buckeye State; Benjamin Harrison, who grew up in North Bend; and William McKinley, who began life in Niles.

"Virginia is famous as 'the Mother of Presidents,' " she excitedly announced to fellow students. "One more good ole Buckeye in the White House will make half a dozen and then Ohio will be famous as 'the Father of Presidents'!" When friends teased and asked what she expected to do about this matter, her eyes flashed fire as she announced without hesitation: "I don't know who Number Six is, but I expect to find out, and when I do, I'm going to marry him!"

NONE OF NELLIE'S FRIENDS were impressed when she introduced them to a Cincinnati Law School student named Will Taft. Almost but not quite six feet tall, to some of them he looked more than a trifle pudgy. Privately, some of them snickered a bit about "Nellie's new catch." They guessed, correctly as events proved, that if a fellow just twenty-two years old weighed well over two hundred pounds, "he'll be a monster when he's fully grown." Some of them learned from former students at Woodward High School that when Taft was there he was widely known as Big Lub. Expecting to have great fun with Nellie, they told her about the early nickname of her new boyfriend. Instead of reacting as they had expected, she took the news in stride, announcing, "Sure; he was real young when some of his friends saw that he would be big enough to hold down the biggest job in the U.S.A.!"

Taft wasn't long in letting it be known that he took a strong liking to Nellie, but the young adult whose baptismal name was William Howard didn't like to do anything in a hurry. It seemed sorta nice to think of himself as being engaged to one of the prettiest and most vivacious females he had ever met, but it took him months and then years to get around to popping the question.

Their first encounter took place in the Mount Auburn suburb where Nellie lived with her parents and a little sister whose name served as a daily reminder of that never-to-be-forgotten White House visit. Neither of them assigned a precise date to the meeting, but since it was at a bobsled party it had to be during the winter of 1879–80. They saw each other infrequently for a time, but by July, Nellie was describing him as "that adorable Will Taft who strikes me with awe."

Although she did not explain the basis of her awe, it may have stemmed from the fact that she had to lift her head sharply in order to converse with him. Always energetic and an enthusiastic organizer, Nellie established a group that she called "a salon." Members met in her home with the avowed purpose of "discussing topics both intellectual and economic." Will was an early member of the group, who hid his feelings if he minded seeing her smoke cigarettes and down an occasional bottle of beer.

He must have begun to hint at the possibility of marriage within a year after they met, but there is no evidence that Nellie encouraged him. In January 1885 the young attorney delighted his friends and acquaintances by telling them that he had received the surprise of his life by being appointed as assistant solicitor for big and wealthy Hamilton County.

This immense upward move must have fortified the man who had reached the height of George Washington—six feet, two inches—and whose horizontal growth was continuing. In June he ceased to hint and came out with a strong marriage proposal. Nellie, who may have seen his

Nellie and Will, and their son Charles. (Library of Congress)

early rise to a significant office as a harbinger of things to come, said she'd become his wife. They married in her home seven years after they met; Will was twenty-nine and his bride, who was nearly four years younger, came close to thinking of herself as mistress of the White House as she walked to the improvised altar.

Their long-drawn friendship, which had gradually evolved into courtship, had little of the zest and fire widely associated with such periods. Had they been endowed with anything like the adolescent passion of Andrew Johnson and Eliza McCartle, they couldn't possibly have waited so long for physical consummation of their love. Their long wait ended with a marriage that was never threatened with dissolution but was notable for its lack of passion. During a period of eleven years they became parents of two sons and a daughter, all three of whom learned early that their mother was ardently eager to see their father inaugurated as president of the United States.

Will never shared that passion; to him, appointment to the U.S. Supreme Court seemed the highest goal to which an attorney could possibly aspire. After barely six years as a married man and a father, he was ecstatic when President Benjamin Harrison picked him as U.S. solicitor general. Two years later, the chief executive whose earliest years were spent in Ohio named Taft as a U.S. circuit judge.

To Nellie's husband, who had surpassed *big* to become positively *huge*, these fast upward moves meant that the Supreme Court was not as distant as it once seemed. She told him over and over, flat out, that he was too good for the court. He should focus his eyes on 1600 Pennsylvania Avenue and never waver from that goal, she insisted without avail. He was thrilled beyond measure to be invited to join the faculty of Cincinnati Law School, where he taught and served as dean for four years.

That period, which to Will seemed idyllic, came to an abrupt end when fellow Ohio native William McKinley persuaded Nellie's husband that six months of hard work on his part would establish civil government in the newly acquired Philippine Islands. Taft and his wife went there in June 1900 with the expectation that he would resume teaching at the beginning of the next calendar year.

The task of bringing order to the Philippines proved far more difficult than it had seemed to be when viewed from Capitol Hill and the White House. Will and Nellie threw themselves wholeheartedly into the work and became so deeply involved that he did things his friends back in Cincinnati would have regarded as impossible. In 1902 and again in 1903 he declined appointment to the Supreme Court.

Taft believed he had accomplished a great deal in Manila, he explained on both occasions, but he would be a quitter if he left before finishing his job there. Nellie, who must have been patting her foot in triumph on both occasions, had warned him not to hint that a seat on the high court might not be a good springboard for a presidential try. His refusal of the Supreme Court spot was largely due to her adamant insistence that he must do nothing that might endanger the realization of her girlhood dream to be mistress of the White House.

Theodore Roosevelt did not send to Manila a mildly worded request that Taft should consider becoming a member of his cabinet as secretary of war. In characteristic blunt and enthusiastic fashion, the twenty-sixth president simply told the big fellow from Ohio that he was needed and should report for his new post immediately. Nellie offered no objection to this abrupt termination of their stay in the Philippines. She knew enough about politics to be sure that a secretary of war would be highly visible, causing his name to become a household word because of publicity about his dealings with leaders of other nations.

One of Nellie's girlhood dreams was fulfilled in Chicago when delegates to the Republican National Convention gave her husband 702 votes on the first ballot. His supporters warned that he should not become overconfident. Nellie, however, never doubted for an instant that November would bring another big victory despite the fact that her Will would have to defeat resilient Democrat William Jennings Bryan in order to win.

Some candidates who rode to victory in the electoral college did not fare well at the polls. That was not the case with the man whom a wealthy girl from Cincinnati had pushed toward the White House for years. Taft won 1.2 million more popular votes than Bryan and swept to an easy win in the electoral college.

Soon after the second half of her girlhood dream came true, the new mistress of the White House and her husband boarded the steamer *Sylph* for a visit to Mount Vernon. If either of them knew about the earlier ill-fated Potomac River voyage of the USS *Princeton*, they were not deterred by what many persons would have viewed as an ill omen. This time, tragedy struck long before the residence of George Washington came in sight.

Gasping and clutching at her throat, Nellie collapsed as the *Sylph* was leaving the dock. Since she was still conscious, experienced fellow voyagers quickly concluded that she had suffered a severe stroke. Maj. Archibald Butt, Taft's military aide whose destiny was to go to the bottom of the Atlantic with the *Titanic,* described the afternoon in detail in his journal. According to Butt, the dazed president "seemed like a great stricken animal" whose face showed his agonizing fear about the future of his beloved wife and advisor.

It took more than a year of convalescence and therapy to restore the woman from Cincinnati to reasonably good health. During most days her husband spent several hours at her bedside. He brought her flowers from the greenhouse, read to her from novels, and never lost patience as he worked to help her regain control of the intricate network of muscles by which speech is produced. When they agreed with each other that she had fully recovered, the president dashed off a joyous note to one of his brothers. In it he said that his wife was now "quite disposed to sit as a pope and issue directives, which is an indication of the restoration of normal conditions."

Despite the fact that high drama was missing from their courtship, their marriage, and Will's rise to the highest office in the land plus later service as Chief Justice of the United States, the two Buckeyes racked up a surprising number of first achievements while in the White House. As the first president who weighed substantially more than three hundred pounds, it's no wonder that he became stuck in the bathtub and ordered a monstrous new one as soon as he was extricated. Earlier, she had been the first wife of an incoming chief executive to ride to his inauguration at his side.

Will was the first presidential golfer, and he claimed that his immense size gave him an edge when he used a driver. (George G. Bain photo)

With Nellie's warm encouragement even during weeks when she spoke only in monosyllables, Taft agreed to establish a precedent by throwing out the first pitch of the baseball season. He bought the first White House automobile and authorized the first U.S. Army purchase of an airplane. He was the first president to regularly play golf—and she was the last first lady to keep a cow on the White House lawn so the place would never be without fresh milk.

Although much of what they accomplished resulted from Nellie's gentle prodding that never degenerated into nagging, she and Will did more things together than typical married couples. He became restless if separated from her for more than a few hours, and she suffered torment if she went very long without a gentle caress from his big hand and a word of endearment from his surprisingly gentle voice.

As mistress of the White House, Nellie fell far below the standard set by some of its earlier occupants, and Will does not come close to reaching the top of the chart when chief executives are ranked by historians. If, however, their union were to be measured by mutual dependence and domestic tranquillity over a period of many years, the big man and the little lady from Cincinnati would put multitudes of once-passionate lovers to shame.

28

Woodrow, Ellen, and Edith Wilson

Y ou must have had a mighty good time with her . . ."

"Who?"

"You know perfectly well who I mean—Mary Peck!" exclaimed Ellen Wilson.

"She's just a casual acquaintance; I wrote you all about her from Bermuda."

"I have every one of your letters in a locked box, and I have gone over them two or three times. You didn't mean to do it, but you let it slip that you were having a fantastic time with that woman."

"My dear," responded the president of Princeton University, "your imagination is running wild. You know perfectly well why I was on the island; Mrs. Peck did not arrive until I had been there for at least a week."

"Maybe. But you met her there a year earlier. That's when the two of you laid your plans to get together again this summer."

Woodrow Wilson assumed his most austere look, stood silently for an instant, and then went to his bedroom without another word. He had become accustomed to accusations by his Georgia-born wife of twenty-three years and was sure she'd calm down during the night.

Normally, that's what the sequence of events would have been on the heels of his return from a trip ostensibly taken for the sake of his health. This time, Ellen did anything but cool down. At breakfast she was so hot under the collar that she barely spoke to her husband. As she rose from the table, she signaled for him to stop and demanded: "How many times has she been married?"

Trying to control his anger in order to seem to be casual, Woodrow snapped: "If I've told you once, I've told you a dozen times. She has been married twice, but was not divorced. She lost Tom Hulbert quite suddenly ten years ago."

"Suicide, or murder?"

"Don't be ridiculous, my dear. He died of natural causes—a heart attack, I believe. Please do not start throwing around accusations about things you know nothing about."

185

"You forget that I grew up in Savannah, where everybody who was anybody knew what was going on around town. This is the third year in succession that you've gone off to Bermuda without me. I wasn't born yesterday. She smokes cigarettes—you told me so, yourself."

"My dear Ellen," Wilson nodded in agreement, "that has nothing to do with us. I begged you to go with me in 1907 and again in 1908, and you refused."

"You know perfectly well that my skin can't stand the summer sun there. I offered to go to Michigan with you, and you said that didn't suit you. You had your heart set on Bermuda and Mrs. Peck."

Grim faced, the educator terminated the argument by striding toward his office. After having suffered an extremely mild stroke in 1906, he and his doctors had come to the conclusion that rest and relaxation in a semitropical climate would do him more good than medicine. He liked the island so much that he returned the following summer and then became more than casually acquainted with the vacationing wife of a Pittsfield, Massachusetts, businessman.

Mary Peck was attractive, vivacious, well-read, and intelligent. Ellen Wilson had all of these attributes also, but in adolescence she learned how to scold and seemed to have honed her skill in this art as the years slipped by. They had now been married long enough, her husband realized, to become thoroughly accustomed to one another—perhaps so thoroughly that it was easy for him to take her for granted. Swallowing his pride, he resolved to tender an apology that evening. He could have saved his breath. Ellen remained in a huff for days—longer than at any previous time during their years together.

Although born in Staunton, Virginia, he had lived in both Georgia and South Carolina when his Ohio-born father, a Presbyterian minister, moved from one church to another.

Ellen spent much of her girlhood in Savannah, which she never tired of telling new acquaintances was the second largest city in Georgia. Because Ellen was the daughter of a Presbyterian minister, Woodrow felt instant affinity when they became acquainted. After graduating from the College of New Jersey, later renamed Princeton, he planned to study law at the University of Virginia but had to withdraw because of ill health.

He and a friend he met in law school hung out their shingle in Atlanta, but their practice was so unsuccessful it lasted only a year. Woodrow became a graduate student at Johns Hopkins University, where he completed a book on *Congressional Government* published by the noted Houghton Mifflin Company of Boston. Six months after it appeared, he

Princeton University president Woodrow Wilson, his wife Ellen, and their three daughters.

and Ellen married in Savannah, after both of them had apparently decided they were not likely to do better.

Their early marriage was harmonious and might have been happy had his health been better and had he not sometimes looked at other women in a fashion Ellen seldom evoked after their first few months together. She was confident that he had never entered into a physical relationship with someone else, but she didn't like his frank revelations about luncheons or conferences with other women. She bristled and became furious at the very thought of Mary Peck, who was well connected socially and politically in Bermuda.

Attempting to be furtive but never having learned how to keep his mouth shut, Woodrow continued to exchange letters with Mary. Some of his letters to her have been preserved and they show more flair and élan than any existing letter he sent to Ellen from a distance. After Mary lost her second husband, Wilson's pen pal managed to magnify the differences between her and his wife. Despite his poor health, Mary encouraged his ambition to seek a political office; Ellen tried hard to persuade him that no prize was worth the race if the race seemed likely to cost him his health.

George Harvey, editor of *Harper's Weekly* and head of the publishing house of Harper & Bros., was responsible for driving this wedge between the two women who were then central to Wilson's life. Delivering a speech at New York City's Lotus Club, Harvey went to considerable length to tell his listeners that a scholarly southerner who was now president of an ivy league university would make an ideal Democratic candidate for a high office. Barely two years after having floated this idea, Harvey wrote a *New York World* editorial in which he said that Woodrow Wilson of Princeton should become the next president of the United States.

Against the wishes of Ellen, her husband became a candidate for the governorship of New Jersey and resigned from the presidency of Princeton just two weeks before chalking up a stunning first victory at the polls. He had hardly taken over the reins of his adopted state before a "Wilson for President" club was organized in Virginia. Eighteen months later delegates to the Democratic National Convention in Baltimore stalled in their attempt to select a presidential nominee. Desperate, some of them turned to Wilson and others followed. Subsequently, he was nominated on the forty-sixth ballot. Ellen shook her head in dismay when she heard the news and confided to intimates, "The pace is too much for him; if he wins, he'll be dead within a year."

Ellen was wrong. Having been born just one year before the start of the Civil War and having known the meaning of Reconstruction at first hand, she died in the White House just eighteen months after having become its mistress. Woodrow showed what seemed like inconsolable grief, even though he may already have been occasionally seeing the forty-three-year-old widow of longtime capital resident Norman Galt. Like the president a native of Virginia, Edith Bolling Galt moved in Washington's top social circles and was at ease when acting as hostess or guesting at a formal dinner.

In some respects more like Mary Peck than Ellen Wilson, Edith loved politics and was full of insider information. She knew that Woodrow was not physically strong, but she discounted notions that the stress of his office would prove detrimental to his health. Sixteen months after Ellen was buried at Rome, Georgia, the widow Galt became Mrs. Woodrow Wilson. Since Edith's second husband actually was frail and about to celebrate his fifty-ninth birthday, mutual friends agreed that theirs was "a marriage of common interest" that included little or no passion. Regardless, the two of them displayed public affection in a fashion that made her seem to be more loving than Ellen had ever been.

LONG BEFORE WEDDING BELLS rang after a private ceremony held in Edith's home, gossip mills had begun to turn out grist. Since Ellen's health had seemed to be better than Woodrow's, a rumor circulated that he and Edith had conspired to poison his first wife. Purists for long-established convention added, "It was unseemly of the president of the United States to stop grieving for his dead wife so quickly; he must have been glad to see her go."

Wilson, who made no public statement about his second marriage, had always been eager for female companionship. That accounts for the manner in which he entered into a long relationship with Mrs. Peck. Commenting to Edith about the way in which they were portrayed in the press, he observed, "In this place [the White House] time is not measured by weeks, or months, or years—but by deep human experience."

Advisors sensing that Wilson's popularity had begun to wane warned the chief executive that he should do something spectacular to regain the hearts of the masses. That advice, combined with his strict Presbyterian upbringing and perhaps other unknown factors, soon led him to make a radical departure from the ways of his society-loving second wife. Almost as though he were Moses on Mount Sinai, he began labeling himself as a prophet chosen by Almighty God to keep America out of war. Having made what seemed to be a promise to that effect, he ran for and won a second term—despite being discouraged by his physicians but enthusiastically encouraged by his second wife.

Despite Wilson's promise, the United States was drawn into "the European war" in 1917. Following the defeat of Germany, the president and his wife went to Europe and received a tumultuous welcome in Paris. A first-draft treaty was hammered out, but when the former academician returned home he found the U.S. Senate stubbornly opposed to its ratification. It was at this point that his sense of divine leadership led him to formulate plans for creating the body that became the League of Nations.

Edith did her best to see that he did not exert himself unduly during this turbulent period, but he suffered a stroke that left him partly paralyzed. Aides wanted him moved to a hospital, but his wife wouldn't allow it. She said he was too weak to leave the White House and saw to it that he was put in bed on September 26, 1919. Within a week she had assumed the role of protectress.

No one, regardless of rank or the urgency of an impending decision that required presidential approval, was allowed to see the chief executive, his vision blurred and left side paralyzed. Literally, Edith stood guard outside his bedroom in order to shoo away cabinet members and other dignitaries. When Vice President Thomas Marshall appeared to make a courtesy call, she barred him from the sickroom and ordered him not to return to the mansion until her husband had recovered.

Within days after the president's wife had assumed her new role, the press was airing criticism. Some brief messages, ostensibly from

As the second Mrs. Wilson, lovely Edith Bolling Galt ran the nation during weeks in which her husband was incapacitated.

Wilson, filtered out of his sickroom, although everything that came from there was censored, if not prepared, by Edith. Soon she began to be ridiculed as "Acting First Man," but she paid no attention. Her own explanation of the most unusual role ever filled by a first lady was simple and straightforward:

> I examined every document sent to the President from the various Secretaries [that is, cabinet members] and Senators. Then I digested into tabloid form the matters that I knew should receive the attention of the President.
>
> I, myself, never made a single decision concerning the disposition of public affairs. The only decisions I made were with regard to what was so important that he must know about it and give his verdict. Of course, I also was responsible for the crucial matter of deciding when to present anything to my husband.

Her explanation, framed after Wilson had begun to recover, was widely criticized as being lame and inaccurate.

During the first few days of Wilson's illness, only those persons with White House access knew the seriousness of his condition. A bulletin, issued after it was approved by Edith, merely said that the chief executive was "briefly indisposed." Admiral Cary T. Grayson, the president's personal physician and a close friend of Edith's, confided to a few influential congressmen that Wilson's strenuous efforts to achieve world peace had left him exhausted. Nothing was said about the incapacitating stroke, however. Around the middle of October, Grayson repeated and slightly amplified his statement in a press release.

Although the measures taken by Edith and by Grayson were unofficial and not based on legislation, their effect was to put her in charge of the nation. One of her most furious critics was Senator Albert Fall of the foreign relations committee concerning a multitude of postwar issues. "This nation is now under petticoat government," Fall exploded to his colleagues in the vital committee. "Woodrow Wilson is gone, and Mrs. Wilson is the nation's chief executive."

Robert Laning, then serving as secretary of state, went one step further. He brought cabinet members together to discuss the crisis and decide what to do about it. Edith discovered what was taking place before the meeting adjourned, so in her husband's name she demanded Laning's resignation—which came within a matter of hours. Again acting in Woodrow's name, she saw to it that a man inexperienced in foreign affairs filled Laning's vacancy. Although Edith knew that she was being widely criticized and that pressure for temporary relinquishment of power by Wilson was mounting, she refused to change her procedures.

After a little more than a month, Grayson was gratified to report significant improvement in his famous patient's condition. His recovery was slow, however, and a full year after having suffered the stroke Wilson still moved slowly and awkwardly with the help of a cane. If he was troubled by the fact that urgent messages from foreign leaders had failed to reach him, he never admitted it.

Having been frail all of his adult life, our twenty-eighth president decided to remain in the capital after his term of office expired. Edith took him to a home on S Street, where he soon became an invalid more dependent on her than ever. Alarmed when her husband experienced a severe bout of indigestion, Edith again called Grayson for help. Although on vacation, he immediately returned to the capital. Questioned after Wilson's death in February 1924, the U.S. Navy's top physician said that when he reached his bedside, the former president managed to stammer only, "Grayson, I am a broken piece of machinery."

Edith, who survived the loss of her second husband by thirty-seven years, never wavered in her insistence that she had done precisely the right thing during weeks in which Woodrow was unable to function. That interval in which a president's second wife was for practical purposes the head of government helped prod Congress into shaping and enacting legislation dealing with such an emergency if it should ever again arise.

29

Warren and Flossie Harding, and Company

J im, you need to let your body get itself in order. If you don't, you're going to have a heart attack or something."

"I'm in bad shape, but I can pull out of it."

"That's exactly what I thought when I was about your age. But I kept on getting worse. You're heading in the same direction."

"Maybe so," mused Jim Phillips. "I sure don't know. One thing I do know, when you had your trouble you hadn't just lost a little boy."

"No, that was a couple of years before I even got married. You're in worse shape than I was. But little Jim Junior isn't going to come back. Both of us know that. You owe it to his memory to get yourself in shape again."

"I've already been to the doctor twice, and he didn't do me a bit of good."

"Of course not," responded Warren G. Harding, "two of them made me worse instead of better and the *Star* was dying fast. Two other fellows had gone in with me. We put three hundred dollars into it and took over the mortgage. I thought I'd soon put it on its feet, but the paper kept losing money until I got some of the Republican business. By the time it started to break even, I was just about dead."

"Is that when you went to Battle Creek?"

"Sure. Seemed like every doctor I tried made me worse instead of better. Somebody told me about John H. Kellogg, and I lit out for Michigan because I knew I had to do something."

"What kind of medicine did you get there?" Jim asked.

"Nothing. Not a drop of any kind. John Kellogg just put me on a diet, sent me to the baths twice a day, and made me exercise. I was back in Marion, fit as a fiddle, in three or four weeks. It won't take you long to get yourself straightened out after you get there. Don't wait, though. The worse you are, the harder it will be for you to pull out of it."

Decidedly reluctant but persuaded, the successful dry-goods merchant set out for the famous sanitarium that began soon after the Civil War as a water-cure center. His train was barely out of sight when his close friend, who had been to Battle Creek earlier, was knocking on the front door of Jim's house. Carrie Phillips, expecting Warren, threw her arms around his neck, gave him a lingering kiss, then led him into the bedroom.

For more than a month, they and their mates had been riding around the county almost daily in Harding's huge green Stevens-Duryea. Subtle signals exchanged between them had led each to know that the other was ready for an affair. With Jim out of the way for several weeks and Flossie Harding busy at the circulation desk of the *Marion Star*, their illicit romance got off to a roaring start.

Good-looking Harding was hailed by the press as being just like average American males of his age.

Like most marriages, the extra-marital affair of the future president did not always remain on an even keel through its fifteen years. There were periods, sometimes several months in length, when the lovers saw each other only occasionally or not at all. At other intervals they were together constantly—sometimes with their unsuspecting mates tagging along.

It would be wonderful, the pair agreed in the spring of 1908, for the foursome to take a European Grand Tour of their own planning. Jim Phillips and Florence Harding liked to go to bed early, and both were sound sleepers. In European hotels their mates could take an extra room and meet in it at 10:30 or 11:00 o'clock. Warren and Carrie could spend an hour or two together many nights a lot more safely than at home; besides, the frequent change of scenery would give new zest to sexual encounters that had sometimes seemed a bit mundane.

Once the idea was broached, their mates endorsed it with enthusiasm. As usual, Florence Harding—whom her husband typically called "the Duchess" because she made firm decisions from which she seldom wavered—took charge of the planning. During a period of more than ninety days, she spent all of her spare time with travel brochures and pamphlets about art galleries and opera houses. She decided that it would be thrilling to start in Madeira, then move down to North Africa long enough to see what it was like before turning northward to Spain's museums and music halls. Proceeding leisurely through Italy and Germany, they could spend a few days in Switzerland before returning to humdrum little Marion, Ohio.

When the foursome sighted the *Deutschland* in February 1909, all of them became visibly excited about the ninety days that lay ahead of them. Standing in line waiting to get on board, Warren and Carrie brushed against each other in apparently casual fashion and he managed to squeeze her hand.

They had such a roaring good time that within a few months Carrie began wheedling Jim for another tour. Although he thought they ought to wait a few years, he said he'd go if Warren liked the idea. Harding, who didn't want to appear too eager, said he'd leave the decision up to the Duchess. She approved, but said they couldn't afford another long stay in Europe and suggested that Bermuda could be a nice, inexpensive vacation spot. Late in March 1911 the illicit lovers and their spouses—who seem not to have had their suspicions aroused—boarded the *Bermudan* for a brief stay on the island already famous for its hospitality.

Bermuda hotels, tiny compared to those they had visited in Europe, didn't offer the same opportunities Warren and Carrie had enjoyed earlier. Thus, they came home disappointed and didn't suggest trying some other place. Increasingly dissatisfied with the merchant she had married largely in order to get out of her tiny hometown village, Carrie became bold, almost aggressive in her attitude toward her lover.

Carrie's new pattern of behavior confirmed what the Duchess must have suspected much earlier. Warren initially denied his wife's accusations, but during a particularly violent session he stormed at her. He never would have given the wife of Jim Phillips a second look, he protested, if his wife had provided him with satisfaction. Grim-faced, she forced him to go with her to a divorce lawyer to discuss a settlement and to start proceedings.

At some point in the conference, questions raised by the attorney caused the woman named Florence, but widely known as Flossie, to become flustered. She stammered that as a very young girl she had run off with Marion DeWolfe. They found a justice of the peace somewhere on the way to Galion, she said, but for the life of her she couldn't remember the name of the town.

Soon after a baby boy came along, her husband took off during the night and never came back. Because she couldn't make it on her own, she dragged herself back to Marion and began giving piano lessons on a borrowed instrument. After her divorce, she explained, she had become interested in Warren. He didn't seem to mind that she was five years his senior, and he quickly made friends with her ten-year-old boy.

Florence had brought along her papers from the divorce, but she had searched high and low and had failed to find a certificate from her first marriage. This dilemma seems to have brought an end to her plans to divorce Warren. If they went to court, all the messy details about her teenage indiscretion would come out. Subsequently, her wealthy father, Amos Kling, with whom she had become reconciled, would be more angry than ever in knowing that his daughter might not have been legally married to DeWolfe.

Many clues suggest that Warren had taken the Duchess as his bride because she seemed to be the sole heir of Kling, a banker and merchant believed to be the richest man in Marion. An astute businesswoman, she took over some departments of Warren's newspaper and worked fifty or sixty hours a week until she turned it into a success. Her husband, who never spent more than half that much time at the newspaper office, became interested in Carrie Phillips about the time the *Star* rounded a financial corner.

If word that he had been threatened with divorce got out, it would nip Warren's fast-growing political career in the bud. He wanted to move upward in elective offices, but he didn't want to sever ties with Carrie. Hence, for a period of several years, their most frequent contact was by means of correspondence. Their handwritten passionate love letters, sometimes forty pages in length, included pet names for their sexual organs plus passages so explicit that they would today be widely regarded as constituting personal pornography.

Carrie, nine years younger than Warren and fourteen years younger than the Duchess, eventually tired of a relationship that could not lead to lasting satisfaction. She began pleading with her lover to divorce his wife and marry her, but Harding wouldn't budge. Warren's refusal to dump his wife so infuriated Carrie that she decided to launch a new life. Parting company with Phillips, for whom she never seemed to have cared deeply, she moved to Germany, the region of Europe that had most enthralled her during their Grand Tour. It lost much of its charm during the Kaiser's final push that led to World War I, so she returned to the states and her husband while resuming her intimate correspondence with Harding—now a member of the United States Senate.

When it became clear that Woodrow Wilson was tilting toward support of war with Germany, Carrie pleaded with her lover to use his influence to block this move. Probably because public sentiment was overwhelmingly in favor of war, Harding ignored Carrie and cast his vote in favor of sending troops against Germany. She did not carry out her threat that she would make his love letters public if he voted for war, but her pro-German activity became so conspicuous that she was investigated by the Secret Service.

Known to her husband as "the Duchess," Florence Harding often looked as though she had dressed for that role.

DELEGATES TO THE REPUBLICAN National Convention of 1920 nominated Harding for the presidency on the tenth ballot. A few astute political leaders, some of whom had begun working for his nomination many months before the convention convened in Chicago's Coliseum, feared that his illicit love affair would be revealed. These men supposedly were instrumental in raising enough money to give Jim Phillips and his wife about twenty thousand dollars in cash plus tickets for a lengthy trip to Japan.

With Carrie still out of the country and Warren established in the White House having Flossie at his side, his lengthy relationship with the wife of a close friend came to an end. Jim Phillips dropped completely out of sight, and as a senile pauper Carrie eventually entered a state-supported haven for the aged. A pro bono attorney assigned to look after her interests opened a closet after her death and found it packed with Harding's love letters. At least two persons read most or all of the letters before a suit brought by the Harding estate led the court to seal them until 2014.

A handful of letters managed to find their way into print despite the legal seal. One of them, published in 1976 by the *Washington Post*, suggests that Harding's fondness for Carrie's sexual charms did not exhaust his interest in her. Francis Russell read reams of letters written by the Ohio native who brought the state's long chain of chief executives to an end. In her judgment, the young and sensuous wife of his friend was the only woman with whom our twenty-ninth president was ever in love.

Warren's relationship with a girl thirty years his junior has been the subject of at least as much interest as his romance with Carrie Phillips. There is a striking difference between the two affairs, however. Nan Britton, a Marion schoolgirl of about fourteen, was deeply smitten by Harding when his picture began appearing on campaign posters. She cut several of these out and arranged them in such fashion that anywhere she turned in her room, she saw the political candidate.

A gulf between ages of these "consenting adults" made their affair somewhat like White House scandals that rocked the entire world close to the turn of the twenty-first century. There was another resemblance, a bit surprising in nature. Job hunting on the part of Nan Britton was a key element in her early relationship with Harding, who was a senator when they first became acquainted.

Ostensibly interested in nothing but an opportunity to find suitable work, Nan approached Warren from New York by means of a letter that was a plea for help in finding work after she had completed a secretarial course. His initial response seems to have been little more than a typical Capitol Hill reaction to a constituent asking for a favor. If Nan is to be believed, however, he foolishly met her in New York soon afterward and she threw herself at him with such fervor that he couldn't say no to her invitation to help himself to her charms.

The influence wielded by the senator reputedly was such that Nan soon got a job at the U.S. Steel Corporation. A book she published some years later, entitled *The President's Daughter*, declares that she became pregnant by Harding on a couch in his office. Her account abounds with graphic details of sexual encounters in such places as a White House closet plus stories of how she and her high-placed lover, nearly old enough to be her grandfather, giggled when they eluded the Duchess. If she told the truth and nothing but the truth, Harding's steamy affair with her was launched before his ties with Phillips were severed.

The Duchess, highly intelligent and perceptive, must have known a great deal more about her husband than some of his biographers think. Once in the White House, she demanded and got a significant "first"—a Secret Service agent assigned to her only. Having this trained operative at her beck and call, she obviously could keep a better eye on her husband than was possible back in their Marion days. Nan Britton's lurid account cannot be dismissed out of hand—but it cannot be taken as wholly factual unless significant new corroborative evidence is found.

That's the case with the last highly questionable episode in the life of the president who was permanently tarnished by the roles his subordinates played in the Teapot Dome oil scandal. His administration, say historians, is the only close competitor with that of U. S. Grant for rank as the most corrupt in the life of the republic. Largely for that reason, a brilliant political leader whose roving eye led him to at least one and possibly to two voluptuous women is all but forgotten today.

Strangely, in the light of what happened to the body of Zachary Taylor, there has been no publicized effort to solve the final mystery of this energetic man's life. Seeking to improve his public image, he set out with the Duchess on what he termed a Voyage of Understanding. He desperately needed to make fresh contacts with common folks and learn from them what they thought about his leadership and the country in general, he said.

After making dozens of stops during a month of leisurely movement from city to city, the presidential party veered northward. This enabled Harding to become the first president to visit Alaska. Earlier having complained that he felt tired and "generally run down," Warren became quite ill on the return trip from Alaska. During the evening of July 29, 1923, he repeatedly rubbed his abdominal area in an attempt to get rid of severe pain but did not succeed. Surgeon General Charles Sawyer, on call during the entire journey, knew that Harding had an enlarged heart and that his blood pressure was dangerously high. After an examination, he diagnosed the president's condition as a mild case of indigestion and advised him to sleep it off.

Although still not feeling well, the chief executive was able to go to his room in the Palace Hotel without assistance after the train reached San Francisco, but he soon returned to a sickbed with nurse Ruth Powderly in attendance. Forty-eight hours after entering the hotel, Harding was dead. The Duchess haughtily refused to give permission for an autopsy, so her philandering husband was listed as having suffered a stroke, and he was buried without a medical examination. Some of Harding's enemies floated a supposition that his embittered wife must have managed to poison him and then placed his unexamined remains into a brown metal casket. No evidence to support this charge has ever surfaced, but, unlike the body of Zach Taylor, Harding's remains have never been subjected to a late but high-level postmortem of sorts. Consequently, the death of the president who yielded to high-level lust remains a subject of speculation.

30

Calvin and Grace Coolidge

G race Goodhue stared incredulously and did not realize she had relaxed her grip on her watering can until a foot signaled "Wet!"

Flushed with embarrassment, the teacher at Clarke Institute for the Deaf in Northampton, Massachusetts, started to turn her head in order to pretend she had not been looking. Her move came too late; the slender male across the way casually doffed his hat, bowed, and resumed shaving. Calvin Coolidge showed no sign of being perturbed at having been caught shaving dressed only in his underwear and a black hat.

In 1904 it was impossible to be a member of a family without sometimes seeing an adult male wearing only what was then called a union suit. This form of underwear united a covering for the lower and the upper body in a single piece, hence its name. Omnipresent though the union suit was, it was rarely glimpsed outside the home.

Shaking her head with disbelief that a man clad in a union suit would stand by an open window in order to shave leisurely with a straight razor, Grace refilled her watering pot. When she finished looking after the plants whose blossoms she often took into her classroom, she began shaking with laughter as she turned back into the institute.

Coolidge, who had saluted the dark-haired young woman with his hat, was well acquainted with one of the instructors at Clarke. Halfway through his description of the woman who had caught him without his pants, his friend gestured for him to halt. "The teacher you saw watering flowers was Grace Goodhue. Couldn't possibly have been anyone else. Come on down the hall; I'll introduce you to her right now."

After the most bizarre first encounter of any couple who eventually went to the White House together, Calvin and Grace saw each other frequently. He learned from her that work at Clarke was the fulfillment of her early ambition. Grace went to school with a deaf girl who understood very little of what was going on and had a terrible time in class. Very early, Grace decided she'd like to help the deaf learn to read lips well enough to know what others were saying. Her work at the institute took nearly all of

Grace Coolidge and Rob Roy.
(Howard Chandler Christy,
the White House)

her time, and until Calvin began asking her to go to walk with him, she rarely encountered an eligible male.

His mother had died when he was a small boy, Calvin explained. His father, a storekeeper and farmer who barely earned enough to keep bread on the table, considered moving to some other location in Vermont.

"He decided to stay at Plymouth Notch. Folks call it Plymouth, but that's not right," he explained.

After finishing at Amherst College, Grace's new acquaintance told her, he decided to stay in Massachusetts. When he proudly informed her that he was reading law with Hammond and Field, her ears perked up. She had never had reason to become acquainted with an attorney, but she knew the firm was regarded as the best in Northampton. A man who had been accepted there must be plenty smart, she realized.

After half a dozen leisurely walks, she screwed up her courage enough to speak of the day she first caught sight of Calvin and inquired: "What makes you put on a hat in order to shave?"

"Hair," explained her friend who often answered questions with a single syllable. Noticing the bewilderment written on Grace's face, he offered a rare burst of words. "Got a little forelock that wants to curl. My hat keeps it in place."

Although Grace mentally filed that explanation as far-fetched, she nodded understanding and fell silent for a long time. During their half-hour walks, interspersed with an occasional ride and two memorable picnics, they exchanged only a handful of words. Occasionally, Grace couldn't restrain herself and let sentences bubble out one on the heels of another. Calvin typically nodded comprehension or encouragement, but when he spoke he said very little. Even when they spent an evening playing whist, their conversation—if it could be called that—was extremely one-sided.

When they saw signs that the relationship between Grace and Calvin was slowly progressing beyond casual friendship, some of her coworkers made fun of "the way your beau lets you do all of the talking." She tossed her head and responded that since the bulk of her time was spent with deaf children, she was accustomed to silence.

Despite the fact that he seldom said much, Coolidge was not nearly so slow to act upon a good thing when he found it as were some other men destined to occupy the White House. He and Grace were married about eighteen months after she first laid eyes on him. They lived in a Northampton duplex, where the rent was thirty-six dollars a month and a hand-painted plaque over the mantle read:

A big brown owl lived in an oak;
The more he saw the less he spoke.
The less he spoke the more he heard,
So he was soon a wise old bird.

Calvin was chairman of the Hampshire County Republican Council when they married, so Grace was not surprised when he decided to run for a seat in the Massachusetts House of Representatives. Some of her relatives in Burlington, Vermont, laughed when they learned of his ambition and joked that he'd never make it because no one would know what he thought about anything.

Eyes flashing, Grace came to the defense of her taciturn husband. "That's exactly why he will win!" she exclaimed. "He never says anything to offend anyone."

TO SOME OUTSIDERS, THEIR marriage seemed as austere as Calvin's speech. Living on an income of two thousand dollars a year, they managed to put a little money in the bank every year. Grace, whose father held views almost identical with those of Calvin's, seems never to have questioned the prevailing marital pattern in which the male was breadwinner and the female took charge of the house and children.

Florence Harding once casually told a group of her friends that she habitually went over Warren's speeches and made many changes in them. Grace Coolidge wouldn't have even thought of doing such a thing: Calvin's decisions concerning anything but needs and activities of their two boys were final. She completely agreed with him that hard-earned money should never be thrown away on luxuries and trifles. Yet she must have rejoiced that he always wanted to see her looking her best and encouraged her to buy relatively expensive clothing.

As tight-fisted as he was personally, professionally, and politically, Calvin never begrudged what it took to feed and care for the numerous pets that Grace accumulated. Although he didn't care to ride in parades, attend luncheons, and greet strangers, he encouraged Grace to do so as strongly as he supported her in playing baseball with their two sons. In his autobiography, his summary of their marriage was terse but perceptive: "For almost a quarter of a century she has borne with my infirmities, and I have rejoiced in her graces."

As Massachusetts governor, Calvin faced an explosive situation in 1919. Members of the Boston police department, thwarted in their effort to organize a union, voted 1,134–2 to strike. With the city in turmoil and looters having a field day, Coolidge balked at endorsing a compromise measure drawn up by Mayor Andrew J. Peters. A conference of leaders degenerated into a shouting match, during which the mayor of Boston punched the governor in the left eye.

Peters, who found that he had authority to call out national guard units stationed inside the city, put them on patrol. A clash between men in uniform and rioters, combined with belligerent strikers, led to an exchange of gunfire in which six persons died. Grace barely referred to the matter when Calvin came home that evening, and offered no opinion about what he or anyone else should do.

The next morning the governor called out the national guard and put the police department under his control. Samuel Gompers of the American Federation of Labor issued a formal protest to this "unwarranted infringement upon the rights of workers seeking to be unionized." Still, without having given any hint to Grace of what he might do in such a situation, Calvin issued one of the most lengthy statements of his career. In it he said, "There is no right to strike against the public safety by anybody, anywhere, any time."

Jeered by some but cheered by multitudes of others, the man who habitually acted without getting input from his wife became a national

Silent Cal sometimes worked outdoors with nothing on hand except writing materials and the presidential seal.

figure overnight. Supporters soon nominated him for the presidency. They got nowhere, and so they then consulted him about taking the second spot on the Republican ticket. Grace didn't want him to become a candidate for the vice presidency, because she thought he was too good for the post. When he gave the nod to his backers, however, she accepted his decision without question or hesitation.

During months after the inauguration of Warren G. Harding, the pair of Vermonters spent as little time in Washington as they decently could. With the parlor of his father's home lighted only by oil lamps, Calvin took his oath of office as president at 2:30 A.M. on August 3, 1923, in Plymouth Notch, Vermont, following Harding's death. The elder Coolidge, a justice of the peace, was the only man who administered this oath to his son. Although the ceremony was legal and binding, for the sake of appearances Calvin repeated his vows before Justice Adolph Hoehling eighteen days later.

Grace rejoiced that her husband had been careful to avoid dealing with men whose conduct had made the Harding administration seem permeated by graft and corruption. She bristled when shown a clipping according to which noted satirist H. L. Mencken had called Calvin "the greatest men ever to come out of Plymouth, Vermont," and was tempted to scold him in writing. When she confided about the matter to her husband, he grunted only two words: "Forget it."

Tragedy struck the close-knit family from Vermont when sixteen-year-old Calvin, Jr., developed a serious infection after a blister on his foot burst. He survived only a few days, and "Silent Cal" did not issue a statement to the press. Grace, described as being friendly and outgoing to the point of gregariousness, didn't hesitate to show her grief in public. She refused, furthermore, to retreat into isolation as did some earlier first ladies when tragedy struck.

Grace never so much as whispered a word of advice to her husband, and she stayed fully occupied with her own special interests. Baseball fans adored her because she was an outspoken follower of the national pastime and an articulate admirer of the great Babe Ruth. Unlike Calvin, she was enamored of the very latest innovation in communications—radio. No other first lady had brought one of these clumsy contraptions into the White House, but Grace turned hers on during most mornings and let it run all day.

Several times, students at the Clarke Institute visited Washington at the invitation of Grace. She also persuaded actor Spencer Tracy and other notables to help her raise $2 million for the formerly obscure school for the deaf. Even her husband was deeply impressed, although he said little about it, when the former teacher placed her fingers on the lips of Helen Keller in order to tell others what she was saying.

Although he seldom gave other than terse replies to a few questions, Silent Cal adopted one practice that to some seemed strangely incongruous. He held press conferences regularly, frequently as often as three times a week, and he never tried to dodge a challenge. Unlike her husband, Grace refused to talk to reporters, but she was at ease in front of audiences. She once gave a luncheon for pioneer female members of the White House press corps and was urged to share with them some little tidbit of news not yet made public. Virtually pushed to her feet under the splendid old magnolia tree planted by Andrew Jackson as a tribute to Rachel, she stood silent and motionless for an instant. Then she lifted her arms and for five minutes used her hands to "speak" in the sign language she had learned in Massachusetts. Some of her guests later confessed that they did not catch a single word Grace signed, but a few prided themselves on having under-stood entire phrases. When Grace ended the communication session that topped even those held by Silent Cal, her guests erupted in ecstatic applause.

GRACE DIDN'T ASK CALVIN'S permission to offer at an auction some of the things she had knitted. She brought in $250, having learned in advance that the proceeds would benefit Washington's home for needy Confederate women. She entertained Charles A. Lindbergh, Gen. John J. Pershing, Will Rogers, Sergei Rachmaninoff, and other international notables at state dinners. Knowing in advance that her husband would have little or nothing to say, she always tried to arrange the seating in such fashion that he would feel no embarrassment at eating and drinking while uttering only an occasional brief comment.

Without letting his wife know what he was doing, the president made arrangements for noted artist Howard Chandler Christy to execute a formal portrait of Grace. For her sessions in front of the canvas she wore a striking red gown and sat with one of the six dogs, two cats, and a raccoon that were White House pets. Christy praised the patience of their white collie, Rob Roy, but Coolidge refused to say that he liked one of the most famous of all portraits painted at 1600 Pennsylvania Avenue. In a rare exhibition of near petulance, the president protested that if the artist wanted color contrast, Grace should have had Rob Roy's hair dyed red and she should have worn a white evening gown of which he was especially proud.

Calvin's mild protest concerning his wife's attire while having her portrait painted was one of no more than a few dozen instances in which he or she voiced a contrary opinion or offered unsolicited advice. Few cou-ples who spent years in the spotlight talked so little with one another as did the Coolidges—but the number whose love was not known ever to have been disturbed by a single tiny ripple was far smaller.

31

Herbert and Lou Hoover

Are you making fun of me?"

"Certainly not, Bert. I got acquainted with the young lady I want you to meet when I went to Pacific Grove to deliver a talk. She's as much an Iowan as you are."

Intrigued that two persons born in the state of tall corn should have come together at Leland Stanford Junior University, Herbert Hoover thanked Prof. John C. Branner for having introduced him to Lou Henry. Soon he and his fellow Iowan left the geology laboratory together, talking animatedly as they walked.

"My father took the family to West Branch before I was born; where did you grow up?"

"In Waterloo, where my father ran the bank."

Tugging on the facial hair that he grew in a futile attempt to look older, a boyish Herbert Hoover mused: "We were in the same state but we grew up in different worlds; my father was a blacksmith—but he served as a town councilman and as an assessor."

"What brought you to Stanford?"

"A train of circumstances, I guess. My father's heart gave out when I was just six years old, so I grew up with relatives. One of them is a doctor in Oregon. A man who had come there from the East took an interest in me and let me go with him when he was surveying land. He told me a lot about his life, and said he thought I would make a good mining engineer. I guess I'm in debt to Robert Brown. How did you land here?"

"Father brought us to California because he thought the climate would be good for my mother's health. We lived for a while in Whittier, then went north to Monterey," Lou explained.

"Never went to Monterey, but I've been to Whittier two or three times to see some of the Friends there."

"I was reared in the Episcopal Church, but at heart I guess I'm a member of the Society of Friends; I think Quakers are the best people in the whole world."

"My uncle John has been a Friend all his life. He's a mighty good man, but he doesn't go along with everything that others believe. He wanted to be a surgeon in the Civil War, but they turned him down; too old."

"Are you sure it was his age and not his religious beliefs that kept him out of the Civil War?"

"Positive. He was a fighting Quaker, I guess. When I came home one day and told him about a bigger boy who pushed me against a tree, Uncle John gave me some advice. 'Bert,' he said, 'be sure to turn your cheek once—but if a fellow smites you again, you must punch him hard.' "

Lou got a laugh out of her new friend's boyhood memories and seconded Uncle John's advice before wondering, aloud, if the two of them had anything else in common.

"Geology!"

"You're right," she admitted. "Of course!"

Hoover, self-conscious about his round face and ruddy complexion, blushed a trifle as he probed: "How did you become the only girl in the department?"

"Professor Branner's responsible. Our family went to hear him talk about 'The Bones of the Earth' one evening, and he fired my imagination. That's why I came to Stanford—to study under him."

"So you plan to take up mining engineering, like me?"

"Not on your life!" Lou responded. "I'm in the geology department at least for now, because of Professor Branner. Without him, I'd be somewhere else, and I'm not sure I'd like that. Once I got started here, though, I found that my real interest isn't geology."

"Exactly what are you really interested in?"

"Language . . . !" his fellow Iowan exploded.

"That's my hardest field," Herbert mused. "Guess I ought not to tell you, but I was 'conditioned' in English when I was admitted. Matter of fact, that condition wasn't removed until this year."

"Well, we have a lot in common but I see we're a long way apart about language. I simply love to explore ways to use nouns and verbs, adjectives and adverbs. If it wouldn't offend Professor Branner, I think I might switch to the English department; I'm just getting started, you know."

Hoover, who in 1891 was the youngest member of Stanford's first class and was unusually shy, had tried to size up the bright-eyed fellow student. "You must have stayed out of school for two or three years," he probed. "You make me feel like I'm not old enough to be here."

"Ha! I'm a freshman, too, born way back in 1874."

"When?" Hoover blurted.

Lou Henry Hoover at the White House.

"March 29. Why?"

"We have something else in common; I was born in 1874. But I didn't come along until August 10. You really are older than me . . ."

"Four whole months," Lou scoffed. "Gee, fate—or something—must have been at work. Both of us are from Iowa, and here we are at Stanford. Both in geology; one a Quaker and the other a Quaker in beliefs . . ."

"Only one of us likes language, but that ought not to be come between us; when can I see you again?"

Although both later insisted that they did not experience anything approaching "love at first sight," Lou and Bert saw each other regularly during the remainder of his stay in California. By the time he walked across the platform to accept his diploma, they had arrived at what they described as "an understanding." That is, they were seriously interested in marriage, but had no intention of entering into it until Lou had also graduated.

By the time Lou was a senior, Bert was in Australia having the time of his life except for being very lonely. Although he was only twenty-three years old, he was beginning to make a reputation for himself—and was accumulating money faster than he dreamed possible. As graduation approached, he sent Lou a one-sentence cable from Down Under. She promptly responded to his proposal from halfway around the world with a simple "Of course."

Bert sent his resignation to London, wrapped up his work, made arrangements to start a new job soon, and returned to California for a simple marriage ceremony early in 1899. Almost immediately afterward, the bride and groom boarded a steamer for the long journey to Tientsin, China. This major port, located about fifty miles south of Peking, held far more foreigners than any other Chinese city.

Hoover's work for the Chinese Department of Mines and Railways required extensive travel, so the childless Lou had spare time on her hands. Encouraged by her husband, she decided to put her energy to novel use— by learning the language of the Chinese people among whom they lived. Lou quickly mastered some of the distinctions between Chinese consonants and vowels, but she had trouble with tones that serve to distinguish words in the spoken language. After her husband discovered immense deposits of coal, of which the Chinese were not aware earlier, he spent longer and longer periods in the field. That gave Lou freedom to devote many days to her study of language. Before she had been in Tientsin a year, she had mastered the rudiments of both spoken and written Chinese.

Half teasing but also serious, she suggested that her husband should follow her example. Herbert at first shook his head in dismay, but he eventually spent many hours being tutored by Lou. She never lost patience with him and prodded him to keep practicing until he had mastered a few dozen common words. Neither of them dreamed how their knowledge of Chinese would later be used.

Until June 1900 neither Lou nor Herbert realized that her increasing mastery of the Chinese language would be anything but a self-chosen discipline. Her new skills proved to be invaluable, however, in the wake of an uprising known in the West as the Boxer Rebellion. Finding it impossible to topple the empress dowager T'zu Hi, members of the Society of Boxers turned their wrath against foreigners in Tientsin.

When the city came under siege, Hoover's wife was the only person in it who knew English, Latin, French, Chinese, and a bit of German. Serving as interpreter, she played a significant role in preventing the massacre of non-Chinese residents during a three-week siege of the city. A military force that included units from England, Japan, Germany, the United States, Russia, and France drove off the insurgents and the siege was lifted. Most foreigners left in the wake of this development. Instead of returning home, the Hoovers settled in London.

Years after leaving China behind, as residents of 1600 Pennsylvania Avenue in Washington, President and Mrs. Hoover spoke to each other in Chinese when they wished to prevent members of the Secret Service and other intimate aides from learning what they were saying.

Long before they went to the White House, Herbert expressed interest in making a classic work on geology available to English readers, but he was handicapped by his limited knowledge of Latin. Written by a sixteenth-century German, *De Re Metallica* was famous as the only work describing the course of geology and mining from the earliest times to its 1556 publication date. Lou volunteered to make the translation, then wrestled with obsolete and archaic technical terms for nearly a decade. The only joint scientific work ever published by a future president and his wife came off the press shortly before the outbreak of World War I.

Although Hoover campaigned for re-election, his bid was doomed by the nation's financial crisis before it started.

OUR THIRTY-FIRST PRESIDENT, who spent a small fortune on his pet project of a self-published book, was open-handed concerning the White House and its furnishings. When Lou decided that the dreary Red Drawing Room needed a complete restoration job, it was restored to emulate the era of James Monroe at their expense rather than with funds provided by taxpayers.

Lou labeled a home without plants as "hopelessly sterile," so she devoted many days to transformation of the second-floor West Sitting Room. Again at the expense of the mansion's occupants, it was transformed into the Palm Room. Palms and semitropical vines, plus a variety of songbirds, made the once-commonplace room into what a newspaper reporter called "a kind of indoor-outdoor paradise at the nerve center of the nation's capital."

Members of the household staff sometimes complained that it was not proper to treat visiting dignitaries like ordinary folks, but Lou Hoover made few concessions when the prime ministers of Great Britain, France, and Italy were their guests. Everything she did as mistress of the White House was marked by elegant simplicity without a trace of pretense.

Like her husband, Lou was nearly numb with unbelief when the 1929 stock market crash plunged the nation into the Great Depression. Working closely together as they had for decades, Herbert and Lou did their best to turn things around but failed. She never became reconciled to the fact that one of the most talented and skilled executives ever to head our nation would become the victim of forces he could not control.

Although their marriage lacked what some commentators called "the fire and ice" of the union between Grover and Frances Cleveland, it was stable and solid. Apparently neither of them showed serious interest in another member of the opposite sex before their marriage, during it, or after they were parted by death.

Lou was stricken by a heart attack at the Waldorf-Astoria hotel in New York City early in 1944 and was buried in Palo Alto, California. Herbert survived her by two decades but never even considered taking a second mate. After World War II he devoted much of his time and energy to relief efforts and headed two separate commissions that succeeded in effecting major reforms in the operation of the federal government.

Upon Hoover's death in 1964, members of the family decided to lay him to rest in West Branch, Iowa. They then brought Lou's remains to West Branch for reinterment in the only spot she ever truly wanted to occupy—very close to the husband she loved quietly but devotedly for forty-five good and mutually fulfilling years.

32

FDR, Eleanor Roosevelt, and Their Playmates

Polio got his legs, but it sure didn't whittle him down other places. If it had, we wouldn't have been in such a hurry to get Lucy out of Georgia before some of you fellows got to Warm Springs."

"What do you really think of your boss?" a reporter inquired.

"You gotta hand it to him. He's dead now, but he sure was alive and kickin' a few hours before he went. Talk about a real man . . . !"

"What do you mean by 'a real man'? "

"If you coulda seen him crawlin' on the bed and hoppin' on Lucy with just one flip, you'd know what I mean," responded a member of the Secret Service who agreed to talk anonymously long after the 1945 death of Franklin Delano Roosevelt at the cottage he lovingly called his Little White House.

"Don't look at me that way, mister! If you'd ever been in that little shotgun house he called his hideaway, you couldn't have helped seein' him in action any more than I could help it."

"Since you saw him together with Lucy, are you trying to tell me she was his mistress?"

"Nope. Not tryin' to tell you anything. You have to make up your own mind. But I know what I saw. All of us thought we were helpin' to hide a secret for him, but Eleanor found out right away—if she didn't know all the time."

The principal subjects of that brief interview, the thirty-second president of the United States and the former social secretary of his wife, were together at Warm Springs, Georgia, when the chief executive died on April 12, 1945, very early in his unprecedented fourth term of office. At his rustic rural retreat, Roosevelt kept an old car that had been rigged so he could control everything by hand without having to try to use his legs and feet.

He had planned to take Lucy for a drive that afternoon, but begged off by saying he had a bad headache. Shortly after 3:00 P.M. he suffered a massive cerebral hemorrhage that killed him almost instantly and brought to an end an extramarital relationship that had started a nearly unbelievable twenty-nine years earlier.

Members of the public knew nothing about the illicit romance, but some details about it were familiar to nearly every member of the widespread Roosevelt family, to say nothing of Secret Service operatives guarding the president. None of the latter knew what Eleanor Roosevelt had learned as soon as she peeked into the first of a bundle of letters packed in her husband's luggage.

Back home from Europe late in the summer of 1918, Franklin was extremely pale and weak. At first it seemed likely that he had a bad case of seasickness, but a doctor looked him over carefully, shook his head and solemnly pronounced *pneumonia*. Unpacking for him while he lay on his bed with a high fever, his wife discovered letters that revealed he had been unfaithful to her. To complicate a situation that would have been bad enough under any circumstances, the twenty-two-year-old woman in the case had become acquainted with Franklin while working as Eleanor's social secretary.

As soon as her husband had recovered sufficiently to be confronted, Eleanor told him exactly what had happened and said that if he didn't love her, she'd give him a divorce so he could marry Lucy Page Mercer. Although Franklin urged delay because he was in no condition to make a life-shaping decision, it seemed to Eleanor that he was leaning toward taking up her offer.

A servant must have told Franklin's mother what had happened, for Sara Delano Roosevelt came storming into the house the next morning. She shook her finger in her son's face and announced that if he cut his ties with Eleanor, she'd cut him off without a nickel. A conservative estimate placed her holdings at well over a million dollars during an era when the nation had only a handful of millionaires. She had total control over the fortune and never let anyone think otherwise.

With Sara standing over his bed Franklin cringed, tried to cry, and whimpered that he was sorry for what he had done. He had learned a lesson the hard way, he said, and solemnly promised that he would never see Lucy again. From early boyhood, when he signed his name in full he had always written "Delano" with a special flourish because it might come to Mamma's eyes. To annoy Mamma was dangerous; to make Mamma angry was foolhardy.

Eleanor, whose youngest child was barely two years old at the time, had never pretended to enjoy the marital bed. She delivered a baby at least six times because she had been taught that it was part of a woman's duty to bear children. A daughter and four sons lived to maturity; as mature adults,

Largely in her own right rather than as mistress of the White House, Eleanor became world-renowned as a crusader, columnist, and lecturer.

to the surprise of their intimates two of them said they didn't blame their father for having cheated on their mother.

"She liked the idea of being married and felt that it was socially essential," one of her sons has been quoted as saying, "but she didn't like to respond to our father's most primeval urges."

Franklin kept his distance from Lucy for a few months after nearly losing his inheritance, but they secretly resumed the relationship as soon as he thought it safe. By the time he went to Washington for a seven-year stint as assistant secretary of the Department of the Navy, Eleanor had become deeply involved in numerous and varied projects of her own. That meant she was away from home a great deal, and she was unlikely to discover that her husband and her former secretary were once again meeting at every opportunity.

Soon after Franklin's relationship with Lucy surfaced, he and Eleanor reached a working agreement. They would go their separate ways, but for the sake of appearances they would maintain a marriage of mutual convenience. He'd continue affectionately to address her as "Dear Babs"—an abbreviation for "Baby"—and she'd keep on submitting to sex because both of them sincerely wanted children. This arrangement was not worked out in detail before taking effect; instead, it took form gradually without being made articulate. It matured during World War I, was taken for granted by everyone close to them, and continued for the rest of their years together.

Both grew up in wealth, with servants omnipresent to look after all their needs and wants. Eleanor never pretended to having learned to cook; an omelet was her most complicated dish. When she entertained members of British Royalty at her Val-Kill retreat, she served hot dogs to them and pretended that she did so in order to give them "a taste of what the average American eats."

Her childhood appearance was so homely—downright ugly according to some—that her wrinkled little face caused many relatives to address her as Granny. Very early, it was apparent that Franklin would be handsome and tall. By the time he reached late adolescence he exhibited infectious charm that was all but irresistible. Females whom he met for the first time were bowled over by him—but no more so than new male acquaintances.

Franklin had private tutors until age fourteen, then enrolled at Groton and prepared for Harvard. Eleanor, Teddy Roosevelt's niece and Franklin's sixth cousin, also studied under tutors until age fifteen, when she was sent to Madame Marie Silvestre's posh Allenswood finishing school for girls, near London. After three years there she returned to New York for her debut, which she dreaded immensely because in England she had discovered that her teeth protruded, her lips were entirely too thick, and her voice was far too shrill.

FRANKLIN AND ELEANOR HAD known each other since early childhood; both lost parents very early and were reared by a grandparent. Eleanor, three years younger than her good-looking cousin, began to show signs of being interested in him while he was at Harvard. Family ties quickly brought them closer and closer together, and their 1905 wedding was a massive family affair dominated by Uncle Teddy.

Franklin's mother selected what she judged to be a suitable house, rented and decorated it, then staffed it with some of her servants. Domineering Sara Delano Roosevelt had little patience with the wishes of her son or her daughter-in-law if they differed from her own. She virtually pushed Eleanor aside when the children began to come along, and she had a continuous major hand in rearing them.

Soon after the Democrats nominated Franklin for the vice presidency in 1920, he resigned as assistant secretary of the navy and became a partner in a New York law firm. Eleanor played the part of the ever-faithful wife when Franklin was stricken with poliomyelitis at age thirty-nine. She had her hand on his shoulder to steady him and keep him from engaging in a characteristic outburst when doctors reluctantly gave him their verdict. He'd never walk again, they said, but hastened to add that his brain and other organs were not affected. Sara directed her son not to worry; he must retire to Hyde Park and become a country gentleman in the real sense of the word.

For the first time in their relationship, Eleanor forcefully refused to accept the dictates of her mother-in-law. Franklin, she insisted, must learn to use crutches and a wheelchair, and he must at all costs maintain his interest in national affairs. To facilitate achievement of the latter goal, she persuaded Louis Howe to move into the house with her husband. The former Albany correspondent of the *New York Herald*, Howe became the most trusted confidant and advisor of the aspiring politician who had begun to refer to himself simply as FDR.

After being examined by another team of doctors, Roosevelt flashed his famous smile when they told him his illness had not made him sexually impotent. With his legs made rigid by heavy steel braces, he learned to crawl so he could escape if he should find himself alone in a burning building.

Eleanor, already managing a small furniture plant at their Val-Kill retreat near Hyde Park, had ambitious plans about providing for the physical needs of every impoverished family in the nation. She mastered shorthand and touch typing in order to keep up with her fast-growing volume of correspondence and took over the editorship of the *Women's Democratic News*. To the surprise of family members dependent on their chauffeurs, she learned to drive cars with stick-shift transmissions because she wanted to help transport voters to the polls on election days.

All of these frenetic activities were simply a prelude to her accomplishments as first lady. She successfully campaigned for better care of veterans, became an early and articulate spokesperson concerning civil rights, wrote regular magazine and newspaper columns, visited far-flung military bases during World War II, demanded that women of the South pay higher wages to household helpers, insisted that women everywhere be given equal wages, held regular press conferences, often gave radio talks, launched or promoted dozens of projects for the unemployed, refused to let the chief usher of the White House push elevator buttons and operated it herself, dealt with a stream of letters that reached three hundred thousand per year, and under the tutelage of Howe managed to lower her high-pitched voice.

Bess Furman, then an Associated Press reporter, surveyed Eleanor's multitudinous accomplishments and wrote a gushing testimony of the first lady, writing, "Under her impact, Washington will never be the same." Furman probably had no idea that Eleanor's husband was maintaining a relationship with Lucy Mercer of such intimacy and that she sometimes came to the White House—sometimes with the connivance of FDR's daughter Anna.

Only a handful of trusted servants who knew how to keep their mouths shut were positive that the president had formed an intimate bond with a second woman who functioned as an aide when he traveled. Missy LeHand—whose formal name was Marguerite Alice—met Roosevelt when he made his first try for the vice presidency in 1920. At about age twenty-three she quit her job at Democratic campaign headquarters in order to become his personal secretary. Eleanor, who knew that Missy swam with her husband and spent many hours with him during his sessions of rehabilitation from polio, seems to have regarded the girl as her husband's casual mistress.

The first lady's innumerable activities and interests did not prevent her from devoting time to a relationship that may account for some of her indifference about male-female sex. At least as early as 1932, she became acquainted with Associated Press reporter Lorena Hickok. Despite the fact that colleagues saw Lorena as being far too fat and too lazy or too indifferent to wear smart clothing and keep her hair tidy, Eleanor soon made her an intimate. Their close relationship lasted practically as long as that between FDR and Lucy.

Nearly always jaunty when he made a public appearance, FDR in private struggled mightily with programs such as the massive Works Progress Administration.

The two professional women become so intimate that after having visited the White House regularly for many weeks, Lorena moved into the mansion and was assigned a room. She quit her job in order to be free to travel with Eleanor and became so fully "a member of the family" that the president often joked with her. He once heard the intimate friends engaged in argument, and when it was over gestured for Lorena to step to his wheelchair. Leaning toward her he cautioned in a stage whisper: "Never get into an argument with my wife; you can't win!"

Eleanor's close ties with Lorena lasted for fully three decades. Since they were sometimes separated for extended periods, the woman who never forgot that as a child she was called the ugly duckling of the family wrote hundreds of letters to her friend. Many of these were donated to the Roosevelt Presidential Library by Lorena, under conditions that made it impossible for them to be seen until 1968.

Surviving letters reveal that Eleanor often addressed her as "Hick Darling" and "Dear One" or simply "Dear," but no direct references to a lesbian relationship are found in them. If explicitly sexual letters were exchanged between the two women, they were presumably destroyed as soon as they were read. In a passage highly suggestive that such a bond existed, Eleanor raved about a "a soft spot just northeast of the corner" of Lorena's mouth. She remembered how distinctive it felt against her lips, she wrote, and delighted that in a little more than a week she expected to kiss it—clearly not for the first time.

FDR'S DISABILITY MAY HAVE prompted him to prove that polio had not reduced his virility by even a tiny bit. Having been pushed away by Eleanor, even his ever-faithful Lucy's constant availability did not prevent him from dallying with Missy for about two decades.

Secret Service agents who drove hell-for-leather for hours on a steamy April day in order to get Lucy away from Warm Springs, Georgia, might have saved themselves the trouble. Eleanor pretended to be indignant when she learned her husband had died in another woman's arms. Whatever else she may have been, the ceaseless bundle of energy who was mated to the architect of the New Deal was highly intelligent. Her relationship with Lorena plus her innumerable and ceaseless crusades couldn't possibly have blinded such a woman to what her husband was doing behind her back.

The many-faceted and less than fully known doings of the distant cousins who made a marriage of sorts did not come to light until after both had died. With their secrets well hidden during Eleanor's later life, the loss of her husband served to give her an even larger share of the limelight than she enjoyed during her White House years.

Instead of fading into obscurity, Mrs. Franklin Delano Roosevelt blossomed. She became a six-year delegate to the United Nations, chief author of the International Declaration of Human Rights, and a powerful force in the successful movement to create the nation of Israel.

33

Harry and Bess Truman

Henry R. Luce of *Time-Life-Fortune* magazines didn't know whether to take offense or be puzzled. In this dilemma he posed a direct question to our thirty-third president: "Why is my wife [Clare Booth Luce] never invited to the White House despite the fact that she is a sitting member of Congress?"

"I have a wife, too," replied the man from Missouri. "She has never been in politics and has always watched her conduct carefully. Your wife has repeatedly referred to her in print as Payroll Bess because she did secretarial work for me while I was in the Senate. No one has a right to smear my wife. As long as I am in residence in the White House, your wife will not be on a guest list."

Sneering at his lack of high-level experience, some of his critics called Truman "the haberdasher from the sticks." Many of his supporters cringed when he became angry with a high-ranking military officer or the head of a governmental department and lashed out as him as an SOB. His wife, the former Elizabeth Virginia Wallace, universally known simply as Bess, frequently gave him a tongue-lashing when she learned that he had used profanity. He always meekly nodded contrition—then turned around and soon did the same thing again.

Their sometimes fiery exchanges, which often made it into the news, suggest that they might have been incompatible and spent much of their time squabbling. Nothing could be farther from the truth; they had a complex working partnership in which neither pulled any punches but both relied heavily upon the other. When Bess died in 1982 as the oldest woman who had ever been mistress of the White House, a *New York Times* headline told the nation that "Bess Truman Is Dead at 97; Was President's Full Partner."

When word of FDR's sudden death reached Washington about 7:00 P.M. on April 12, 1945, hasty arrangements were made for Harry to take the oath of office and become chief executive. Bess sobbed quietly throughout

Truman shortly before being hand-picked by Thomas "Boss" Pender-grast to wage an uphill battle for a seat in the U.S. Senate.

the ceremony, overwhelmed at the thought of what her husband would have to endure. Grim-faced, he showed no sign of weeping but shortly afterward admitted, "I felt like the moon, the stars, and all the planets had fallen on me."

They had been together only thirteen years at that time, but had much earlier arrived at a relationship having few parallels with those of other first families. She was extremely careful to stay in the background except for brief appearances on Harry's arm. He was more than simply ready to speak his mind at the drop of a hat; his salt-sprinkled language erupted so violently that some Republicans called him "the foul-mouthed donkey from the hinterlands."

Bess constantly offered her opinions to her husband on matters of state and wasn't easily silenced when she expressed views opposite of his, yet she never gave a public hint that she was the president's most trusted advisor. He sometimes lashed out at her in spite of the fact that he didn't want anyone else doing the same thing.

Their only daughter aspired to be a professional singer but was widely considered to have mediocre talent. Her father, described as "being as protective of Margaret as a hen with a single wet chick," became furious when the *Washington Post* published a disparaging review of a performance. Seizing stationery headed only "The White House," Harry dashed off a blistering handwritten blast at the music critic who had dared to suggest that his daughter was less than the very best.

The on-again, off-again relationship of Harry and Bess as man and wife was a holdover of sorts from their highly unusual courtship. It was completely lacking in fervor and was incredibly long due to financial problems plus Harry's term of service in World War I. He didn't have the nerve to propose in person, so he wrote a letter in which he asked Bess if she would wear a ring. Her mother discouraged her from sending a quick reply. She knew the suitor's background and suspected that a man who had once been a poor dirt farmer couldn't support a wife in the style to which Bess was accustomed.

HARRY HAD IT VERY hard from the very beginning. His life got off to a most unusual start when a baptismal name was given to him. Because his parents were torn between honoring a relative named Shippe and another named Solomon, they conferred on him the most distinctive of presidential middle names—simply S, without the period.

At age six the spindly boy, already wearing thick-lens glasses and destined to go through life explaining the S in his name, was taken to Sunday school at the Presbyterian church in Independence, Missouri. There he caught a good look at a radiant girl, one year his junior, whose sparkling blue eyes and dainty golden curls he couldn't forget.

The electrical current generated that Sunday morning seems to have promptly grounded, however. Harry and Bess didn't marry until twenty-nine years after the first time he laid eyes on her at an age when he "was a lot too backward to dare to speak to her." When their knot was finally tied, they were years past the usual age of marriage in that period—thirty-five and thirty-four years old, respectively.

Neither of them had received even a tiny bit of advice about sex, but both knew they couldn't waste a great deal of time if they expected to become parents. They never developed a burning desire for frequent and passionate physical union, so their only child didn't come along until they had been married for five years. Except for the fact that Margaret was conceived when her father was thirty-nine years old and her mother thirty-eight, and that neither of them ever ogled a person of the opposite sex, absolutely nothing is known about their conjugal relations.

Their working partnership was a different matter.

Because his $10,000 salary as a member of the U.S. Senate didn't cover the cost of living in one of the most expensive cities of the world, Harry hired Bess to be his secretary at $4,500 a year. Many Republicans shouted, "Nepotism!" and some Democrats hinted that maybe he had made a mistake and had better find someone else to look after his correspondence and records.

The Senator stormed that "the Missus," as he often called his better half, was far more competent than most professional secretaries and did two or three times as much work as the best of them. He refused to remove her from the payroll and said she deserved a pay scale far above "the piddling allowance" customarily paid by the U.S. government that he derided as being "a twentieth-century Midas—only more so."

Clare Booth Luce dipped her pen in venom when she wrote about this squabble over a salaried job for Bess, thereby triggering Truman's later refusal ever to invite her to the White House. One of his foes was accurate when he observed that "Harry never forgets a grudge; he waters it daily, fertilizes it regularly, and delights in seeing it grow bigger and stronger during each new season."

Bess always defended her husband as passionately—but with more guarded language—than he defended her, and rarely said no when he begged her to

Bess and Margaret Truman, who were given quarters in Blair House while the White House was undergoing renovation. (Harry S Truman Library)

do something for him. Reluctant as she was to play a public role of any sort, she went with him on the campaign trail in 1948 and stepped out in front of crowds more than three hundred times. She rarely said a word, however, and after she had been introduced as "the Missus," she habitually stepped from the spotlight.

During that memorable thirty-thousand-mile journey by train, they did their best to stick to long-established routines. They tried always to go to bed at the same time and to get up together. Harry never had a bosom pal, and Bess avoided intimate relationships with other women. A White House servant queried about the fact that they spent so much time together explained, "The only close companion either of them wanted was the other."

UNLIKE MANY MEN WHO very early chose to make politics their career, Truman was satisfied to run a small business, sell memberships in the Kansas City Automobile Club, and fill low-level public offices. Because he was an ardent lifelong Democrat, he was for a time associated with Michael Pendergrast, whose brother Thomas was widely known as a powerful political boss.

Probably because of Harry's ties with his brother, "Boss" Pendergrast sought him out and promised his all-out backing if he'd run against Senator Roscoe Patterson. Since an incumbent nearly always has an advantage over an opponent—especially if that opponent has never held a major office— Harry indicated interest, but he also expressed hesitation to become committed. He and Bess talked things over at length and largely because she thought it would do him good to get out before the voters, he decided to toss his hat into the ring. November 1934 saw him win an astonishing 262,000 more votes than the incumbent—largely because of the power of the Pendergrast political machine from which he quickly divorced himself.

Because Bess sorted mail and handled many routine matters without bothering her husband, she is believed to have been the first person of influence who spotted what seemed to be extravagance on the part of contractors building military bases. At her instigation, Harry observed closely during a tour of Fort Leonard Wood at Rolla, Missouri, and came back to Washington steaming mad. Soon he delivered a speech, much of which was the work of Bess, in which he denounced wasteful spending for military purposes.

It took only a few months for Bess and Harry to realize that both of them had grossly underestimated the extent of fraud and waste in the hasty buildup stemming from the war in Europe. It looked as though it would spread. A report of the Truman Committee, to which Bess supplied vast quantities of data, detailed waste of $100 million and made the name of "the tough little haberdasher from the West" familiar throughout the nation. Having butted heads with the top brass in the military establishment, Bess convinced her husband that he would soon be pilloried if he did not push forward with the investigation.

He encountered stiff opposition on Capitol Hill, so at the insistence of his wife, he released additional committee findings in a national radio broadcast. Ordinary citizens and officials of the government, at first reluctant to believe that overpricing plus shoddy work was rampant, eventually came to accept reality. As a result, work of the Truman Committee was estimated to have saved the federal government at least $14 billion to $15 billion. Although radiantly happy when she learned the results of a survey taken among newspaper correspondents in the capital, Bess said to her husband simply, "Looks like they've finally begun to sit up and listen to you."

With the election of 1944 fast approaching, Harry told his wife that he'd like to have a major hand in the Democratic convention at Chicago. She gave him her unqualified support, so he went there in order to nominate James F. Byrnes as running mate to the man sure to sweep to an overwhelming victory on the first ballot. FDR had revealed that after eleven years in the White House, he wanted another term "in order to bury the Great Depression so deeply that it cannot be dug up."

As expected, Roosevelt sailed to an overwhelming renomination, but Harry's rousing speech in support of Byrnes failed to generate support for his candidate. Since it looked as though delegates might become hopelessly divided in their search for just the right running mate for FDR, the president stepped in. "Put Truman on the ticket," he directed.

Bess Truman dolled herself up for this formal portrait by Greta Kempton. (Harry S Truman Library)

Bess was surprised and angry when she learned that her husband had been nominated for a new office on the second ballot. "He's much better off in the Senate where he can do some good," she said. Events had moved so swiftly in Chicago that Harry had no chance to seek or get her views, so he offered profound apologies when he returned home. Less than ninety days after having reluctantly found herself wedded to the vice president of the United States, the death of FDR made Bess mistress of the White House.

She did not welcome the role, telling Harry that she couldn't possibly be like Eleanor Roosevelt if she tried—which she did not want to do.

Showing surprising patience in a difficult situation, the new chief executive listened carefully to everything his wife said during a number of evenings. "Forget about Mrs. Roosevelt," he finally advised. "Just be yourself, and don't worry about what folks will think of you."

After having been badgered by female members of the White House press corps, Bess had reluctantly agreed to continue holding conferences in the fashion launched in 1933. Hours before her first scheduled appearance, she took Harry's advice and notified women who had expected to question her that she had not been elected to any office and had nothing to say. Although she frequently met socially with members of the press corps, she accepted written questions only and in response to them typically wrote: "No comment."

Yet many capital insiders saw the subtle hand of the first lady in a bizarre chain of events. Author Merle Miller advanced persuasive arguments that the new field of oral history seemed as though it had been tailor-made for blunt-speaking Truman. During one of many sessions that were conducted in relaxed fashion, the chief executive let it be known that Gen. Dwight D. Eisenhower's private life was deeply offensive to him.

Having no idea of what the man from Missouri meant, the writer probed and evoked from Truman a story about a letter he was positive Eisenhower wrote to his commander, Gen. George C. Marshall. Refusing to refer to the Texas native as Ike, the president exploded at remembering that "the fellow wanted a leave so he could come home, divorce his wife, and marry an English woman."

Evidence that is impossible to refute points to Capitol Hill gossip picked up by Bess and passed along to her husband as the source of his implacable animosity toward the man he was sure had wronged Mamie. Had Truman's wife not relayed to him stories that she heard from wives of other lawmakers, there is no reason to believe that the final and damning account by Summersby would have been made public.

A supreme irony of the Truman administration that lasted nearly eight years lies here. A spotlessly clean White House pair who violently hated personal attacks were central to a lasting assault upon the character of our thirty-fourth president.

34

Ike and Mamie Eisenhower, Plus "That Girl Kay"

How do I know he gave it his best? Because I was there, remember? He tried so hard I was afraid he might have a stroke. When he finally realized he couldn't make it, he rolled over on his back, put his head between his hands, and moaned over and over, 'O, God! O God!' "

"Was this the only time?"

"No," responded Kay Summersby, "but after two or three failures he gave up trying. I think the man's body was worn out and his mind was spinning from poring over maps and charts all day."

"Was this after he was made supreme commander of the AEF?" inquired Captain Summersby's longtime friend who, unknown to her, was working for a British tabloid.

"No, it was right after the invasion of North Africa. He was still a lieutenant general then and hadn't been here very long. President Roosevelt didn't make him the supreme commander until December of '43."

Her suspicions suddenly aroused, the red-haired Irish woman, a jeep driver for the man everyone called Ike, demanded, "Why are you asking so many questions? I jolly well don't want to talk about it any more."

"Oh, just say I have a woman's curiosity. Besides, I read every issue of *Stars and Stripes* and it uses lots of jokes about you and the general."

Mamie Eisenhower, who had stayed in the States against her will, scanned one of the latest terse accounts of her husband's affair with a girl she had never seen. "Hogwash!" she exclaimed, and she threw the offending newspaper clipping into a trash basket. To the end of her days, she vehemently denied that there was ever a strong relationship between her husband and "that girl Kay." Deep down, however, she was never absolutely sure. Her wartime letters reveal that she was deeply troubled for months.

Ike and Mamie on their wedding day, when he refused to sit down because he thought he might spoil the crease in his trousers.

ON JULY 1, 1916, it didn't occur to Marie Geneva Doud that her future might some time include a love triangle. At her father's home in Denver, Colorado, the daughter of a prosperous meat packer looked lovingly at First Lt. Dwight D. Eisenhower as she spoke her vows. Six years his junior and universally known simply as Mamie, she knew that a U.S. Army post wouldn't bear much resemblance to Miss Wolcott's finishing school. To her, that didn't seem to matter even a tiny bit; she was in love, in love, *in love*, and knew beyond a shadow of a doubt that Ike was interested only in her.

It was simply wonderful, she told friends earlier, that her sweetheart announced he didn't want her to be married to a second lieutenant. At his urging, the date of the wedding was scheduled to coincide with his promotion to first lieutenant that came barely a year after his graduation from West Point.

Starry-eyed and eager for Ike to return to their Fort Sam Houston quarters so she could throw her arms around his neck and give him a big kiss, she could tell something was wrong when he walked in a single day before their "one-month anniversary." After embracing Mamie with a lot less enthusiasm than usual, he didn't say a word but began getting his things together.

"You can't be leaving me this soon, can you?" she demanded.

Standing with his hands on his hips, Ike waited for what seemed an eternity and then spoke quietly but firmly. "You married an officer of the United States Army," he responded. "We might as well get one thing straight, right now. As long as I'm in uniform, my country has to come first. It can't be any other way."

Devastated by her bridegroom's indirect manner of saying that she would always be second, Mamie retreated to the bedroom and sobbed. Ike completed his packing, patted her, and told her he was sorry, but he couldn't change things. Then he threw straps across his shoulder and strode away without closing the door.

"Ike is one of the best men who ever lived," Mamie told reporters years later in divulging that their marriage "got off to a pretty rocky start." She was still of the opinion that he shouldn't have gotten miffed with her that day at Sam Houston. "I was just nineteen and had barely begun to learn a little about how a soldier's wife has to live," she explained.

"Later, I became reconciled to long separations and frequent changes of quarters, but I never liked them. One year, Ike and I went to seven different posts—and I was by myself most of the time." She said nothing about it during an early interview as mistress of the White House, but she always believed that her husband's early life had prepared him for a military career. She grew up in opulence and found it hard to adjust to an entirely different lifestyle. Ike had been born in a rented room near the railroad tracks in Denison, Texas, and had enjoyed none of the amenities that Mamie's father had provided for her.

During early months of her marriage, Mamie found it almost impossible to do everything around their quarters, for she had grown up with several servants at her beck and call. Gregarious and vivacious, it was difficult for the young officer's wife to adapt to a pattern of change so frequent that she could not form any lasting friendships. They'd been married only nine months when the United States entered World War I. Ike was not sent overseas, and Mamie told him that this made up for a lot of things.

Their union improved when Doud Dwight was born in September 1917. Ike had encouraged Mamie to go home to have their baby, saying that at Camp Meade the best quarters he could possibly get were likely to be rough and uncomfortable. She was thankful that he had urged her to go to Denver, for their little boy was not strong and had to have frequent medical attention. His death at age four left an enormous vacuum that was partly filled by the arrival of another son, but Mamie never completely got over the loss of her first child.

Like Doud, John was born in Denver rather than on an army post. He was still tiny when his father was sent to the Panama Canal Zone, but he went with his mother to join Ike at Fort Leavenworth, Kansas, when he was three years old. One of Mamie's proudest moments of her early marriage came when her husband, who had been picked to study at the Command General Staff School, was honored as first in his class of 275 men.

It didn't eliminate any of the factors that put a strain on their marriage, but Ike's stay at Leavenworth proved to be a springboard toward special assignments. In 1928 he attended the Army War College in Washington, then was made an aide to the assistant secretary of war. Mamie reveled in the

Petite and charming as she had been years earlier, Mamie later gave her inaugural dress to the Smithsonian Institution.

two years her husband spent in the capital on Gen. Douglas A. MacArthur's staff. By this time she could identify herself to a new acquaintance as "just an army wife" without bitterness, but she was never happy that the U.S. Army had first dibs on her husband.

When MacArthur went to the Philippines in 1935, he insisted on taking his brilliant young aide with him. Ike's stint there stretched out to nearly four years—the longest period he spent in one place until he entered the White House. Actively encouraged by Mamie, he took to the air and earned his pilot's license. His wife later liked to point out that no other future chief executive ever matched that achievement.

Returning to the states late in 1919, the family of three went to Fort Lewis, Washington, and then back to Fort Sam Houston, Texas, where Ike was stationed when he and Mamie married. This time, however, he escorted her to elegant quarters set aside for the chief of staff, III Army Corps, instead of a cubicle in a dreary barracks. They spent much time together during their second tour of duty at Sam Houston and found fewer things to quarrel about than during previous periods.

When she heard that the Japanese had bombed Pearl Harbor, Mamie instantly realized that their good times were over, but she said nothing to Ike. Moving rapidly up the chain of command and in rank, he took command of the European Theater of Operations in June 1942. His London office became the center of a fast-growing military network. Its goal was to get a stranglehold on Hitler's forces, which threatened to overrun all Europe and to engulf the British Isles. At home Mamie followed heavily censored war news as best she could and wrote letter after letter to her husband who was at the eye of the hurricane.

She was confident that Ike, temporarily serving as a lieutenant general, would soon become our nation's twelfth full general. She fervently hoped that her letters, filled with news about family and friends, would fill some of the void created by physical separation.

Since *Stars and Stripes* failed to give significant space to a report that General Eisenhower had been assigned a pool of carefully picked drivers, Mamie knew nothing about the matter until much later. Sgt. Leonard D. Dry, who had responsibility for Ike's transportation, took charge of the only drivers he could get—members of the Women's Army Corps, commonly designated as WACs.

Pearlie Hargrave, a slender blonde of twenty-five, was highly experienced and was much tougher than she looked. Dry believed she could sit behind the wheel all day, then step out of a jeep looking as though she had just come from a beauty salon. Inez Scott had almost as much experience as Pearlie, but lacked her stamina. Elisabeth Duncan, a native of England, had been in uniform only a short time and Dry doubted that she had fully adjusted to her new role.

According to the American sergeant, his fourth driver was in a class all by herself. He considered recently divorced Kay Summersby's most striking feature to be her "blazing auburn hair." Yet he was inclined to believe she could have been a fashion model instead of a jeep driver had it not been for war. Without previous experience in handling the all-terrain vehicle, she mastered it quickly.

Tragedy struck soon after Ike became casually acquainted with his drivers. Capt. Richard Arnold, who had planned to become Kay's second husband, was killed. After crying for hours for many nights, she reported for duty with swollen eyes. In an attempt to show compassion, the general later, as he later told Mamie, assigned secretarial duties to Kay with the hope that additional work would get her mind off her loss. When the prescription failed to cure her malady, Ike doubled the dose.

It took weeks for Kay to gain enough self-control to stop crying every time something reminded her of Richard. Ike piled on more and more work and extended her hours—probably without giving a thought to the fact that she was spending more and more time with him.

Kay Summersby, shown here in a 1940s file photo, later told Parade Magazine *that her relationship with Ike "was a friendship . . . with tenderness and affection, but that's as far as I'm going." (AP/Wide World Photos)*

Mamie's increasingly frequent and pointed accusations from home, based largely on what she interpreted to be veiled allusions in *Stars and Stripes*, made things worse. Repeatedly challenged to tell the truth about his relationship with Kay, he stifled his anger at his wife and wrote her a temperate letter that said in part:

> Darling, stop worrying. I have met very few women here and they mean nothing—absolutely nothing to your husband. Other considerations aside, I don't have the time or the youth to become interested in them. Remember that I love only you—always.

By the time her husband returned home and was literally shoved into the presidency as a military hero, Mamie had practically ceased to think about the seductive-looking colleen who had been one of her husband's drivers during their long wartime separation. She assumed her duties as mistress of the White House with zest, frequently remarking that life at 1600 Pennsylvania Avenue was not monumentally different from girlhood days in her father's Denver mansion.

Kay Summersby, who came to the United States soon after the end of the war, did not surface until 1948. She was briefly in the news that year as

As a civilian chief executive, Ike dispensed with much of the formality that marked his years as a high-ranking military commander.

a result of publishing a volume entitled *Eisenhower Was My Boss*. Mamie grabbed a copy as soon as it came off the press, read it from cover to cover, and then laid it aside with a silent prayer of gratitude that nothing in it suggested that the author had been anything more than one of Ike's many aides and subordinates.

As the election of 1956 (Ike's second) approached, Mamie influenced her husband far more than did his powerful political supporters. She pointed out that during the twentieth century, no Republican had won two successive terms in the White House.

Although he sometimes tried to act as though he was not eager for a second term, Ike secretly feared that Democrats were gaining strength, and he didn't want to risk facing defeat at home after being victorious in Europe. When he became reasonably satisfied that Adlai E. Stevenson of Illinois would give him no more trouble in 1956 than he had in 1952, he became an enthusiastic candidate. Leaving his campaign to seasoned veterans, he romped to an easy but overwhelming victory that made Mamie prouder of him than ever, if that was possible.

After having spent much more time together in their eight White House years than in their first thirty-six years of marriage, combined, they eagerly anticipated retirement to Gettysburg, Pennsylvania. Ike, age seventy, beamed when Mamie frequently reminded him—as though he did not know it—that no other man his age had served as chief executive.

In May 1962 Mamie went with her husband to Abilene, Kansas, for the dedication of the Dwight D. Eisenhower Library. She is credited by some historians with having been the first person to realize that the one

hundredth anniversary of the dedication of the Gettysburg national cemetery by Abraham Lincoln was just around the corner. His wife may have
been responsible for the fact that our thirty-fourth president rededicated
the national shrine at which our sixteenth president had made one of the
most memorable brief addresses of all time.

Nearly a decade after Ike and Mamie adapted to what she called
"wonderfully quiet life without the burdens of the world on our shoulders,"
her husband suffered three heart attacks in fairly quick succession. After
recovering, he personally planned what he privately called "the greatest
golden wedding celebration ever held." Before it was over, he was hard at
work on his third book—a volume of stories he had enjoyed telling to
friends. Soon after it was published, he suffered one heart episode after
another and was taken out by pneumonia that progressed into congestive
heart failure.

To Mamie's gratification, Ike's volume entitled At Ease did not mention Kay Summersby. Without her husband's knowledge, she had earlier
secured a ghostwritten account of the jeep-driver's experiences and had
read every word of it. Then seventy-seven years old and self-described as
"mellowed by time and experience," she had nodded understanding at
some comparatively lurid passages that seemed to confirm her suspicions of
earlier years.

According to Summersby's account, the general who was separated
from his wife by the Atlantic Ocean became interested in his driver and
then fell madly in love with her. She said that he desperately wanted to
consummate their physical union, but was so exhausted that to her ever-
lasting regret he was impotent.

Mamie, who had known for years that there was bad blood between
her husband and Harry S Truman, blamed encouragement by his predecessor in the White House for the second and revised account by Summersby.
She and Ike had plenty of ups and downs, she readily admitted, but she was
positive that the young Irish woman enamored with the general had greatly
embroidered her account of their relationship.

35

JFK, Jackie, and Stable

Jacqueline Lee Bouvier mused to friends that she "had a few doubts" about the wisdom of visiting the Kennedy compound at Hyannis Port, Massachusetts. "One to one, I can take care of little me in just about any situation," she said. "The Kennedys are different, though; there are lots of them, and they form a closeknit clan. I'll be an outsider on their turf—but I'm going, anyway."

"My God! Jack's got a fashion model this time!" Robert Kennedy exclaimed when on Wednesday, July 4, 1953, he caught sight of the woman who despised being called "Jackie" but couldn't prevent others from using that form of her name. Her bearing plus her face, hair, and costume labeled the first-time guest as the society queen she had been her entire life.

An old friend of John Fitzgerald Kennedy's, then working as a Washington-based newspaper correspondent, was instrumental in first bringing Jack and Jackie together. Both were guests at the Georgetown home of Charles Bartlett late in the spring of 1951, and before the evening was over they were acting like bosom friends. After having spent four years in the U.S. House of Representatives, JFK—as he was already known to many—was restless. That evening he casually confided that he was itching to "put his butt in the Senate seat Henry Cabot Lodge had warmed for him," but said nothing else about politics.

He immediately added Jackie to the list of women he planned to have, but at the insistence of his brother, Robert, spent most of the following year preparing for an uphill race. If anyone then wondered what money can do in politics, the Kennedy campaign of 1952 must have been an eye-opener. Henry Cabot Lodge II, whose father had been revered as "Mr. Washington," had been in the U.S. Senate since 1947. He and nearly every other Republican up for election expected to ride to an easy victory on the coattails of Dwight D. Eisenhower.

Most contests went as expected, but during the Republican landslide Jack was the surprise winner in Massachusetts. His margin of victory was only seventy thousand votes, but that was more than plenty. By midnight

Joseph Kennedy, flanked by members of the dynasty he formed and headed.
(JFK Library)

on November 2, 1952, Joseph Patrick Kennedy was nearly as happy as any member of the family had ever seen him. He had expected to put his oldest boy into the White House, and he never completely recovered from the death of Lt. Joseph P. Kennedy Jr., lost in a dogfight over Suffolk, England, during World War II. Jack, who was now first in line for the throne his father boasted he could buy any time he was ready for a Kennedy to occupy it, would soon be positioned to take the prize.

Senator Kennedy managed to begin seeing Jacqueline with some frequency as soon as he took over "the Lodge seat" on January 3, 1953. By spring he had decided that she had everything a wife could bring to an aspiring politician—beauty, brains, and social standing that money couldn't buy. She also had that somewhat detached point of view that prevailed among members of what was then called "the upper crust."

Having already decided to make her his wife, he invited her to "come meet the whole family and have the greatest weekend of your life." Through mutual friends, Jackie had learned quite a bit about the Kennedys,

but she was not prepared to see Pat and Eunice in shirts and sneakers looking as though they had spent all day on the tennis courts. Along with their
sister Jean, they made little effort to hide their disdain for her costume and
demeanor. Behind her back they experimented with mocking her wispy
voice and decided that she must be a real-life version of a then-popular doll
that could say a few words.

Rose Kennedy, a devout Catholic who attended daily Mass, was
openly delighted that Jack had this time brought along a girl who knew
her rosary. She and Joseph had long ago set out on widely divergent paths
and although they had nine children they followed their separate interests. Rose, who wouldn't have considered divorce under any circumstances, knew a great deal about her husband's flagrant womanizing but
never tried to interfere. Experience told her exactly what was going to
take place when, talking animatedly, Joseph pointed Jacqueline toward
"the doll room."

A guided tour of the room with display cases holding several hundred
female dolls dressed in costumes of their native countries was part of the
ritual conducted when any likely candidate for marriage into the clan paid
a first visit to the compound. Ethel, now pregnant with Robert's third
child, had passed "the doll room test" with flying colors. "When I had the
top diplomatic post of the United States as ambassador to Great Britain,"
Joseph explained to Jackie, "somebody started the custom of bringing me a
doll as a gift."

Trying to smile but seeming to leer, he reflected aloud that maybe that
custom got started because everybody knew he had been interested in girls
all his life. Jackie nodded understanding and in her little-girl voice said she
thought it was nice that he had put them under glass where they wouldn't
get dusty.

"Don't know why," the elder Kennedy continued, "but these pretty
little things in all kinds of outfits do something for me. When I brought
Gloria Swanson here, they sorta seemed to turn her on, too. The first time
we made love in this room, I found out that once was not enough for her;
she was one hell of a woman who didn't know when to quit."

Joseph didn't bother to try to conceal his pleasure; his judgment
plus reports from his private detectives had been center target. This
twenty-four-year-old "high society dame" had shown no sign of being
shocked or offended by explicit talk from a man nearly old enough to be
her grandfather. Long before he nodded consent to the suggestion that
"Jackie Bouvier might be willing to come for the Fourth," the head of the
clan knew his first-time guest was not a sexual novice. She had spent a
lot of time with Jack Marquand, among others, "and they didn't waste

energy on horseback riding or golf."

After having been screened by the doll room ritual and passing the test with a top score, Jackie didn't do quite as well the next day when pulled into a rough-and-tumble game of touch football. Ganging up on the visitor they scorned as a snob and mocked as "the Deb," Jack's sisters blocked and hit so hard that the girl of whom Joseph heartily approved suffered a more than trivial injury. Although some reports say she broke her ankle, medical records indicate that it was severely sprained.

Barely sixty days after having recovered from her Hyannis Port injury, Jacqueline Lee Bouvier was regal on her own turf at Newport, Rhode Island. It didn't seem to bother her that her once-wealthy father was tanked and didn't show

Chief architect and undisputed queen of America's "Camelot." (JFK Library)

up to see her walk down the aisle to become Mrs. John Fitzgerald Kennedy. Instead of standing before Archbishop Richard Cushing with her head meekly bowed she looked him straight in the eye and tossed him a trace of a smile.

Her thrice-married and very wealthy stepfather, Hugh D. Auchincloss, gave the bride away with what relatives and guests characterized as "unusual flair." Few veteran politicians were on hand that September day, despite the fact that the bridegroom had seen to it that every member of the U.S. Senate had received a personal invitation. If Jack was annoyed, he concealed his feelings by triumphantly waving a document proclaiming that he and his bride were recipients of an apostolic blessing from Pope Pious XII.

AS A FRESHMAN SENATOR, Kennedy was not cordially received by colleagues who prided themselves upon being "elder statesmen." Some of them had sown some wild oats decades earlier, and they had their own sources of information. It was a bit ironic, they agreed, that the brash thirty-six-year-old from the Bay State had married a young woman whose only job had previously been held by one of his mistresses.

Inga Arvad, a former Miss Denmark and Miss Europe whose looks caught the attention of Ensign John F. Kennedy of the U.S. Navy in 1941, had made a name for herself as the Berlin correspondent of a Danish newspaper. That background of experience helped her to land a job as "camera girl" for the *Washington Times-Herald*. It also brought her to the attention of the Federal Bureau of Investigation because she had interviewed Adolf Hitler and some of his aides.

Jack and Jackie, widely admired as looking like motion picture stars, found the mores of Hollywood to be wholly compatible with their own.

Kennedy didn't suspect that Inga—whom he affectionately called Inga Binga—was under surveillance and that her telephone was tapped. They spent a day or two together at irregular intervals for more than two years—during which time J. Edgar Hoover accumulated evidence that guaranteed he'd get a respectful hearing every time he made contact with the thirty-fifth president of the United States.

Since Jacqueline followed Inga at the newspaper of the capital a decade later and held the same job, fellow employees told her everything they knew. She walked into marriage with her eyes wide open. Nearly penniless despite her aristocratic background and knowing that the Auchincloss fortune would go to his own children, Jackie desperately wanted money. A trust fund earlier settled upon Jack was believed to be worth "in the neighborhood of ten million." For now, she seems to have decided, that would have to do.

To a handful of intimates the wife of the aspiring politician confided that going to bed with the Lochinvar of the U.S. Senate wasn't all it might seem to be. Her husband not only craved sex; he demanded it. Yet he had little skill or interest in the art of making love; he did want children, so made Jackie pregnant at least five times during sessions in which he routinely consulted his wristwatch to see how much time he had before his next appointment.

To the nation whose eyes are continually focused upon occupants of the White House, JFK and Jacqueline shaped a make-believe marriage that was central to their Camelot era. Members of the media, their servants, and their Secret Service agents cooperated with this charade without reservation, despite their knowledge that the marriage was never fulfilling and tranquil. At the FBI, Hoover and his agents kept a tight lid on the information they had accumulated; it might be needed in a time when wills were being tested and hence was far too valuable to leak.

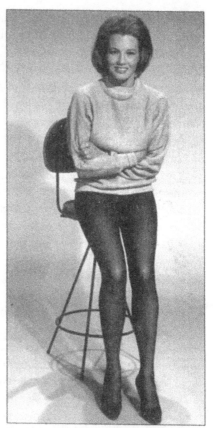

Leggy actress Angie Dickinson's name often comes up when stories of JFK's affairs get bandied about. (AP/Wide World Photos)

It would be pointless to offer yet another compilation of JFK's premarital and extramarital affairs. This has been done many times and the list of documented relationships plus public claims of women is very long. It ranges from White House staffers Priscilla Weir and Jill Cowan to actresses Gene Tierney, Jayne Mansfield, Angie Dickinson—and Marilyn Monroe. Dozens if not scores of other women were with Kennedy for periods ranging from fifteen minutes to "a one-night stand."

According to British tabloids, Jackie's husband rather casually remarked to Prime Minister Harold Macmillan that if he went without sex for seventy-two hours, he would develop a splitting headache that wouldn't go away. Similar comments were reported in American media—but not until long after his death. Some analysts of his brilliantly successful public life and his abysmal failure as a husband believe that drugs administered in efforts to ease almost unendurable back pain contributed to his enormous libido. Interviewed in depth in 1976, Ralph Horton, who knew Jack intimately during his four years at Choate preparatory school, believed his first sexual experience was in a Harlem brothel at age seventeen. That may have been the story Jack's schoolmate told, but it is within the realm of probability that it was Joseph who introduced his son to the joys of the flesh.

Even during one of his numerous comparatively lengthy relationships with women—including his wife—JFK seems to have participated in sex as an end unto itself. His magnetic charm led females by the score to throw themselves at his feet, but even after having accepted those he liked when he looked them over, he treated them as sex objects rather than as persons.

Jacqueline, who was genuinely interested in the arts and languages, was the real author of the Camelot image. Her husband cared little for anything except sex, sports, and politics. Yet he was both brilliant and astute, so he went along with his wife's ideas because he quickly saw that it strengthened his hold upon the public.

Did the queen of the royal court know what her knight errant was doing with other women? Absolutely and incontestably, she did. She and Jack quarreled with some frequency, but neither of them seemingly ever considered a separation that would have led to a messy divorce. Compared to her licentious husband, Jacqueline came close to living as a plaster saint—but never quite made the final leap to that status. Interviewed for a British documentary film in 1995, JFK's former secretary ventured to say that the wife of her boss had all the lovers she wanted.

Evelyn Lincoln's revelation that Jackie may have spent time with a rich and handsome Italian nobleman cannot be documented. Her long-lasting relationship and final public capitulation to Greek shipping magnate Aristotle Onassis is a matter of public record, however. She first became acquainted with him at a party given in honor of Winston Churchill aboard one of Onassis's yachts. During a lengthy period of absence from the White House, the first lady cruised the Mediterranean Sea with Onassis aboard his yacht *Christina*. As a widow of a few weeks, still demurely dressed in mourning, she sought and apparently found comfort in Onassis's arms, plus, presumably, thoughts of his billions.

Jacqueline was always discreet in public; her husband was not. With his connivance if not by his arrangement, Marilyn Monroe was the star performer at the party held in honor of JFK's forty-fifth birthday. Earlier Marilyn had called the White House numberless times, and she apparently had been with him enough to be able to confide to members of the press (who swore their lips were sealed) that "he was hasty and perfunctory in bed."

On the evening of the big bash in May 1962, Marilyn wore a tight, revealing dress. She managed to stumble through "Happy Birthday" in such fashion that many onlookers thought she was offering herself to the guest of honor as a birthday present. Less than three months later Marilyn was dead, reportedly as a result of a massive overdose of sleeping pills. Some cynics have opined that she was murdered because she had been talking too candidly about her relationship with the president as well as one with his brother Bobby.

From the perspective of decades, even Kennedy's open involvement with that era's top female sex symbol was far less dangerous than his liaisons with Judy Campbell over a period of at least two years. White House logs later revealed that she visited the mansion at least twenty times during a period of about three months in 1961, soon after Frank Sinatra allegedly had arranged for them to meet. They held other trysts in big-name hotels, as well as in a Georgetown residence.

This photo of Judith Campbell Exner was taken in 1960, the year she said she met JFK. (AP/Wide World Photos)

Kennedy seems to have had no idea that his newest acquisition was also a mistress of Chicago gangster Sam "Momo" Giancano. Members of the public knew nothing about this complex three-way relationship until Campbell was forced in 1975 to testify before the Senate Select Committee on Intelligence Operations. Her sworn statements were sealed until 2025 by court order, but it is a matter of record that the committee headed by Senator Frank Church was investigating possible involvement of a governmental agency in a plot to assassinate Fidel Castro. No one knows positively whether or not the Kennedy-Campbell-Giancano-Castro matter was central to the still-mysterious assassination of the president.

Gunilla von Post is seldom listed as having been a mistress of JFK. Jack wrote dozens of love letters to her from 1954 to 1956, however, and she saved most of them for forty years before putting them into book form with the help of Carl Johnes. She seems truly to have kept on believing she was young Kennedy's truest love. Gunilla was dead wrong; he probably never loved any woman.

36

LBJ, Lady Bird, and Ménage

C arrying an overnight bag in his left hand, Texas senator Lyndon Baines Johnson gripped the door handle with his right hand and started to turn it. Releasing his grip, he glanced over his shoulder and called: "Gotta spend a couple of hours in the saddle. Be back some time tomorrow."

Without lifting her eyes from *The Wall Street Journal*, Lady Bird Johnson wiggled the fingers of her left hand in a wordless good-bye. He knew that she knew he was not headed to Longlea estate near Culpeper, Virginia, in order to relax on horseback. He'd do that eventually, of course. But his real objective was a curvaceous two-legged filly named Alice Glass, who was simultaneously his mistress as well as the squeeze of another powerful Texan who had made millions in oil.

The senator's wife, baptized Claudia Alta, was still as dainty and bright as the shapely little beetle whose name was conferred upon her in 1912 by an early nursemaid. Unlike many infants, the tiny daughter of prominent rancher Thomas Jefferson Taylor and his wife Minnie Pattillo really was beautiful from birth. Shaped about like half of a pea, the bright red or yellow body of a flying ladybird, dotted with colored spots, makes it among the most colorful of common beetles. Conferred in a gesture of spontaneous admiration, the name stuck to the baby so closely that her most intimate friends never addressed her as Claudia.

Lady Bird grew up not knowing the meaning of wanting something she couldn't have. Her father, who had started in a small way upon reaching Karnack, Texas, from Alabama, never had a huge spread of land. Instead, he owned and operated numerous relatively small tracts. He raised cotton in large quantity and processed it in his own gins. While his holdings were small by comparison with the famous King Ranch, he always had plenty of money to indulge every whim of his Lady Bird, whose mother had died when she was five years old.

Four years before Lady Bird arrived at the Taylor place, Sam Ealy Johnson and his wife, Rebekah Baines, were glad to see that her first pregnancy was over, but neither of them tried to pretend that their male infant was pretty. Ten-pound Lyndon Baines was so eternally long and gaunt that he seemed to have been on a starvation diet in his mother's womb. Every time his father looked at him, Sam was given a vivid reminder of how hard it was to keep food on the table in their run-down, three-room shack on the Pedernales River.

Lyndon's early years were spent in an economic environment 180 degrees away from that of Lady Bird's. There almost always was enough to eat, but he often had to settle for potatoes and corn when he'd rather have had something else. He rarely if ever remembered being without a shirt on his back, but he paid for most of his coarse clothing from his own earnings as a day laborer on nearby farms. He later worked as a shoe-shine boy on some Saturdays at Johnson City's one-chair barbershop and washed cars before landing a job as a highway laborer, where the work was hard but the money was the best he'd ever seen.

His mamma, who spent a lot of time crying or sitting silently at a window, didn't believe in putting up with any foolishness from a boy. If Lyndon's memory was accurate, any time he refused to obey an order, Rebekah would walk around the house for a day or two acting like he didn't exist. Years of marginal living took a nosedive when a few bales of cotton bought on speculation by Sam at a peak of forty-four cents plummeted to six cents.

Because he was extremely bright and quick to learn, Lyndon went through high school hoping to get into a good college. All such notions were torpedoed along with the price of cotton, so he went to work as a clerk in a store about the time Lady Bird—four years younger—was beginning to think about choosing between Baylor and the University of Texas.

Work behind a counter didn't suit Lyndon, so he got together with some of his buddies who had a Model-T Ford and lit out for California. It didn't take him long to find out that "the Land of Opportunity" wasn't exactly what it was cracked up to be. He didn't have enough money to get back home, so he took any odd job he could find. Two years of mopping restaurant floors, picking fruit, and washing dishes were all he could take. He bummed his way back to Texas and reached the little house on the Pedernales without a nickel in his pocket.

Pushed hard by Rebekah, he decided to give college a try, even if he'd have to work his way through by collecting garbage. That's how he really started at Southwest Texas State Teachers College in 1927. Lady Bird was at the University of Texas and finding it a breeze before Lyndon began making what seemed to him to be good money as an assistant to the secretary of the college president. By then he was Big Man on Campus, six feet, three inches tall, and president or vice president of nearly every student organization. He'd learned how to run for office, and every win gave him a

From infancy, Claudia Alta Taylor Johnson has merited the compliment of being called as "pretty as a lady-bird."

feeling he experienced from no other activity—not even the successful pursuit of girls. Several he knew in high school remained his close friends in later years.

THIN AS A RAIL but already towering over high school classmates, Lyndon had an indefinable magnetism that drew girls to him. Louise Casparis didn't try to hide the fact that she was crazy about him, and she considered it a triumph when he briefly wore her class ring. Her family wanted nothing to do with "the no-account Johnsons," so their relationship endured for less than a year.

Kitty Clyde Ross was different; instead of being pursued by her, Lyndon went about fervently trying to win her affection. His success, if that is what it really was, lasted only briefly, but it made an impact so lasting that he was bound and determined that she should attend his inauguration after he won the 1964 election. It wasn't enough to send one-of-a-kind invitations to Kitty and her husband; the president-elect wangled a favor and had them brought to the capital aboard *Air Force One.*

Although he never forgot Kitty Clyde, by the time he was twenty Lyndon was madly in love with Carol Davis of Kerrville. She was a raving beauty who was light years ahead of him in music and literature, but to her suitor Carol's most desirable trait was her absorbing interest in politics. He often talked of having fallen in love with her the minute he first laid eyes on her and swapped a few sentences with her.

Carol was in the notion of getting married before they had been together a dozen times, and Lyndon told her he was more than willing. They discussed running off to a justice of the peace, but gave up that idea because it would have deprived Carol of "a real wedding in a church." Hand in hand, they confronted her father, a Ku Klux Klansman. He listened to them for less than two minutes before spitting out a few expletives and calling his daughter's suitor "nothing but a young sprout raised by a no-good cattle rustler." He'd known a lot of folks like the Johnsons, he said, and had learned that "They never change from generation to generation. They don't know a thing except how to be shiftless dirt farmers and penny-ante politicians."

Stung by her father's blunt rejection of her would-be husband, Carol renewed talk of running off to a justice of the peace. Lyndon later declared that the relationship ended on the front porch of the Davis home. He broke his ties with Carol, he said, because he "just couldn't stomach the notion of puttin' that girl through hell at home."

Eager to get as far away from Carol as he could, Lyndon landed a job teaching public speaking at $153 a month. He launched his professional career at Pearsall, but all the time had his eyes on a possible opening in Houston. The job materialized, so he moved to the high school named for "the father of Texas." But as desirable as Sam Houston High School had looked from Pearsall, he stayed there only a few months. Always eager for advancement, he turned his back on schoolrooms forever and took charge of the Austin office of Congressman Richard M. Kleburg. As a trusted aide to the lawmaker, he made frequent lengthy trips to the nation's capital and quickly decided that he'd rather spend his life there than anywhere else in the world.

A few months after getting settled into his new job, Lyndon went to breakfast at the home of his friend Gene Behringer and was surprised to find another guest there. By the time they had finished their bacon and grits, Johnson had made up his mind that Lady Bird Taylor was going to be his wife. He proposed less than twelve hours after seeing her for the first time, and casually shrugged off her instant refusal. "She'll come around," he confided to Kleburg. "Women always do—that's their nature."

After seven weeks of incessant begging, the rancher's daughter, who had many male acquaintances but no previous lover, capitulated. She took him to her father's home, more than a trifle afraid that he would frown on their proposed union. Instead, Taylor was impressed by Lyndon's size, bearing, and inside knowledge of events in Washington. Once he gave his approval, the engaged pair drove for ten hours in order to reach San Antonio to be married at a spot where Lady Bird's college roommate could be her maid of honor.

Lyndon's political associate Dan Quill, San Antonio postmaster, had received a quick telephone call in which he was ordered—not requested—to make all the necessary arrangements. He made plans for a wedding at Mark's Episcopal Church, rented a hotel room for the newlyweds, and rounded up attendants plus a handful of guests. Yet he forgot one thing Lyndon had demanded—a wedding ring.

With the sun setting early in November, the pair of lovers reached their hotel and learned that no ring was on hand for the ceremony that

Alice Glass, simultaneously the mistress of two powerful Texans, eventually became the common-law wife of Charles Marsh.

would be held that evening. Quill raced across the street to a department store, found a tray of rings priced at $2.50 each, and took a dozen of them to the hotel so Lady Bird could find one to fit her finger.

House hunting was comparatively easy during the heart of the Great Depression, so they soon found a one-bedroom apartment in Washington that was fully furnished. Located at 1910 Kalormara Road, the neighborhood was a bit rundown, but Lady Bird didn't care; she was thrilled that their rent would be only $42.50 a month. Before reaching the capital, they had reached an agreement that was never broken. Lyndon would take care of his professional responsibilities and wouldn't have to be bothered about household matters. Lady Bird would keep a close eye on their pocketbook and see to it that they would never be in debt. Knowing that she'd come into a sizable inheritance sooner or later, Lady Bird stretched Lyndon's $267 a month far enough to enable them to put $18.75 of it into a government bond every thirty days.

They had been at the center of the national whirlwind for only a year before Lyndon, who made it his business to know every Texan of importance in and around Washington, spent an entire afternoon with Charles Marsh. After having made millions in oil, Marsh had acquired a string of more than two dozen newspapers. That meant he controlled a communications empire of which Austin was the center.

Marsh immediately soared to the top of the list of men Lyndon wanted to cultivate. When invited to visit his new friend's nine-hundred-acre estate, Johnson accepted without an instant of hesitation. He wasn't prepared for what he found there—a tall Texas-born beauty for whom Marsh had abandoned his wife and children. Alice Glass saw the visitor to the estate as being fully as attractive as she was to him. According to long-time Johnson associate John Connally, "Lyndon and Alice hit it off the first time they laid eyes on each other. Some kind of chemistry or magnetism or something else went to work when he hadn't been at Longlea an hour. Before dinner they were making plans to get together when Marsh was away on business."

Lady Bird, who occasionally went to Longlea for a morning or an afternoon, knew exactly what was happening there when her husband stayed overnight "in order to work out a few kinks on top of a fine chestnut-colored horse." In a fashion that is difficult or impossible for an outsider to understand, early in her marriage she learned to cope with the fact that Lyndon would never be hers alone. To a friend she once confided that he wanted a lot more sex than she could willingly provide, but "after all, I'm the only wife he has ever had or ever will have."

LYNDON NOT ONLY PERMITTED his wife to manage their finances; he actively encouraged this practice. When she came into an inheritance big enough to where she now had to decide between competing investments, her husband gave his enthusiastic support when she decided to buy a failing radio station in Austin. Once the station belonged to her, she set out to get it into the black. During a period of more than six months, she functioned as station manager and made only occasional brief trips to Washington to see Lyndon. Once KTBC began turning a small profit, its owner began thinking of expansion and soon went into the brand-new field of television.

Lady Bird's long stay in Austin gave her husband plenty of opportunities to be with Alice Glass, who later strongly encouraged him to take the second spot on the Democratic ticket in 1960. His wife was not sure that he should give up his seat in the U.S. Senate in order to become "a

In 1965, Lady Bird had to be watching with interest as her husband danced in the White House with Princess Margaret of Great Britain.

yes-man if Joseph Kennedy succeeds in buying the White House." Although he had serious reservations before the election was held, very early on the morning of November 9 Johnson told Lady Bird—as though she didn't already know it—that the narrow Democratic victory over Richard M. Nixon and Henry Cabot Lodge meant her husband was "only a heartbeat away from the oval office."

Along with Jacqueline Kennedy, Lady Bird was aboard *Air Force One* departing Dallas in the aftermath of Kennedy's assassination when Lyndon took the oath of office and became our thirty-sixth president. Unlike the Kennedys, who had separate White House bedrooms, the two Texans slept together in a wide bed.

No one knew better than Lyndon that he would have been lost without a faithful wife. He gave every evidence of being deeply in love with her from the morning on which he first saw her until his death after having become embittered over his failure to achieve military victory in Vietnam. His public embraces and kisses inside and outside the White House were not staged for the benefit of onlookers, but were outward signs of deep and lasting love.

LBJ's intimate bond with Alice Glass is believed to have lasted at least a quarter of a century. During much of that period, however, she probably was not his only longtime mistress. In 1987 Steven Brown, age thirty-six, filed a multimillion-dollar lawsuit against the Johnson estate. Through his attorneys, he claimed to be the son of the former president and hence to be entitled both to monetary compensation and the right to change his name to Johnson. During legal arguments, evidence was produced to support Steven's claim that his mother, Madeline, became Lyndon's mistress shortly before he entered the U.S. Senate. This liaison lasted for at least two decades, according to the man who wanted compensation for the infidelity of the lawmaker he said had sired him. Brown's sudden death from cancer left unanswered the question of whether his mother had really shared Johnson with Alice Glass plus Lady Bird for a period of twenty years.

Johnson boasted so often and so loudly about his third set of relationships with women that dozens of former associates have attested to their existence. Prone to brag about and possibly to exaggerate the size of his male member, he frequently used it on the nearest available female. Some of these encounters took place almost through chance, but others were planned when he personally selected young women whose work would place them close to him. How many of the tales he told about "quickies on White House desktops" and similar hastily chosen spots are true and how many such accounts were embroidered, it is impossible to determine.

Lady Bird reportedly walked in during more than one such session of impromptu sex, but she did not let her husband's promiscuity bother her. Aside from being the almost universally admired first lady of the land, she proved herself to be a financier with few parallels. Fourteen years after having become Lyndon's widow, she sold her television and radio interests for more than $27 million.

All evidence supports the conclusion that Lyndon and Lady Bird communicated with each other freely and effectively throughout their years together. She reacted calmly if not casually when she learned about one of his new warts or blemishes, and his enthusiastic yearning to have her as an integral part of his life never flagged.

37

Richard and Pat Nixon

P at Nixon slipped into the tiny kitchenette of their private railroad car as soon as she noticed a change in the pitch of her husband's voice and the tempo of his speech. That nearly always happened when he was angry, and she didn't want to listen to one end of a long-distance conversation. Richard remained on the telephone for nearly half an hour, then moved slowly into the kitchen. His downcast eyes signaled serious trouble: When confronted by a minor problem the senator from California typically stared without blinking.

"It's all over," he muttered. "I'm out of politics for good. Maybe it's for the best. You never have liked this rat race."

"But you love it; it's become your life. What in the world has happened?"

Still looking at the floor, the man who had received the Republican nomination for the vice presidency of the United States in Chicago on July 11, 1952, was silent for what to his wife seemed to be an eternity.

"It's that piddling expense fund!" he finally blurted.

"What about it? All the money came from California, and you can account for every cent."

"Sure! That's not the issue. Some egg-sucking reporter has been digging into it and claims I put it in my pocket. The *New York Post* has run a front-page story saying rich men support us in a style way beyond my salary. Ike wants me off the ticket."

"You mean you won't be running with Eisenhower, after all?"

"Absolutely not! I'm through with politics, for good!"

Pat brewed a fresh pot of coffee and plied him with questions while he downed three cups. Bit by bit the story came out, and when the parts were assembled into a coherent whole, the wife of the nominee learned that supporters in California had sent more money directly to Nixon than she earlier thought. He should have returned it, but carelessly or foolishly had spent it himself. All of it and more went into printing, postage, telephone bills, and travel expenses. Since he depended on aides to keep books, he hadn't bothered to hang on to receipts and records.

"What the hell? It's a stinking eighteen or twenty thousand. I told 'em to tell Ike I'd give headquarters my check for the whole thing, but they said he'd never agree to handling it that way."

Pat knew from experience that her husband listened to her in times of stress and crisis. They were often poles apart in their opinions, but he always let her have her say. Usually, he modified his position by the time they stopped talking, and sometimes he made an about-face because of her arguments.

In this emergency, she stressed her complete loyalty to Eisenhower but reminded Richard that the general was a political novice. Directing the war in Europe had not prepared the man who had never shown any interest in politics to direct campaign strategy. Eisenhower headed the ticket, of course, but that didn't mean he had the background or experience to make every major decision, she suggested.

Body language having confirmed her feeling that Richard was softening a little, his wife, toughened by firsthand experience with hard times and hard work, added that a lot more than his reputation was at stake. He should take into consideration what capitulation would do to their daughters, before she tossed out a suggestion about a novel course of action.

"Tell 'em you have no intention of resigning," she insisted. "Go on national television and give the voters the whole story. Any network you approach will offer you half an hour, because that California money is going to be all over the news."

"God! That would make Ike boiling mad. But it just possibly might work."

"You can make it work. I know you can."

Noticeably calmer than he was when he hung up the telephone, Richard mused that the course his wife suggested would be a big crapshoot. It could put the matter of the expense money behind, if he could compose exactly the right speech. But if he blew it, he might as well forget about ever escorting his wife into the White House in order for her to become its mistress.

Pat, keenly aware of the high risk involved, tried to laugh but couldn't. "Remember the days when both of us were in show business?" she prodded. "Write the best speech you've ever put together, then go out and act like you're on stage and speaking the lines that were given to you. Put everything you've got into it, and you'll get a standing ovation!"

Definitely interested but still wary, he pointed out that he'd have to bare their personal finances—tell the world how little they had and how much they owed. Pat's voice quivered as she asked if she'd have to be with him when he bared his soul.

"Without you by my side, it won't float," Richard insisted. "You've gotta be there, showing how much you love me and believe in me."

Tearfully, Pat nodded understanding and agreement. "Let me wash my face and fix my hair. We'll have a nice, quiet luncheon right here. Then you can start working on that speech!"

After the watershed decision had been reached, Nixon wavered only occasionally and briefly. A wire service story that the Nixon home held lavish draperies that cost ten thousand dollars would be easy to refute; an experienced decorator could take one look and see that they had been handmade by Pat for a pittance. A *Washington Post* editorial demanding that he resign from Congress was waved aside as "just what to expect from that bunch of communists."

IT WASN'T AS EASY to deal with a *New York Herald Tribune* editorial that said he should get out of the upcoming race, however. Since the publisher of the newspaper had close personal ties with Eisenhower, it was likely that the general had been consulted before the piece was written. On the heels of seeing the blistering *Herald Tribune* editorial, Richard received a two-page telegram from party stalwart Harold Stassen. In it, he urged the vice-presidential nominee to withdraw from the race "for the good of Republicans everywhere." Had it been received the day the story broke, it might have tipped the scales. Since it did not reach him until the candidate had decided to plow ahead, it was pondered briefly before being tossed aside as not meriting a reply.

Pat was wrong about easily getting free TV time, but when all the networks turned down that idea, the Republican National Committee decided it was worth seventy-five thousand dollars to try to get the issue out of the way. A careful analysis had convinced professionals that the charges wouldn't stand up under scrutiny, and it was public knowledge that Adlai Stevenson had squirreled away a substantial sum left over from his last campaign. When questioned, the Democrat smiled and casually responded that he used it "to supplement salaries of underpaid officials" without offering any details. Key campaign leaders encouraged Nixon to go for broke—and then ask listeners to take part in a call-in vote asking what course of action to take.

A few hours before the scheduled speech, Thomas Dewey called and aides put him through; he was too powerful to be shunted aside. Top Eisenhower backers had held a conference, he informed Nixon, and they had concluded that he should proceed with his speech—but, just before going off the air, he should submit his resignation to the presidential nominee.

Sixty million persons had their eyes on television sets when Richard Nixon's face hit the tube during prime time on September 23, 1952. Speaking from the Los Angeles studio of the National Broadcasting Company, he repeatedly referred to and gestured toward his wife who sat silently in an armchair close to the desk he chose in preference to a podium.

He admitted that $18,235 had been improperly handled, but insisted that not one penny of it went into his own pocket. It was used for expenses incurred as senator above the total allowed by law. Cost of things done for his constituents "should not be charged to the taxpayers of the United States" he insisted. Every dime that belonged to him and Pat, he said, was honestly their own. But all of the assets they held jointly were less than their liabilities—which would have been reduced if he had used expense money for personal purposes.

Pat Nixon hung stockings for both of her daughters every Christmas.

"The Checkers Speech" became the informal but lasting title by which his make-it-or-break-it television address was remembered. Checkers, a black and white spaniel, was the biggest personal gift that had been accepted, he said. The animal was sent by a Texan—not to Richard and Pat, but to their daughter. Six-year old Tricia just didn't have it in her heart to send the lovable little fellow all the way back to Texas, so she had been feeding it and was trying hard to house train it, he explained. "Regardless of what they [political foes and critics within the Republican party] say about it," he thundered, "we're going to keep the puppy!"

Minutes after he and Pat were off camera, motion picture producer Darryl Zanuck called to congratulate the candidate. His self-vindication had constituted "the most tremendous performance ever seen," he said. At its Washington office alone, the Republican National Committee received three hundred thousand messages, most of which had multiple signatures. Multitudes of telegrams and letters poured into offices of state committees throughout the nation. Long before the last were tabulated it was apparent that respondents were nearly 350 to 1 in favor of retaining the man from California on the ticket.

Eisenhower seems to have been offended by the notion that the Republican National Committee should decide who would be his running mate, however. He wanted a one-on-one conference before making up his mind and suggested a meeting in Wheeling, West Virginia. Again urged by his wife to stick by his guns, Richard sent the general a telegram saying he had to resume his campaign tour. *"I will be in Washington five days from now, and will be delighted to confer with you then,"* he wrote.

Key aides, almost out of suitable words with which to congratulate Richard on his speech and his nerve, quietly reminded him that Eisenhower would get the message via public response to the speech. In order to permit the general to save face, they advised Richard to meet him in Wheeling and effect a reconciliation.

When he and Pat stepped off the plane in West Virginia, Eisenhower was there to greet them with a big smile and hearty handshakes. The general didn't say a word about seeking a new running mate. Instead he congratulated Nixon on his speech and urged him to make "a few more just as good as it was, even if you aren't in front of a camera."

UNTIL CONFRONTED AND OVERWHELMED by the Watergate affair, the matter of a few thousand dollars sent directly to Nixon by his backers created the biggest crisis of his political career. He owed his surprise victory as much to Pat as to his own ability to deal with issues. Although neither of them said anything about this aspect of the matter, both of them knew that teamwork was a hallmark of their entire married life. Both had been reared under circumstances that today would make their families borderline candidates for federal aid, and that strong bond strengthened their stable marriage.

In Yorba Linda, California, Richard had helped wash dishes and sweep floors by the time he was big enough to use a broom. Before reaching school age he learned how to wash produce so it would sell in Nixon's Market. After age six, he customarily looked after this chore before heading off to school.

His wife's earlier years were even tougher than Richard's. Because her father's health had been ruined by years of working in Arizona copper mines, the family moved to California and tried to exist on meager profits from a truck farm. Then usually known as Thelma or Thelma Catherine, the girl learned to plant and tend tomatoes, potatoes, cauliflower, potatoes,

Richard Nixon normally looked both friends and foes directly in the eye.

and other vegetables when barely past toddler age. She later walked a mile in each direction in order to attend the Artesia public school. Her mother died when she was an eighth grader, so the entire responsibility for housekeeping fell upon her. Soon her father's silicosis made him bedfast, so for two years she nursed him. Because he was a first-generation American who had come straight from Ireland, she dropped Thelma in favor of Patricia and the affectionate "Pat" he habitually used became standard long before she was well known.

After squeezing every penny for two years during which she worked hard after graduation from high school, Pat paid her own way through Whittier College. It was there, while as a member of the cast of a play performed by the community drama group, that she met Richard M. Nixon, who had also been chosen to take part in a melodrama entitled "the Dark Tower."

For him, it was deep and lasting love at first sight, but she was reluctant to risk the rest of her life with an aspiring young lawyer who had only a handful of clients. Half in jest, perhaps, he proposed marriage a few hours after they met, but Pat refused to take him seriously. Their courtship lasted for nearly three years, during which she became a Quaker because Richard had been reared in that tradition. For their honeymoon, they drove a battered old car to Mexico and spent $178 dollars during two weeks there, often driving most of the night in order to avoid having to pay for lodging.

Their first home was a rented garage apartment, and they considered a visit to a nearby ice cream parlor as a veritable night on the town. He probably could have avoided the military draft during World War II, but he decided that it was his patriotic duty to quit his $90-per-week job with the Office of Price Administration in order to fight for his country. Pat, who much earlier had decided to speak her mind freely in private but to support whatever decision he reached, found work at the OCA before he sailed for the South Pacific. He started in the U.S. Navy as a lieutenant, junior grade, but had been promoted to lieutenant commander by the time he was discharged four years later.

Their financial woes should have ended about this time but did not. Always relying on Pat for advice and criticism, Richard launched his political career with a surprise victory in California's Twelfth Congressional District. Soon he and Pat discovered that the cost of rearing Tricia and Julie made it impossible to break even on the salary of a congressman or a senator. After having been defeated by John F. Kennedy in a 1960 try for the White House, he and Pat set their eyes on the mansion of the California governor. When beaten by incumbent Edmund G. Brown, the disgruntled Republican held a press conference at which he lashed out at representatives of the media. "You won't have Nixon to kick around anymore," he told his largely male audience, "because, gentlemen, this is my last press conference."

Had it not been for the continuous vigorous encouragement of Pat, that prediction might have come true. Both of them refrained from demonstrative affection in public, but they were devoted to each other.

Publicly repudiating patterns of conduct in which "people slobbered around about how much they love each other," Nixon insisted, "Love can be a lot stronger when you don't make a big point of showing it off." Privately, he drew upon Pat's strong will and strength of character during their entire time together.

38

Jerry and Betty Ford

Visibly shaken, assistant White House press secretary John W. Hushen reportedly made his way to the Oval Office as the official workday was about to end. He was surprised to find the president—not behind his desk, but sitting with his arm around his wife who was at his side. Gerald R. Ford's face betrayed his emotional turmoil, but the first lady appeared to be calm and relaxed.

"Yes?" said the chief executive.

"I'm afraid there has been a leak; word of Mrs. Ford's impending surgery will be all over the papers tomorrow morning."

"Do correspondents know what I will be going through?" Betty Ford inquired.

"No, they only know that Dr. Lukash has referred you to Dr. Thistlewaite."

"Then I want you to get a press release together tonight," she said. "Tell the truth and the whole truth—but try to keep Susan and our boys out of it."

"Do you really mean you are willing to let the public know that the wife of the president faces a possible mastectomy?"

"Absolutely," Jerry responded for her. "Betty and I are honest-to-God Republicans and we don't believe in keeping secrets from the public. We don't know much, yet; the biopsy will tell the story. Whether it comes back positive or negative, Betty or her surgeons will make a statement as soon as it's all over. We've worked together without a serious quarrel for twenty-six years, and we are in total agreement about what must be done now."

Decades earlier, Grover Cleveland, our twenty-fourth president, had taken great pains to hide his surgery for cancer of the jaw from the public. In the opinion of Cleveland and his top aides, potentially ominous news from the White House could create all sorts of trouble on Wall Street and elsewhere. That was the Democrat's rationale for having his July 1, 1893, surgery performed on a vessel moored in Long Island Sound instead of in a hospital. Dr. Joseph D. Bryant and all who were to assist him were sworn to secrecy before they boarded a yacht lent by E. C. Benedict.

During a second secret surgical procedure on July 17, Cleveland was fitted with an artificial jaw of hardened rubber, making it possible for him to address Congress on August 7. That day, as he had throughout his life-threatening ordeal, Cleveland gave no hint that he and the nation had gone through a time of extreme trauma.

Betty Ford, who had spent days becoming familiar with the lives of her husband's predecessors and their wives, knew all about the veil of secrecy that had prevailed ninety years earlier. Outspoken in her belief that "new times call for new ways of doing things," she had no intention of slipping into a car after dark and riding for hours in an attempt to shake off White House correspondents. She and Jerry had agreed that they must bare intimate and delicate details, rather than take part in a charade.

Both of them had just learned that about one-third of all cancers developed by females are in their breasts. The Fords were keenly aware that although mastectomies were performed thousands of times each year, most persons who were key figures in such surgery were reluctant to speak of it, even to their intimates. Many persons wouldn't understand their departure from the norm, and some might even criticize them. These possibilities did not drive Betty and Jerry apart. Instead, they were pulled closer together than ever when they determined to share the full truth with Americans at large, no matter what the consequences.

Betty's condition had not been suspected. A secretary, Nancy Howe, had casually remarked one Wednesday afternoon that she was scheduled for a routine physical at Bethesda Naval Medical Center the following morning. Making a spur-of-the-moment decision, the first lady had decided that she would go along and get her routine six-month gynecological examination over with. She had not been alarmed when her personal physician brought Dr. William Fouty to look her over after having checked her breasts for lumps.

But before she returned to the White House, Dr. William Lukash called and said he'd very much like to see her at 7:00 P.M. that day. That meant something was wrong, but she did not know what it might be. When she was introduced to a member of the faculty of the George Washington University Medical School and told that he was to examine her breasts, she suspected the worst. By the time she came out of the dressing room, her husband—who had come directly from the Oval Office—was waiting outside.

As gently as he knew how, Dr. Lukash informed them that a lump had been found and that he'd like to schedule surgery at once. That evening they talked things over with their daughter. Between sobs, Susan nodded understanding and agreement to plans that Friday would go forward in a normal way without any change of schedule and that surgery would take place early Saturday.

By 6:30 A.M., family members had gathered at the hospital. Alerted by a news bulletin late Friday, their longtime friend the Rev. Billy Zeoli had made a hasty trip from Ohio in order to be with them. As soon as Betty came out of the anesthesia, faces of those who had gathered in her room told her that she had lost her right breast. Jerry gave her a long, silent hug and she said, "I'm thankful they found it early." Her husband then hurried off to speak to delegates who had assembled for a major economic conference. Knowing that they would want to know about Betty, his voice broke as he told them that she had undergone surgery that had been pronounced a success.

While still in bed, the famous patient turned on her television set to get the news. She was astonished to hear that her announcement had created "a wave of public interest with few parallels." In several major cities women were standing in line outside clinics in order to get breast examinations. Nothing quite like Betty's candor and the response to it had ever been experienced, the news anchor told his national audience.

During Betty's recovery, fifty thousand pieces of mail came to her, as well as thousands of telegrams. Dozens of these messages included effusive thanks for what she had done, and women ranging in age from nineteen to ninety-three said that after having had examinations they were ready to face mastectomies of their own. Deeply moved, the first lady gave an interview in which she said that the response to her public statement "more than made up for disappointment at having failed to achieve some early personal goals."

PEOPLE WHO KNEW THE woman baptized Elizabeth Anne Bloomer, but who grew up as Betty, rejoiced at the good news. Most of her early life had been spent in Grand Rapids, Michigan, and from age two she was described as "unable to be still when exposed to rhythmic music." When nearly all of her little contemporaries were absorbed with dolls and tea sets, Betty's most passionate interest had centered around dancers whose pictures she saw and the clothing they wore.

Because William S. Bloomer drank heavily in secret, his family had little extra money and Betty didn't get to take dancing lessons until she was eight. Once she began to receive professional guidance, she made up her mind to become "the best dancer in Grand Rapids" and soon become locally celebrated. By age fourteen, she was giving lessons to other girls and was dreaming of a career on the stage.

Elizabeth Anne "Betty" Bloomer went through a short marriage and an amicable divorce before becoming Mrs. Gerald R. Ford.

Later she spent two summers at Bennington, Vermont, where she studied dance and became acquainted with the great Martha Graham. Following Graham to New York, Betty paid her way by appearing in fashion shows and by modeling for the John Powers Agency but failed to become a regular in Graham's famous troupe. That led her to return to Grand Rapids to teach dancing and organize her own troupe.

Leslie Lynch King Jr. had a much more tempestuous childhood and youth than did Betty. His father, for whom he was named, ditched his mother, who fled to her parents in Grand Rapids when the boy was three years old. In later life, the two males met briefly only twice. Adopted by merchant Gerald Rudolf Ford when he married little Leslie's mother, the youngster was formally adopted by his stepfather. His name was soon changed and in the process Rudolf became Rudolph.

Eager to study law after his graduation from high school, young Ford went to the University of Michigan and found the football field almost as enticing as the law library. He was picked as the outstanding freshmen of the Wolverines, and three years later was named the team's most valuable player. Offers from the Detroit Lions and the Green Bay Packers would have persuaded many a college senior to forget about his long-term goals. Jerry rejected the opportunity to play professional football, went to Yale as a coach, and took moonlighting jobs as a male model.

Jerry Ford, a star football player at the University of Michigan, received two offers to turn pro but turned them down. (University of Michigan)

When Coach Ford took one of his teams to Connecticut for a match with men of the U.S. Coast Guard Academy, he met a beautiful female student at a nearby college. Smitten almost instantly, he spent the next four years in ceaseless pursuit of Phyllis Brown. Later describing their relationship as "a torrid love affair that matured him," they might have married had they been able to agree upon a place to live. Phyllis wanted nothing but New York, while Jerry was chomping at the bit to return to Grand Rapids and hang out his shingle as an attorney. Although they had been pictured together in both *Look* and *Cosmopolitan* magazines, they split over their geographical preferences, and he went home to Michigan.

Meanwhile, Betty Bloomer had become Mrs. William C. Warren. A furniture salesman who seemed to have numerous traits in common with Jerry's father, he had no interest in dance or fashion. After three years, he and his wife decided that they had too little in common to spend a lifetime together, so in 1947 they went through an amicable divorce. A friend who knew both Betty and Jerry thought that "those two would be perfect together," so arranged a meeting.

At thirty-five he was only five years older than Betty, and they hit it off extremely well. Soon talking of marriage, they didn't schedule a ceremony until eight months later, after the prospective bridegroom had virtually ended his first campaign for public office. Weeks earlier both had decided that the other would be a perfect mate, and neither of them seemed to waver in that verdict.

When the former Betty Bloomer Warren became the bride of a freshman member of the U.S. House of Representatives, she hoped to stay in Washington at least eight years. Her husband was re-elected time after time, and during his sixteenth year in the lawmaking body became minority leader. After he had spent more than seven years in that key post, Vice President Spiro Agnew resigned in the face of charges of bribery, extortion, tax fraud, and conspiracy.

The vacancy left by Agnew's sudden departure from Washington forced Richard M. Nixon to nominate a new vice president. He found the choice difficult, since numerous notables, including governors Nelson Rockefeller of New York and Ronald Reagan of California, were potential candidates. After a great deal of scrutiny and consultation, Nixon turned to the minority leader of the House of Representatives, who won quick and overwhelming confirmation in both houses of Congress. Nixon's own subsequent resignation during impeachment hearings put Jerry and Betty into the White House.

Jerry became vice president as a result of the first use of the Twenty-fifth Amendment, which had been ratified in 1967. He then became the eighth chief executive not chosen for that post by voters—and Betty became the first divorced woman to preside over White House receptions and dinners. Knowing that he would be crucified by the press, he became the first president to pardon an accused ex-president—with Betty's support. He did it, Betty explained time after time, because the two of them decided that the nation's business would be delayed for months if he didn't take action to free his time from dealing with legal jeopardy faced by his predecessor.

Jerry and Betty stayed silent on one subject for years—Betty's drinking. Although mutually dependent upon one another, his intense work schedule enabled him to stay on an even keel even when separated from his wife for a considerable period. Not so Betty; in Jerry's absence, idle time combined with self-pity at being left alone led her to "develop a problem." When both of them realized that it was serious, she began watching her alcohol intake carefully and for two years stayed away from it entirely.

Her tendency to turn to alcohol was magnified by arthritis and muscular pains being treated by drugs. After she and Jerry retired to Palm Springs, California, her dependence on alcohol increased rapidly. Initially shocked when confronted by recollections of loved ones about times when she was in an alcoholic daze, she reacted by collapsing in tears. Vehemently insisting that all of her problems stemmed from use of prescription medications, she initially refused even to consider the possibility that alcohol was heavily involved.

Soon, however, she forced herself to go to the Long Beach facility headed by Capt. Joe Pursch. She "signed herself in" voluntarily, saying that she was there to lick her drug dependency. Gently but firmly she was urged to face reality and admit that she had become an alcoholic. What's more, they reminded her of the impact of her frankness about her mastectomy and insisted that she go public again.

Jerry took her hand, soothed her, and urged her to follow the advice of the doctors. "Go ahead," he urged, insisting that a public statement from her would not embarrass him in any way.

She burst into tears and sobbed so hard that she found it difficult to get her breath. "I hope I never have to cry like that again," she wrote in The Times of My Life. "It was scary, but once it was over, I felt a great relief."

That night she prepared a handwritten statement for release to the press and decided to commence a rehabilitation program the following day. Her husband and their daughter also spent two weeks in a course designed for relatives of recovering alcoholics. Instead of being widely condemned, she found herself praised for her courage in admitting her addiction and setting out to master it. An editorial in the Washington Post described her as being determined to overcome her problem and being "unafraid and unembarrassed to say so."

Upon being discharged from the Long Beach facility after four weeks, she decided to investigate the work being done at the Eisenhower Medical Complex in Rancho Mirage, California. Always with the unqualified love and support of Jerry, she not only "made it" to complete recovery: She also

The president and first lady watched election returns on November 2, 1976, as Ford went down to defeat to Jimmy Carter. (The White House)

helped to fund, launch, and manage the Betty Ford Center as an adjunct to the Eisenhower complex. There, scores of women have found help in their struggle to free themselves from dependence on drugs and alcohol.

By 1983 surgeons generally agreed that it was seldom necessary to perform a radical mastectomy. A much-less-drastic procedure, lumpectomy, involves removing cancerous portions of the breast plus lymph nodes, leaving most of the breast tissue intact.

No other first lady and her mate have had a comparable impact upon public attitudes and treatment of two unrelated maladies—breast cancer and drug/alcohol dependence.

39

Jimmy and Rosalynn Carter

Christ set some impossible standards for us. Christ said, "I tell you that anyone who looks on a woman with lust has already committed adultery." I have looked on a lot of women with lust; I've committed adultery in my heart many times . . . [God is the judge, not me, so I cannot] condemn someone who not only looks on a woman with lust but leaves his wife and shacks up with somebody out of wedlock. Christ says don't consider yourself better than someone else because one guy screws a whole bunch of women while the other guy is loyal to his wife. The guy who is loyal to his wife ought not to be condescending or proud because of a relative degree of sinfulness.

Jimmy Carter's fervent but awkwardly expressed attempt to explain his Bible-based personal views concerning sex constituted the most unusual public statement ever made by a candidate for the presidency about the dominant theme of this book.

Religion was central to the life of the Democratic candidate from southwestern Georgia. Baptized at age eleven, he briefly felt so strong a sense of invulnerability that he believed he could step in front of a moving car and not be injured. Less than a year later most Sunday mornings found him behind the wheel of his mother's car, driving around to pick up acquaintances who didn't have transportation in order to go to the Baptist church of Plains.

Jimmy Carter later became a deacon in that church and a Baptist lay preacher who dared to espouse racial integration long before that movement gained widespread support. Heavily laced with his personal brand of mysticism, his abiding reverence for Scripture plus his fervent espousal of Christianity led him to say things whose double meanings were easily turned against him.

Here condensed from Peter G. Bourne's biography of him, Jimmy's comments came after he believed a series of interviews had ended. Freelance writer Robert Scheer had gained the candidate's consent to air his personal views in *Playboy* magazine. Ten days before the issue carrying the Carter interview hit the newsstands, Scheer and *Playboy* editor Barry

As governor of Georgia, Jimmy Carter signed into law a bill that raised the price of cigarettes by four cents—not to discourage smokers but to raise revenue.

Golson appeared on television's *The Today Show*. Their comments, combined with the published interview that came out four days before Carter's first television debate with Gerald R. Ford, contributed largely to a sudden and sharp drop in Carter's poll numbers.

Every time the candidate's wife held a press conference, inevitably the first question she faced dealt with her husband's "lust in his heart." Rosalynn Carter quickly shaped a stock answer, saying, "Jimmy talks too much, but at least people know he's honest and doesn't mind answering questions."

She denied becoming angry with her husband since it had never entered her mind to worry about his "lust for other women." He was using language that the youthful writer could understand, she said, in an attempt to communicate his religious values. "The only lust that bothered me was that of the press and our opponents who were out to get us because of that blooper."

One day after *The Today Show* focused on the fashion in which Jimmy seemed to have equated "lust in the heart" with adultery, syndicated columnist Jack Anderson spoke out. His report, televised by the American Broadcasting Company, persuaded Rosalynn that the only lust she worried about was real. According to him, Republican campaign workers had been digging very hard into Carter's past in hope of uncovering a sex scandal. These zealots, charged Anderson, had attempted to use him "in a scheme to get the story published."

According to the columnist, Republicans had given him the name of "a woman with whom Carter had an affair" and soon added four other women's names. This action led him to launch his own in-depth investigation, Anderson told the nation. When all available facts had been assembled, he reached the firm conclusion that there was "no truth to the sex charges against Carter."

Carter went to great length in an attempt to explain precisely how he came to say what he did. In his final televised debate with Ford he told the

American people that "According to the Bible, which I believe in, adultery is a sin. For us to hate one another, for us to have sexual intercourse outside marriage, to engage in homosexual activities, to lie and steal is to sin. We all sin, but Jesus teaches us not to judge other people."

Scheer, he repeatedly explained, seemed to have ended his five hours of questioning and to have turned off his tape recorder. Pausing as he went out the door, the writer tossed a final question that evoked Jimmy's spur-of-the-moment provocative answer.

Shortly before her husband made the statement that Rosalynn dubbed "Jimmy's blooper," former White House counsel John Dean had written an article for *Rolling Stone* magazine. Dean's piece was constructed in the aftermath of a freewheeling conversation with Pat Boone, Sonny Bono, and an unidentified member of Ford's cabinet. During the session, someone asked the cabinet member for his personal explanation for why Republicans attracted so few black voters. Referring to African Americans as "colored," the high-placed official gave his personal opinion of them. His language was offensive even to some persons who admitted they were prejudiced on the subject of race.

This excerpt from the Dean article was so explosive that it was briefly the top topic of commentators, editorial writers, and columnists. Within days after *Rolling Stone* appeared, U.S. Secretary of Agriculture Earl Butz was identified as having made the racist statement that was sprinkled with vulgarity. He tried for a few days to ride out the scandal, but could not and submitted his resignation from the cabinet.

JIMMY KNEW A LOT more about blacks, firsthand, than did Butz. Growing up on extensive farms near the village of Plains, he was in intimate daily contact with blacks from infancy. His mother, widely known and called simply Miss Lillian by blacks and whites alike, was a registered nurse who ministered to members of both races without charge. Rusty railroad tracks overgrown with vines and weeds ran along one side of Main Street, whose tiny bank held some of Earl Carter's wealth.

Earl didn't believe in spoiling children by letting them lie around doing nothing, so he put his son to work on one of his farms by the time he was old enough to go to school. Always eager to the point of being impulsive, Jimmy moved around so rapidly that he was dubbed "Hot-Shot," but was usually called simply "Hot." On many a blistering torrid and humid afternoon, Hot worked in the fields long after adult black workers had gone home.

During numerous interviews after he became nationally known, however, Jimmy emphasized that he did not have a boyhood of "all work and no play." An ardent lover of things of nature, he nearly cried his eyes out when he saw his father shooting sparrows. Maybe to make up for that incident, he was allowed to keep a pair of baby squirrels he found in the woods. After being fed with an eyedropper when tiny, Pete and Repete, as they were called, perched on Jimmy's shoulders as he went about his chores.

Every December Jimmy spent parts of three or four days searching nearby woods until he found a cedar tree of exactly the right height and shape. Cut and lugged to the Carter home, it was decorated and stayed fresh until well after Christmas. Jimmy became an avid fisherman very early, and once managed to wangle a trip to Florida so he could try his hand in unfamiliar waters. He caught only a few fish, but he returned home with a baby alligator and kept it under his bed for weeks.

Jimmy's sister Ruth often visited a girl whose father, a mechanic, drove the school bus and attended the Methodist church. Rosalynn Smith, who began nursing her invalid father at age thirteen, treasured Ruth as her best friend. She sometimes went home with her and didn't think it unusual that Ruth's brother paid no attention to her. Since villagers often had little else to do when sitting around on afternoons when the heat drove them out of the fields, some of them experimented with her name and began calling her "One Perfect Rose."

Jimmy's uncle Alton, the oldest member of the family and noted for his keen mind and ready wit, praised "the Smith girl" because she didn't make a nuisance of herself talking, and she wore clothes that were obviously handmade. He didn't know it for years, but Allie Smith was not responsible for everything her daughter wore. Rosalynn became an expert seamstress during years when girls in larger towns and cities were becoming Girl Scouts.

Later she found a job in a beauty shop where she could work after school. Saving every penny she earned, she soon bought her own sewing machine and was so proud of it that for once she talked freely about it to everyone she encountered. When she went to Washington to become mistress of the White House, that sewing machine was the only personal possession she took along.

Miss Lillian, who never bit her tongue on any subject, scolded young Jimmy for not eating enough. He was so thin he'd never make it into Annapolis, she warned. Perhaps the result of going barefoot most of the time until he was fifteen or sixteen years old, Jimmy's feet were so flat that she said he'd better do something about them. Her obedient son found glass Coca-Cola bottles that were just the right size and shape, using them to extend his arches by rolling them under his feet while he ate bananas in an effort to put on weight.

When he returned from Annapolis in his eye-catching white uniform, he sometimes noticed that Rosalynn was there with Ruth, but he paid hardly any attention to her or the clothing she had made for herself. Later he learned, probably from the sister destined to become famous as an evangelist, that Rosalynn had left home in order to attend Georgia Southwestern College at nearby Americus.

Since virtually all males of her age were in uniform by that time, Rosalynn later described her social life during college days in a single word—bleak. That didn't prevent her and her classmates from indulging in what she called "adolescent fantasies about love and romance." Along with her college friends, Rosalynn swooned and squealed "over a new singing idol, Frank Sinatra."

Sinatra's appeal seems somehow to have been transferred to a photograph on the bedroom wall of her friend Ruth, whom she still visited frequently despite the fact that the Carter girl was still in high school. In her autobiographical volume entitled *First Lady from Plains*, Rosalynn made an unusual confession. According to her, she fell in love with Jimmy's picture on Ruth's wall and saw him as unbelievably handsome and glamorous.

At this stage in her life, Rosalynn the college student didn't remember ever having spoken to Ruth's older brother except during one summer when he was an ice cream vendor on the main street of Plains and she was an occasional purchaser. Ruth, who soon discovered her friend's fantasy, took delight in urging Rosalynn to come to her house every time Jimmy came home from Annapolis. Ruth's plots fizzled, however, because Jimmy would already have departed to see a friend every time Rosalynn—sure she wouldn't be able to say a word to him—got up enough courage to visit the Carter place.

Just before the end of Jimmy's summer leave, Fate took a hand in the life of the girl who had a secret crush on "an older fellow." Years earlier, Earl Carter had built a community gathering place that everyone called the Pond House. Ruth informed Rosalynn that the Pond House and its yard could use a good bit of cleaning. Most members of the Carter family intended to get involved, she said, and she urged Rosalynn to go along and help.

Vividly remembering the day ostensibly devoted to raking the yard and sweeping the Pond House, Rosalynn said that Jimmy took delight in constantly teasing her. To her surprise, she found that she could give him as good as he dished out. Late that afternoon the girl whose tongue was suddenly loosed was at the Methodist church waiting for a youth meeting to start. A car drove up, Jimmy got out, and invited Rosalynn to join him, Ruth, and her boyfriend to go see a movie. Her emotional whirlwind was of such intensity that she had no idea what movie they saw, but before they

Jimmy and Rosalynn on their wedding day in 1946.
(The Jimmy Carter Library)

parted Jimmy kissed her. As a result, she said, "I was completely swept off my feet."

When Jimmy came back to Plains during his Christmas holiday wearing his dress blues, he proposed marriage—and Rosalynn shook her head in refusal. She agreed to wait, however, and they exchanged letters on an almost-daily basis. During the weekend marked by observance of George Washington's birthday—then a national holiday—she paid her first visit to Annapolis. He again proposed, and this time Rosalynn accepted. She had been home only a few days when a package arrived; Jimmy had sent her a copy of *The Navy Wife*, an unofficial guidebook.

The "togetherness" of Jimmy and Rosalynn led her to become a volunteer construction worker because of Jimmy's passionate interest in Habitat for Humanity projects.

They married on July 7, 1946, in the Methodist church of Plains. Neither had an attendant, and no invitations had been mailed. Although they didn't know it then, the simplicity of their wedding was symbolic of their austere White House years. Members of the press, who didn't realize that Rosalynn was painfully shy and believed her to be haughty, dubbed her the Steel Magnolia. Our thirty-ninth president learned of his wife's new moniker and held a press conference in which he insisted, "There's nothing harsh or insensitive about her. She's very soft and reticent."

Assigned to duty as electronics officer aboard a submarine soon after graduation from Annapolis, Jimmy took his wife and their young son to Plains and then flew to Honolulu. He boarded the USS *Pomfret* at Pearl Harbor and with his shipmates began a routine voyage to China. Hours after leaving port, the sub was hit by one of the fiercest storms ever to be brewed over the Pacific Ocean. Seven ships went down, but the *Pomfret*—and her electronics officer—survived.

In order to recharge the ship's batteries, the vessel had to surface each night. Jimmy was on the bridge high above the water when a thirty-foot wave smashed against the *Pomfret* and knocked him into the sea. After swimming for what to him seemed an eternity, another huge wave lifted him up and deposited him on a gun located some thirty feet aft of the bridge.

Any religiously oriented person saved from a watery grave by a huge wave (and who had earlier spotted and reported a Unidentified Flying Object) would likely regard his wife and children as gifts sent him by Almighty God. Without quite using that terminology, neither Jimmy nor Rosalynn has ever wavered from a life-shaping conviction that, somehow, they were made for each other.

40

Ronnie, Jane, and Nancy Reagan, and Their Bunch

Metro-Goldwyn-Mayer "starlet," or ingenue, Nancy Davis, was devastated that her career might be over. With the nation's Communist scare at its height in 1948 and the witch-hunt for "red sympathizers" in full swing, she found her name on a list of "suspected entertainers." That's the story she seems to have told biographers who cooperated with her prior to writing accounts of her action-filled life. According to several of these biographies, she went to director Mervyn LeRoy practically in tears, choosing him because she had nowhere else to go.

LeRoy, doubtful that Hollywood's "pink fringe" was significant in size or influence, was instantly sympathetic with the actress from Illinois. He tried to soothe her with assurances that having been named as a suspect didn't mean there was substantial evidence to support the charge. "I can't tell you exactly what to do," he admitted after half an hour. "But I can put you in touch with a fellow who can. Ronald Reagan is president of the Screen Actors Guild, and he doesn't stand for any foolishness from persons who are out to nail members of the guild."

Surprised and delighted but also a bit bewildered, the actress blurted a statement to the effect that LeRoy's idea was great, but she had absolutely no idea how to get an appointment with so important an actor. Besides, he was likely to be fully occupied with his own problems, since newspapers were full of stories about the failure of his marriage to Jane Wyman.

"Don't worry your pretty head about that," the director said. "Just go home and try to get a good, long sleep; I'll take care of the appointment for you. You'll get a call from him right away."

Delighted, Nancy went home but did not try to sleep. Instead, she sat close to her telephone and waited for it to ring. Finally she gave up and turned in, only to be awakened early the next day by a call—not from the actor, but from LeRoy. According to the director, the president of the guild kept close tabs on its members. He had checked Nancy out carefully and

273

was sure that she didn't have the faintest taint of Communism in her background.

Another day passed before Reagan contacted her, but she took solace in the fact that he said he'd like to discuss her situation at dinner that evening. She hardly knew what to think when a tall, handsome man appeared at her door on crutches. Laughing at her obvious bewilderment, he introduced himself and explained that he had been seriously injured in a charity sports event recently.

"That's enough about me," he said. "Let's go down to Sunset Strip and find a nice, quiet place where we can talk while we eat."

The president of the guild had done his homework carefully, he told her, and he had been surprised to find four Nancy Davises in his files. He thought it might be a good idea for her to take a new professional name so as to avoid confusion on the part of investigators or reporters. She shook her head vigorously at this proposal and turned the conversation toward his recent injury.

Until he broke into movies, the easiest money Dutch Reagan ever made was a reward for retrieving a swimmer's false teeth.

In order to raise money for the City of Hope hospital, at which many Hollywood hopefuls received gratis treatment, a softball bash had been billed as the Movie Star World Series, and games were to be played in Los Angeles. He'd agreed to take part, Reagan said, but he had forgotten about the matter until he bumped into its organizer.

First to bat against pitcher Bob Hope, the actor swung twice and missed. In desperation, he decided to bunt on the third pitch, and as soon as the ball hit his bat he lit out for first base. With the ball in the air the fellow on first base tried to block the runner, who slammed into him so hard that he broke his leg. He was carried off the field on a stretcher, Reagan told his new friend, and had just been discharged from the hospital after a stay of eight weeks.

Nancy showed great interest in his account, and she quickly showed that she knew almost as much about baseball as he did. Quizzed about her background, the young woman, listed in his records as having come to Hollywood from Chicago, confided that she was following in the footsteps of her mother.

"No kidding?" Reagan responded. "Have I ever heard of her?"

"I doubt it, because she hasn't been on a stage or a set in years. But in her heyday she got around a lot. She played with Walter Huston and they became such friends that I've always called him Uncle Walter. My mother's name is Edith, but she's always been known as Deedee."

"That sorta rings a bell with me, but I can't quite place her yet."

"Deedee played opposite George M. Cohan a lot. And she became a close friend of Zim and Spencer Tracy, who's had me over to his place frequently since I came to Hollywood."

"Zim? Don't believe I've ever heard of him; what roles did he play?"

"*I'm sorry*; please excuse me for using a nickname. Zim was a woman, not a man, and she didn't like to be called Nazimova, so she dropped two-thirds of her name."

Reagan threw back his head and laughed until he seemed in danger of losing his breath. "So your mother knew both the great Nazimova and Spencer Tracy? What does she do these days?"

"She lives in Chicago with her husband and my stepfather, Dr. Loyal Davis. He's a famous neurosurgeon."

"Don't have the names of surgeons in my files, but I'm sure surprised that you know Spence Tracy. We've about outstayed our welcome here and it looks like we could talk all night. Tell you what—let's go take in Sophie Tucker's show; how about it?"

Nancy reportedly arrived back at her apartment about 3:00 A.M., went inside, and pulled out the diary in which she made sporadic entries. Refreshing her memory by consulting her diary while William Novak helped her write her memoirs, she confessed that she didn't know whether she had experienced love at first sight, "but it was something close to it."

She and Ronnie, as she had already begun to call him, "were taken with one another and wanted to see more of each other." They went out together regularly, and friendship developed into mutual love so strong that both were soon ready and eager to become man and wife.

FORMER *WASHINGTON POST* EDITORIAL writer Kitty Kelly tells a quite different story in a biography of Nancy that is boldly labeled as unauthorized. According to Kelly, Ronnie often slept with Nancy but did not propose marriage because he hoped to win Christine Larson. In 1951, long after he had developed a close relationship with Nancy, Reagan begged Christine to marry him and sweetened the deal by handing her a diamond wristwatch as a token of their engagement. Possibly because the twenty-six-year-old actress was enamored of Gary Cooper, she turned Ronnie down but kept the watch.

Paula Raymond, at the time a small-time MGM contract player, told Kelly that from her apartment she watched Ronnie and Nancy making love and quickly saw that Ronnie was not nearly as interested as was Nancy. After being rejected by Christine, he continued his relationship with Nancy—but not Nancy alone. One night when a nightclub was about

Christine Larson, an aspiring actress, was Ronald Reagan's first choice for a second wife.

to close, he picked up nineteen-year-old starlet Selene Walter. After a single drink they swapped addresses and telephone numbers, but she didn't expect to hear from him. According to Selene's story, he began banging on her door an hour after they parted, forced himself into her apartment, and pushed her onto a couch. Too tiny and weak to fight the big man off, she said, "In a matter of seconds I lost."

Shortly after an incident that today would be labeled "date rape," Selene read a newspaper announcement of the impending marriage of Ronald Reagan and Nancy Davis. If Kelly's sources told the truth, Nancy informed Ronnie that she was pregnant. He believed her, but confided to a friend that he felt as though he'd been hunted down and cornered and was being bludgeoned into marriage.

Ronnie had been keenly aware that Nancy went to unusual lengths to befriend his (and Jane's) daughter and son when they paid their weekend visits. Maureen, age ten, seemed especially delighted that her father's friend sang with her when they rode in the Cadillac that Jane had given Ronnie as a birthday present. As soon as marriage vows were spoken, wrote Kelly, Nancy started snubbing both Maureen and her brother. In her own account of the lives of the two Hollywood personalities who wound up in the White House, Maureen insisted that she and Nancy liked each other from the start and got along fine, so as a girl she was truly happy for her father.

Convoluted strands of contradictory evidence leave outsiders uncertain about what to believe. This much is clear, however; Maureen has the

April 4, 1952, wedding of Ronnie and Nancy as having taken place in the home of Bill and Ardist Holden. Numerous other biographers insist that the ceremony was conducted in the Little Brown Church in the Valley— with the half-drunk Holden grudgingly present as best man.

Maureen was not the only member of the family who found the distinction between truth and fiction to be fuzzy. When Ronnie and Nancy applied for their wedding license on leap year's day, she shaved two years off her age and said she was twenty-eight—a deception that deceived few intimates despite the fact that she practiced it all of her life.

BORN AS ANNE FRANCES ROBBINS but known only as Nancy from infancy, Ron's second wife was very young when her parents split. The departure of Kenneth Robbins, a Princeton graduate whose only interest was business, forced Edith (Deedee) Lucket to resume her career onstage. Nancy rarely saw her father, and even then their brief times together were not memorable or particularly happy.

As a small girl, she desperately wanted to emulate her beautiful mother. At every opportunity she'd get her hands on her mother's makeup, then don part of a costume in order to strut and preen before mirrors. Play-acting from early childhood, she was enamored with Mary Pickford for months. She even persuaded her mother to buy her a blonde wig, which she would sometimes even wear to bed.

Nancy, at age eight, didn't know what to think when she found out that her mother had made plans to take another husband. Dr. Loyal Davis, a native of Galesburg, Illinois, took his wife and stepdaughter to a Chicago apartment overlooking Lake Shore Drive, and he soon won the heart of the child. Illinois law had a provision under which a boy or girl could choose between a natural and a stepparent at age fourteen. Pleased when she learned that she was entitled to a decision, Nancy chose Davis and changed her name. Soon after entering Smith College, the surgeon's legal daughter made her debut at Chicago's Casino Club.

Through the influence of her mother's friend ZaSu Pitts, Nancy won a role in the touring cast of the then-sensational *Ramshackle Inn*. This and other bit parts led to travels that often included a stopover in New York. There she experienced the thrill of her life when family friend Spencer Tracy arranged for Clark Gable to escort her to World Series games played in the Big Apple. A video of *Ramshackle Inn* sent west was viewed at Metro-Goldwyn-Mayer and evoked interest in her. Tracy quickly arranged for a screen test, and she signed a standard beginner's contract at $250 a week. Before that unforgettable year came to an end she met and fell madly in love with an unforgettable man whom she came to believe was interested only in her.

It took only a few evenings together for Nancy to learn that Ronnie also had strong ties to Illinois, although his were quite different from hers. He was born on February 11, 1911, in a tiny apartment over a general store in Tampico—almost 125 miles west of Chicago. Jack, his father, sold shoes in the store below and drank much more heavily than his wife realized. Jack's wife, Nellie, was an ardent devotee of amateur dramatics and would give one of her own recitals, gratis, at the drop of a hat.

Tiny Ronald had good lungs and used them almost constantly. Annoyed by his screaming, his father contemptuously called him "Little Dutchman." That name, abbreviated simply to Dutch, stuck throughout his life. When Dutch was two years old, his father took the family to a dreary walk-up in Chicago because he had landed a job at Marshall Field's department store. It didn't last long, so the family moved from pillar to post—Galesburg, Monmouth, and Tampico again before finally settling down in Dixon, where Jack succeeded in opening his own shoe store.

By the time he reached high school, Dutch stood only five-foot-three and weighed just a little over one hundred pounds—which is hard to imagine when you later see Reagan as a strapping young man playing the legendary Notre Dame football player George "the Gipper" Gipp in the movies. The young Reagan went out for sports so enthusiastically that, even as small as he was, he might have made a team had he not been too nearsighted to see a ball unless it were very close to him. Defective vision didn't prevent him from becoming an excellent swimmer, however, so he landed a summer job as lifeguard at a civic park on the Rock River.

The pay wasn't great, but the perks included an occasional reward for special service. His biggest one, he said, came to him when he retrieved a swimmer's lost false teeth. Because he was friendly and good looking, girls went gaga over him. Their absorbing interest in the lifeguard, whose name some of them did not know, probably accounts for his record of rescues that Dutch always admitted with a broad smile to be "nothing short of remarkable. Very few young fellows pull a total of seventy-seven persons out of the water during three or four summers," he often said.

Having saved some of his rewards, plus his $15-a-week pay, the still-growing young fellow from Dixon enrolled in Eureka College, near Peoria. He entered with ninety dollars in his pocket—just enough to meet half the cost of a year's tuition. A sports scholarship took care of the rest, but he had to take any work he could find in order to eat. By the time he graduated with one eye on a sports career and the other on the stage, his alcoholic father had gone belly up and his mother was working as a seamstress at a dollar a week less than Dutch had earned as a lifeguard.

Dutch knocked on a lot of doors, but the job market had gone south during the Great Depression. He eventually landed a job in Davenport, Iowa, as a radio sports announcer at five dollars a game. Keen interest plus native ability soon boosted his audience, and his pay quickly jumped to a hundred dollars a month. Radio station WHO in Des Moines lured him to the larger city, where his contacts became wider, although they paled in comparison to those arranged for Nancy by her mother. Through a female hopeful who had performed on WHO radio, Dutch wangled a screen test that brought him an offer of two hundred dollars a week from Jack Warner. Two years and nearly a dozen

Jane Wyman, who bore two of Reagan's children, won an Oscar in 1948 for her performance in Johnny Belinda.

movies later, his pay jumped to five hundred dollars a week; when that happened, Dutch knew his career was about to take off. By the time Nancy lost her heart to him, her career was about over but his was beginning to soar.

Ronnie's thirty-month delay in formally asking for her hand may have stemmed in part from the fact that he was gun-shy about going to the altar again after having been ditched by Jane Wyman. Dutch and Jane met on the set of *Brother Rat* in 1939, not long after she had initiated divorce proceedings against prosperous dress manufacturer Myron Futterman. Both had roles in the farce about life in a military academy, and they soon were deeply interested in each other.

They married in January 1940 and became parents of Maureen and Michael. Partly because their political views were diametrically opposed, their marriage went on the rocks, and Jane filed for divorce in May 1948. She later married band leader Fred Karger, whose first wife was Patti Sachs.

NANCY WASN'T BLUFFING WHEN she said she was pregnant; seven-pound Patricia Ann (Patti) Reagan made her appearance seven months and three

Husband and wife cast ballots one after the other when Reagan made his first bid for public office.

weeks after that hasty marriage ceremony in the Little Brown Church in the Valley. Hollywood insiders later revealed that Ronnie was not on hand for the birth of his daughter; he was off chasing Christine Larson again. According to these sources, he gave up when a French actor clad only in a towel answered his ring at Christine's door.

Although she must have been furious at her husband for not being present at their daughter's birth, Nancy never gave the slightest hint that she suspected Ronnie of being a man about town. At least as seen by the public, the later married life of Ronnie and Nancy was wholly harmonious—with Nancy having a perceptible edge in decision making. He professed total ignorance of the undercover trade by which arms were shipped to Iran and profits were funneled to leaders of the Contra movement in Nicaragua. Nancy supported him, but insiders later said the president had backed the illicit deal so hastily that he may have conveniently forgotten what he knew about it.

Dutch later withdrew entirely from the public exposure that he had always loved and that he handled at least as deftly as any other chief executive. Reportedly suffering from progressive mental deterioration, he has been effectively protected by the one-time starlet he earlier shielded against charges of Communist leanings.

41

George and Barbara Bush

E leven years ago during this season, the Democratic nomination for the presidency was up for grabs. Can you tell me who won?"

Men and women judged to be at least forty years old who stopped in response to a big placard reading "Two-Minute Random Sidewalk Poll!!" were tossed Question No. 1 at a pair of locations. One set of fifty samples was accumulated at a posh mall in northeastern Atlanta; another fifty responses were gathered at the always-busy Asheville, North Carolina, shopping mall on Saturday, May 8, 1999. Although some family members of respondents who were not old enough to vote in 1988 offered opinions, their guesses were not included in the tabulation.

Seventeen percent of respondents remembered that Michael Dukakis was George Bush's opponent that year. A handful of those who recalled his name volunteered, "He was from up East somewhere" or "I think he came from Massachusetts." Two or three commented that "He won the nomination, but he didn't get to first base in November."

Question No. 2 also dealt with that presidential contest, but was of a different nature. Regardless of whether a woman or a man answered "Dukakis" to the first query, the second followed quickly: "Can you tell me the surname of the hopeful who dropped out because of a sex scandal?"

Thirty-nine out of one hundred respondents thought briefly or instantly responded "Hart" or "Gary Hart." About one-third of these knowledgeable men and women added a comment to the effect that "He was a member of the U.S. Senate, and for a while it looked like he had the race sewed up."

Hart of Colorado, who withdrew from the race in disgrace, was remembered by more than twice as many persons as the Bay State politician who had won the nomination in July 1988. Although the data here reported are in no way scientific, they provide a minute sample of how Americans of all political parties reacted to the contest of a decade earlier.

Staff members of at least a score of metropolitan newspapers gathered in small knots during the spring of 1987 to discuss and to debate a related matter. In light of a rumor that Gary Hart apparently had a mistress, editors throughout the nation were not quite certain what to do with it, if anything. Like their counterparts in Denver, Washington, New York, Philadelphia, Chicago, Los Angeles, and numerous other cities, staff members of the *Miami Herald* were deeply interested in the Hart rumor, but they were hesitant to do anything with it.

Hart had boldly challenged the journalistic world earlier. Thrown a casual question concerning his relationship with women other than his wife, the candidate for the nomination had bristled. He had absolutely nothing to hide, he told a *New York Times* staffer, then added a challenge to the effect that "If you don't believe me, just follow me around the country and you'll find out for yourself."

Only the *Miami Herald* decided to take the Democrat up on his challenge. Florida reporters watching Hart's townhouse in Washington around the clock came up empty for several days and nights. Then they hit paydirt with indisputable evidence that the senator from Colorado had holed up with a beautiful model for an entire night. They quickly identified her as Donna Rice, believed to have been just under thirty years of age.

When the story from the *Miami Herald* hit the wire services, Lee Hart quickly issued an indignant denial that her husband had done anything improper. Soon, however, the *Washington Post* found corroborative evidence. Obviously furious during a press conference he couldn't avoid calling, the candidate confessed that he may have made a mistake in his personal life. It was of trivial importance, he contended, by comparison with what the Reagan administration had done by shipping weapons made in the U.S. to Iran and by shredding documents relating to this matter after it came under investigation. But Hart's angry attempt to deflect scrutiny by changing the subject went nowhere.

Voters quickly let pollsters know that they didn't buy Hart's point of view. He made news again by refusing to answer a *Washington Post* question as to whether he had ever committed adultery. By the time Hart had become the talk of the nation, it was widely known that the senator had earlier taken the same young woman on an overnight cruise to Bimini. Females and males alike shook their heads in incredulity when they read that this voyage took place on a yacht called *Monkey Business*. Hart, who earlier had a twenty-point lead according to pollsters, angrily withdrew from the race on May 8. A front-page story in the *National Enquirer* later carried a photograph showing Donna Rice sitting in his lap.

Today Hart is a successful attorney in Denver. Rice, a self-proclaimed "born-again Christian," is widely honored for continuing to wage a crusade against pornography on the Internet. Hart reportedly is still disgruntled over the fact that he was the first candidate for the nation's top office whose personal life became the focus of investigative reporting.

The Gary Hart revelations and their aftermath marked a turning point. Once the media forced him out of contention for the presidency by publicizing illicit sex, every elected official and candidate for office became fair game.

Then the vice president, George Bush picks out his next questioner at a 1984 press conference.

At the time of her reputed affair with Bush, Jennifer Fitzgerald was no spring chicken.

WHILE THE VAST MAJORITY of adult Americans were still talking about Gary Hart, Vice President George Herbert Walker Bush was accused by Louis Field of being in a questionable relationship with one of his aides. Jennifer Fitzgerald was nearly twice as old as Donna Rice, but the informant who for a time held a minor diplomatic post said he had personally arranged joint accommodations for them a few years earlier.

Fitzgerald dismissed the Field story as a ridiculous rumor. Bush, who was put on the spot during a press conference, initially adopted the Jeffersonian technique and said only "No comment" in response to a question about an affair with a subordinate. When a CNN staffer demanded details about the alleged relationship, the vice president heatedly denounced "journalism that thrives on lies and sleazy questions." A few hours later he rebuked an NBC commentator for helping to drag down the political process. During the 1992 campaign, Hillary Clinton deftly fielded questions about her husband's reputed sexual exploits by turning the conversation to the Bush-Fitzgerald story.

To this day, no indisputable evidence, such as was turned up by *Miami Herald* reporters, exists concerning indiscreet dealings between Bush and the woman who was the State Department's deputy chief of protocol. Yet as long as books full of inside information about Washington are available, the charge against the man who became our fortieth president will not die.

There's no way Barbara Bush could have failed several times to be exposed to tales about her husband, but she acted as though they were not in circulation. Queried about her relationship with George, the first lady still known simply as "Bab" or "Barbi" to many relatives and close friends glowed as she spoke of early years in Rye, New York, and adjoining Greenwich, Connecticut.

Our fortieth president and his wife spent their childhood and youth in the lap of luxury. After attending a public elementary school, Barbi was moved to private Rye County Day School. Her junior and senior high school years were then spent at exclusive Ashley Hall in Charleston, South Carolina. By the time Sarah Johnson was making progress in teaching her husband how to read and to write, the daughter of publisher Marvin Pierce was attending prestigious Smith College in Northampton, Massachusetts.

OHIO-BORN PRESCOTT S. BUSH, a Yale graduate and highly successful investment-banker-turned-politician, moved in the same social circles as did the publisher of *Redbook* and *McCall's* magazines. Yet he and his wife Dorothy—who grew up in Kennebunkport, Maine—were less than enthusiastic when their adolescent son developed a serious crush for "the daughter of a pulp magazine publisher."

George's grandfather, who built up the biggest dry goods wholesale firm west of the Mississippi River, was called "Pop" by most of his children. Some of them dubbed his grandson Pop while others called him Poppy, and the nickname stuck for years. U.S. Secretary of War Henry Stimson came from Washington to deliver the commencement address when Poppy and his classmates graduated from Phillips Academy Andover, in Massachusetts.

George had long planned to follow his father to Yale. But in the aftermath of Pearl Harbor, he decided to do a hitch as a U.S. naval flier before going to college. Volunteers under the age of eighteen were not accepted, so George chafed during months of enforced waiting. On his eighteenth birthday he went to Boston and became a seaman second class. His tenmonth period of training began at Chapel Hill, North Carolina.

Very early in their marriage, George and Barbara agreed that it was more important for her to rear their children than to enter the workplace.

Aviators-to-be were shuffled hastily from one special post to another, so George spent time in Minneapolis; Charleston, South Carolina; Corpus Christi, Texas; and Charlestown, Rhode Island, before receiving his ensign's bars in June 1943. During his Christmas leave the previous year he donned a tuxedo in order to attend a dance at the Round Hill Country Club in Greenwich and was instantly smitten when he caught sight of an accomplished dancer. He had seen her occasionally while growing up but they had never met, despite the fact that their parents belonged to several of the same clubs.

A friend introduced him to Barbara and they walked onto the dance floor just as a Glenn Miller tune ended. To the chagrin of Poppy, the orchestra then struck up a waltz that he couldn't handle, so he suggested that they sit that one out and talk. Conversation soon became so animated that a few years later neither could remember whether they ever returned to the dance floor. For both of them, it was a genuine case of love at first meeting.

Soon they were exchanging letters on an almost-daily basis. Nearly a year after they became enamored with each other, Bush went to Philadelphia for the christening of the USS *San Jacinto*. Since this brand new aircraft carrier would be the home of her sweetheart for the foreseeable future, Barbara and his mother accepted his invitation to attend the ceremony.

Dorothy gave no hint to her traveling companion that she was taking along a star sapphire ring that once belonged to her sister, whose husband was a Wall Street broker. Minutes before a champagne bottle was smashed against the prow of the *San Jacinto*, the ring, passed along to George, was offered to Barbara. She was thrilled to accept it, not knowing whether the stone was genuine. Once on her finger, the engagement ring remained there without intermission for many years. Although relatives and friends knew that the pair were now resolved to be married, their engagement was not made public until an announcement appeared in the *New York Times* nearly a year later.

When she realized that George was slipping a ring on her finger, Barbara had a mental flashback to the evening in 1942 when he first kissed her after they had attended a movie. When describing to a professional writer her early years, she admitted that she married the first man she ever kissed, then added, "When my children heard about that memorable evening, they doubled over with laughter at having so naive a parent."

SEPTEMBER 1944 SAW U.S. naval planes strike one of the isolated Bonin Islands for the second time. At the helm of a Grumman Avenger torpedo bomber, Bush was the Navy's youngest pilot. His radio man and tail gunner was Jack Delaney, and Lt. Ted White was substituting for the regular turret gunner. Their assigned target was a Japanese radio center located on remote Chichi Jima Island about six hundred miles from Tokyo. Although sturdy, their craft was much slower than many others in operation at the time.

During the hour it took to reach their target, Bush eased the plane slowly upward until he passed twelve thousand feet and leveled off. The flak was the heaviest he had ever seen during many combat missions, and he later said that a direct hit made the Grumman feel as though "a massive fist had crunched into the belly of the plane." All three men aboard knew instantly that they couldn't make it back to their carrier. Yet the young flier from Connecticut kept on course until four five-hundred-pound bombs had been released. He then dropped rapidly toward the ocean and signaled for Delaney and White to bail out.

Barbara later said that she had "no strange premonitions" about the time her fiancé's plane hit the water. She didn't know for weeks that events of the summer day might have left her waiting hopelessly. George, who managed to hang on to his log book, later showed her its terse last entry: "Crash landing in sea - near Bonin Is. - enemy action."

Slipping out of his parachute harness as his plane hit the water, Bush, the pilot, looked around for his seatback rubber raft and started swimming toward it as soon as he spotted it, swallowing lots of saltwater en route. By that time, some of the Japanese who had seen the plane go down were in two boats and headed toward what they believed to be the crash site at top speed. Their readings were off, so they did not come near the young American who was perched on the tiny raft trying to stop the bleeding from surface cuts.

It took at least ninety minutes for men aboard the submarine USS *Fishback* to pick him up, and it was days before he learned that both Delaney and White had been lost. During the month he was aboard the *Fishback* he was unable to communicate with the outside world, so Barbara walked the floor wondering if he had been killed.

He didn't make it home for the beginning of Christmas festivities as planned, so their wedding was postponed until January 6, 1945. Barbara arrived at the First Presbyterian Church of Rye wearing a veil lent to her by Dorothy Bush. George's dress blues made him look even thinner than he really was, but few persons present noticed this because all eyes were upon his Distinguished Flying Cross.

They never requested or got financial help from their parents, and it took everything George had saved while in the Navy to put himself through Yale. Their first post-college months were spent in Odessa, Texas, where his job as equipment clerk for an oil drilling outfit paid him three hundred dollars a month. Although they were there as a result of influ-

As first lady, Barbara was rarely seen without a smile.

ence exerted by a college pal of Prescott Bush's, they received no favors. A rundown old house had been converted into two apartments by means of a flimsy partition, and they lived in half of the place. The other half, they later vowed when almost casually telling the story of their first Texas stay, was occupied by a mother and daughter—both of whom were prostitutes. Their period in "half of a whorehouse" was brief. Partly because he was bright, hard working, and ambitious but mostly because of his numerous powerful connections, George moved up the economic and political ladders rapidly.

Five children came along during Bush's climb to wealth, which took him from a clerk's desk on up to key appointive posts of the U.S. House of Representatives. As mistress of the White House, Barbara was quizzed about her feelings at having concentrated upon being a wife and mother instead of a career woman. Confessing that times had drastically changed since she was a young adult, she said that she and her beloved husband did exactly the right thing when they decided she would not enter the workplace.

Even the Jennifer Fitzgerald stories failed to rock the marital boat in which Barbara and George had been passengers for more than forty-five years when the tales surfaced. Hence, both of them seem to have been open and candid when they repeatedly insisted that their "picture book wedding" proved to be a prelude to jointly blissful decades together.

42

Bill and Hillary Clinton, and a Few of Many

I want you to listen to me. I'm going to say this again. I did not have sexual relations with that woman—Miss Lewinsky. I never told anybody to lie, not a single time. Never. These allegations are false. Now I have to go back to work on my State of the Union speech, and I worked on it till pretty late last night. I need to go back to work for the American people.

Brief as it was, this address by William Jefferson Clinton was heard and seen by the biggest live audience in history. This transcript, from the *New York Post* of January 27, 1998, is not identical with some versions published in other media, but the differences are minute: " 'til" instead of "till," for example.

Our forty-second president was barely off the air when some analysts began announcing the verdict, saying, "He told the American people a blatant lie, and irrefutable evidence to that effect will soon turn up."

A tiny handful of listeners, mostly college professors specializing in analysis of the meaning of language, were not so sure. Years of study had convinced these men and women that a given cluster of words seldom evokes identical sets of meanings in the minds of all listeners or readers. What's more, some of them have gone on record as being sure that meaning attached to a few sentences by a speaker can be quite different from the sets of meanings at which listeners arrive. These specialists, technically known as semanticists, generally agree that words tend to be somewhat chimerical; connotations evoked by them may vary from one minute to the next in the mind of a given speaker or writer, listener or reader.

Events later proved the accuracy of this somewhat abstruse analysis of the most important speech Bill Clinton ever delivered. A series of fast-moving developments led to the revelation that when deposed to testify in the suit brought against him by Paula Jones, great care had been taken in defining the meaning of *sex*. This caused connotations of the term to be much more narrow than in ordinary speech. As defined in the Paula Jones

Former White House intern Monica Lewinsky was at the center of the 1998 sex scandal that led to an impeachment trial involving President Bill Clinton. (AP/Wide World Photos)

case, a sexual act involved voluntary or involuntary contact between a male and a female genital organ.

It later emerged that the chief executive really did not have "that kind of sex with Monica Lewinsky." All of the lurid details went out in numerous media, by means of which all the world learned he had indulged in what is commonly called "oral sex." From the extremely narrow perspective of the definition employed when Clinton was deposed, and as he said he saw it, he really "did not have sex with that woman." Their indulgence in sexual play-acting could have resulted in the conception of a child only through an inconceivably bizarre chain of events.

Ignoring fine lines of distinction, the vast majority of Americans soon came to agree with commentators who categorized the presidential address—if, indeed, it was long enough to qualify as an address—as constituting a calculated lie. That verdict was both right and wrong. Deliberate ambiguity woven into what was said that January day points to a derogatory nickname by which the chief executive was already designated: Slick Willie. Judge Susan Wright Webber waited months to render her verdict. Like the nation in general, she concluded that the president lied. As a result, another substantial fine was assessed.

Possibly without being fully aware of what they were doing, the persons who first used "Slick Willie" and those who delightedly picked it up had identified one of Bill Clinton's basic traits. Whether as a result of cold calculation or high-level mental processes that are beyond analysis, the man from Arkansas habitually used words in such fashion that two or more sets of meanings can be found in much that he wrote and said.

In a longer message transmitted by television and radio five days before he denied having had sex with Monica Lewinsky, the president said: "There is not a sexual relationship, an improper sexual relationship, or any other kind of improper relationship [between Lewinsky and me]." That time, he deliberately lied; a sexual relationship did exist, and he knew it. Yet that relationship did not mean he had committed adultery—as he interpreted it.

Correspondents who wondered or fumed or marveled at the manner in which Slick Willie used words noted that he employed a present-tense verb in his radio address. Some of them thought that his assertion that "there *is* not a sexual relationship" failed to rule out the fact that earlier there *was* such a relationship. Unless Clinton clarifies this matter some time in the future, it is not possible to know whether he deliberately crafted his sentences so deftly that he said one thing but seemed to say something different.

According to State Trooper Larry Patterson, the wordsmith who was then governor of Arkansas confided to him that he had studied the Bible carefully and had found that Holy Writ does not categorize oral sex as adultery. Patterson concluded that this interpretation of Scripture may have helped persuade Clinton to favor oral sex over open adultery by the time he reached the White House.

More than three years after Paula Jones initiated legal action, Clinton, through his attorney, issued a formal written answer to her charge. This document said that:

> . . . at no time did the president make sexual advances toward the plaintiff . . . At no time did the president conspire to or sexually harass the plaintiff. At no time did the president deprive plaintiff of her constitutional rights. At no time did the president act in a manner intended to, or which could, inflict emotional distress upon the plaintiff.

The truth of this short excerpt from "Answer of President William Jefferson Clinton" is beyond dispute—for at the time the actions with which he was charged took place *he was not the president.*

BEFORE THEIR MARRIAGE, BILL and Hillary decided that when it came to attending church, they would continue to go their separate ways. She was an ardent Methodist who became a certified lay speaker in the movement spawned by British evangelical John Wesley. He was a dyed-in-the-wool Southern Baptist who may have felt that Methodist theology was too liberal for him. Whatever the case, Mrs. Hillary Rodham Clinton attended First United Methodist Church in Little Rock while her husband took his well-worn Bible to Immanuel Baptist Church in the Arkansas capital.

At Immanuel Baptist, Dr. Worley O. Vaught prided himself upon his knowledge of both Hebrew and Greek. He habitually went into considerable detail to explain to his listeners the precise meaning of a biblical term—not as it appears in any English-language version, but in the original. Clinton was both highly intelligent and extremely powerful; it was natural for Vaught often to see him informally and to discuss with him the nuances of issues about which both men were concerned.

On one occasion, they talked at length about a matter with which the governor was soon going to have to deal—capital punishment. Authorization of an execution seemed to Clinton to constitute a violation of the Law of Moses that in English-language Bibles says, "Thou shalt not kill." Vaught dealt with this matter comparatively easily. In the original Hebrew, he said, the phrase actually meant, "Thou shalt not murder." Execution of a condemned felon being an action prescribed by society, it indeed involves killing a person, but it is not by any stretch of the imagination an act of murder by a governor.

According to Pulitzer Prize–winning biographer David Maraniss, Clinton's pastor succeeded in easing his mind concerning the red-hot issue of abortion. Categorizing himself as almost always opposed to this procedure, Vaught pointed out that ancient Hebrew terms dealing with life and human identity carried with them the express connotation of "breathing life into." Since a fetus does not breathe, it follows that life begins when a newborn baby takes its first breath. Prior to that, the fetus is not a person. According to this line of reasoning, abortion does not constitute murder—because the fetus has not yet reached personhood.

Abstruse reasoning, such as that reported by Maraniss, is widely practiced—often unknowingly. Hillary Rodham Clinton was the subject of a case in point. When it became widely known that she had been cited as one of the top one hundred attorneys in the nation, her rating began to soar. Virtually all newspaper and magazine correspondents, as well as the general public, took this to mean that in a courtroom brawl the wife of the president could chop some well-known male attorneys into little pieces and keep a smile on her face.

A reporter for *Time* decided to make sure that this interpretation was correct, so the reporter queried the editor of the *National Law Journal*. That dignitary reportedly explained that Mrs. Clinton was not honored for her skill in prosecuting or defending cases. Rather, she was singled out because she had successfully prodded the American Bar

Association to reduce the degree to which male and female attorneys are treated differently!

Without realizing that his pattern of communication would have such an effect, the chief executive from Arkansas breathed a bit of new meaning into concepts such as "love, lust, and longing." A few chief executives who

Governor William J. and Mrs. Hillary Rodham
Clinton of Arkansas.

seemed conspicuously lustful may have regarded themselves as simply doing what came naturally to them, and, consequently, they might have had no sense of guilt. Some who appear to have exhibited unsullied lifelong mutual love may have been sexually indifferent to each other as well as to everyone else.

Whatever else they may have been up to and through their White House years, Bill and Hillary were not indifferent. Both of them had for years exuded vitality, enthusiasm, and zest for living despite the fact that their backgrounds were poles apart. Born as William Jefferson Blithe, the

Arkansas native lost his father while he was still a baby. His father, who had failed at three marriages before Virginia Cassidy became his wife in a hasty wartime ceremony, spent most of his time in the army before being killed in an automobile accident.

Virginia soon married Roger Clinton, a divorcé who always dressed like a well-to-do gentleman but was a womanizer and wife beater. Growing up in Hot Springs, Bill called himself Clinton but was never legally adopted. At age seventeen the boy who sometimes fought his father figure in order to protect his mother found a hero. As a senator at Boys Nation, he was ushered into the Rose Garden of the White House, where he shook the hand of John F. Kennedy. That day he purchased a photo of the life-changing moment in which he resolved to be like Kennedy and to enter politics from down-at-the-heels Hope, Arkansas.

HILLARY RODHAM, THE ONLY daughter of a textile manufacturer, grew up in elegant Park Ridge, Illinois—a northwestern suburb of Chicago. Described as "an overachiever in the classroom and everywhere else," she went to Wellesley College as a Republican but switched her allegiance because of the Vietnam war. As a student at Yale University Law School, she met Bill Clinton, who was there on a scholarship after having spent two years in England.

He seems to have suggested marriage soon after they became acquainted, but Hillary had no intention of spending the rest of her life in Arkansas. When she later joined him at the University of Arkansas Law School, where both were faculty members, he soon bought a house she said she admired and persuaded her to become his wife. Despite wide criticism she continued to use her maiden name even when they moved into the governor's mansion.

By the time he decided to become a candidate for the Democratic nomination for the presidency in 1992, he was dogged by rumors of extramarital affairs. Referring to the earlier downfall of Gary Hart, he assured reporters that there was no Donna Rice in his past. Gennifer Flowers, a nightclub singer and Arkansas state employee, nearly blew his campaign out of the water, however. She went public in the *Star* tabloid after she had been named as one of five mistresses of Clinton in a lawsuit filed by a disgruntled state trooper.

Desperate, Bill and Hillary appeared on *60 Minutes* just after the Super Bowl. They admitted to having had some marital troubles, but they said these were behind them. Hillary served as what Sam Donaldson later called Bill's "primary defense shield," saying that Flowers was after money. *The Wall Street Journal* estimated that her tabloid revelation brought her at

Little Rock lounge singer Gennifer Flowers claimed she carried on a twelve-year affair with Bill Clinton. Here, Flowers, dressed to look like Marilyn Monroe, recreates Monroe's famous "Happy Birthday, Mr. President" routine in New York during the week of Clinton's birthday in 1994. (AP/Wide World Photos)

least $130,000, but despite this fact she stuck to her guns. Interviewed by Larry King, Flowers said Clinton had been her lover for a dozen years and described him as being a risk taker who preferred to make love to her with Hillary nearby.

Paula Jones of Little Rock waited until Clinton had been in office for a year to file a suit in which she claimed that the governor had sexually harassed her three years earlier, when she was Paula Rosalee Corbin. Unlike Flowers, who described herself as having been Clinton's lover during much of his tenure as chief executive of Arkansas, Jones charged him with a single brief incident. Sex, as later defined by the president, was not involved, but she alleged that he had tried to entice her to perform oral sex on him. Lawyers representing the president fought the Jones case all the way to the U.S. Supreme Court. To the astonishment of hosts of voters, members of the high court voted unanimously to let the suit—the first of its kind ever filed against a sitting president—proceed instead of deferring it until he was out of office.

Kenneth Starr, who had been named as special prosecutor to investigate charges that the Clintons had broken the law during a failed land venture called Whitewater, had spent millions to no avail. Having learned from an informant that the president had been sexually involved with White House intern Monica Lewinsky, he demanded a deposition from the chief executive during hearings related to the Paula Jones suit.

During this deposition Clinton gave what he repeatedly characterized as a truthful answer, but which the public saw as a whitewashed lie. The whole sordid Lewinsky-Clinton story was eventually made public when Starr's voluminous report was sent to the House of Representatives. Reputedly sexually active long before reaching the White House and said to be a veteran of oral sex, Lewinsky apparently chose the president of the United States as a lover of sorts and had little trouble getting him.

As the story unfolded, ordinary folks shook their heads in bewilderment that a man of Clinton's intelligence had been foolish enough to engage in oral sex with Lewinsky—at least having an orgasm whose preserved sperm on a blue Lewinsky dress effectively nailed him. Right or wrong, the general public perceived the nation's second impeachment of a president as being another political vendetta. Hence, no charge was sustained by the necessary majority in the Senate. Some senators felt the pulse of the public, and most of them cast votes on party lines.

Hillary denounced the Starr investigation as a politically motivated witch-hunt and fiercely defended her husband until the sordid truth was revealed. In the light of the revelations about what took place in the White House, the Gennifer Flowers account suddenly became wholly believable. Paula Jones settled out of court but did not get the public apology she had demanded. Complete details about alleged affairs between Clinton plus Dolly Browning, former Miss America Elizabeth Ward Gracen, Lencola Sullivan, Sally Perdue, Connie Hamzy, Kathleen Willey, and numerous others have not been made public. A charge that then-governor Clinton fathered a son by Bobbie Ann Williams was refuted by DNA tests. Yet Larry Patterson, L. D. Brown, and Roger Perry stuck by stories that as Arkansas state troopers they had procured women by the score for the governor.

Clinton is likely to go down in history as having overcome sex scandals and defeated a politically motivated drive for impeachment—only to be widely remembered as Slick Willie.

Conclusion

Twentieth-century explosions of media offering instant communications now allow us to know more about private lives of recent White House dwellers and to find out more quickly than did people of a century ago. Even now, no whisper of scandal is attached to the lives of some recent chief executives and their wives, such as Jimmy and Rosalynn Carter, and Jerry and Betty Ford. Yet flagrant and sometimes open disregard for the mores of society on the part of presidents and occasionally one of their mates has mounted rapidly during the twentieth century.

Is this phenomenon "a product of the times"? Perhaps it is. No mistress of the White House had been divorced until Betty Ford reached the mansion, and no divorced man became our chief executive until the Gipper took his Hollywood charm to the nation's capital.

Lord Acton's famous warning concerning the dangers of power is almost universally familiar. "Power corrupts," he suggested, "and absolute power corrupts absolutely." In more than two hundred years, no U.S. chief executive has exercised absolute power—and we're a long way from having seen absolute corruption in terms of what is usually called morality. Still, there has been a sharp and distinct increase in the power of the presidency, accompanied by a rise in immorality linked with it.

George Washington and his immediate successors were at the apex of power in a relatively narrow strip of land along the Atlantic Ocean. By 1860 the chief executive had considerable power in thirty-four states that stretched beyond the Mississippi River, eleven of which tried unsuccessfully to leave the Union in order to form a separate nation. In a relatively short time after the Civil War, the territory over which a president presided reached all the way from the Atlantic Ocean to the Pacific. Ike Eisenhower had the unique experience of seeing presidential power extended first to Alaska and then to Hawaii.

Similarly, world influence exercised by the United States has mounted faster than its geographical size has increased. Meanwhile, the once-global empires of Great Britain, Spain, and France have shrunk to a fraction of their size at their apex. As a result, it was generally conceded that during the long Cold War of recent decades, only the United States

297

and the U.S.S.R. deserved to be called "super powers." Today, there's only one superpower left—and many decisions concerning its role are made in the Oval Office of the White House or aboard *Air Force One*.

As late as the administration of Andrew Jackson, masses of ordinary folks large and unruly enough to be called mobs converged upon the White House and literally took it over for hours at a time. Until after the assassination of Lincoln, residents of the White House—to say nothing of ex-residents and some contenders for a term in it—were given security that today seems not to have deserved that name. In the early 1860s the mansion had no guards and when the president or first lady went driving they did so at their own risk.

Presidential salaries have lagged far behind earnings of entrepreneurs and heads of corporations, but perquisites attached to the office have soared in number and in importance. Bill Clinton is expected to take with him a mountain of legal fees when he and Hillary vacate the White House. Because an ex-president now wields a great deal of power and has accumulated wealthy and influential friends, we probably shouldn't waste our time sympathizing with Bill about his debts. Some of them will be written off and others can easily be paid from his earnings as an author, lecturer, and member of corporate boards of directors.

All of these factors and numerous others indicate that the power of the presidency today is many times greater than in the day of George Washington, Ulysses S. Grant, or even Calvin Coolidge. Some students of human behavior hold that although power is rarely if ever absolute, it can serve as one of the most potent of aphrodisiacs. Presidential power is now at such a level that a person wielding that power is pushed very hard toward the role of habitual high-level risk taker.

If this unscientific look at what the presidency has become is accurate, the presidency may be the most dangerous post in the world. Those persons who will sit in the Oval Office during the first half of the first century of the third millennium are going to be exposed to pressures and temptations of such magnitude that ordinary folks cannot conceive of them.

Bibliography

I. Individual Presidents, Their Wives, and Their Relationships

1. George and Martha Custis Washington

Callahan, North, *George Washington*. New York: Morrow, 1972.

Cunliffe, Marcus, *George Washington*. Boston: Little, Brown, 1958.

Fay, Bernard, *George Washington*. Boston: Houghton Mifflin, 1931

Ferling, John E., *The First of Men*. Knoxville: University of Tennessee, 1988.

Fleming, Thomas J., *Affectionately Yours, George Washington*. New York: Norton, 1967.

Flexner, James T., *George Washington*. 4 vols. Boston: Little, Brown, 1965–72.

Harwell, Richard, ed., *Washington*. New York: Scribner's, 1968.

Pryor, Mrs. Roger A, *The Mother of Washington*. New York: Macmillan, 1903.

Randall, Willard Sterne, *George Washington*. New York: Holt, 1997.

Thayne, Elswyth, *Potomac Squire*. New York: Duell, Sloan and Pearce. 1963.

_____, *Washington's Lady*. New York: Dodd, Mead, 1954.

Wharton, Anne H., *Martha Washington*. New York: Scribner's, 1897.

2. John and Abigail Adams

Bowen, Catherine D., *John Adams and the American Revolution*. Boston: Little, Brown, 1950.

Burleigh, Ann H., *John Adams*. Boston: New Rochelle, New York: Arlington, 1969.

Chinard, Gilbert, *Honest John Adams*. Boston: Little, Brown, 1933.

Levin, Phyllis L., *Abigail Adams*. New York: St. Martin's, 1987.

Nagel, Paul C., *John Quincy Adams*. New York: Knopf, 1997.

Smith, Page, *John Adams*. 2 vols. New York: Doubleday, 1962.

Wentworth, "Mrs. Abigail Adams," *The Ladies' Repository*, 1876.

Whitney, Janet, *Abigail Adams*. Boston: Little, Brown, 1947.

Withey, Lynne, *Dearest Friend*. New York: Free Press, 1981.

3. Thomas and Martha Jefferson, and Company

Brodie, Fawn M., *Thomas Jefferson*. New York: Norton, 1974.

_____, "Thomas Jefferson's Unknown Grandchildren," *American Heritage*, 1976.

Cooke, J. E., "Jefferson as a Lover," *Appleton's Journal*, 1974.

_____, "Thomas Jefferson," *Southern Literary Messenger*, 1860.

Cunningham, Nobel E., *In Pursuit of Reason*. Baton Rouge: Louisiana State University, 1987.

Ellis, Joseph J., *American Sphinx*. New York: Knopf, 1997.

Malone, Dumas, *Jefferson and His Times*. 6 vols. Boston: Little, Brown, 1948–81.

_____, and Steven Hochman, "A Note on Evidence," *Journal of Southern History*, 1975.

Mapp, Alf J., Jr., *Thomas Jefferson*. New York: Madison, 1991.

Randolph, Laura B., "Thomas Jefferson's Black and White Descendants Debate His Lineage and Legacy," *Ebony*, 1993.

Wilson, Douglas L., "Thomas Jefferson and the Character Issue," *Atlantic Monthly*, 1992.

Woodman, Charles H., "Love a Hundred Years Ago," *Appleton's Journal*, 1876.

4. James and Dolley Madison

Banfield, Susan, *James Madison*. New York: Franklin Watts, 1986.

Brant, Irving, *James Madison*. Indianapolis: Bobbs-Merrill, 1953.

Hamilton, Alexander, James Madison, and John Jay, *The Federalist Papers*. New York: New American Library, 1961.

Ketcham, Ralph, *James Madison*. New York: Macmillan, 1971.

McCoy, Drew R., *The Last of the Fathers*. Cambridge: Cambridge University Press, 1989.

Madison, James, *Papers—Congressional Series*. 17 vols. Chicago: University of Chicago Press, 1962-97; Charlottesville: University Press of Virginia, 1977–91.

_____, *Papers—Presidential Series*. 3 vols. Charlottesville: University Press of Virginia, 1984–96.

_____, *Papers—Secretary of State Series*. 4 vols. Charlottesville: University Press of Virginia, 1986–98.

Moore, Virginia, *The Madisons*. New York: McGraw-Hill, 1979.

Rutland, Robert A., *James Madison*. Columbia: University of Missouri Press, 1987.

Thane, Elswyth, *Dolley Madison*. New York: Crowell-Collier, 1970.

5. James and Elizabeth Monroe

Ammon, Harry, *James Monroe*. New York: McGraw-Hill, 1971.

6. John Quincy and Louisa Adams

Adams, John Quincy, *Diary*; Robert J. Taylor, et. al., editors. Cambridge: Belknap, 1981.

Bemis, Samuel F., *John Quincy Adams and the Foundations of American Foreign Policy*. New York: Knopf, 1949.

_____, *John Quincy Adams and the Union*. New York: Knopf, 1956.

Faulkner, Leonard, *The President Who Wouldn't Retire*. New York: Coward-McCann, 1967.

Hecht, Marie B., *John Quincy Adams*. New York: Macmillan, 1972.

7. Andy and Rachel Jackson

"Andrew Jackson—A Matter of Character." Westerhoff Publishing, 1997. www.historyclub.com/journal/excerpts/Jackson.html.

"Andrew Jackson: 7th President." http://broadcast.webpoint.com/wphl/lewinsky/pres/html/b.htm

Curtis, James C., *Andrew Jackson and the Search for Vindication*. Boston: Little, Brown, 1976.

Davis, Burke. *Old Hickory: A Life of Andrew Jackson.* New York: Dial, 1977.

Hoffman, William S., *Andrew Jackson and North Carolina Politics.* Chapel Hill: University of North Carolina Press, 1958.

James, Marquis, *The Life of Andrew Jackson.* Indianapolis: Bobbs-Merrill, 1938.

Jones, Cranston. *Homes of the American Presidents.* New York: Bonanza, 1962.

Latner, Richard B., *The Presidency of Andrew Jackson.* Athens: University of Georgia Press, 1979.

Marszalek, John F., *The Petticoat Affair: Manners, Mutiny and Sex in Andrew Jackson's White House.* New York: Free Press, 1997.

"Rachel Donelson Jackson: 1767–1828." http://www.whitehouse.gov/WH/glimpse/first ladies/html/rj7.html

"Scandal of the Century! Rachel Donelson Robards Jackson." www.sticc.cc.mo.us/fv/users/afoster/bc/ad/html

Remini, Robert V., *Andrew Jackson.* 3 vols. New York: Harper & Row, 1977, 1981, 1984.

Schlesinger, Arthur M., *The Age of Jackson.* Boston: Little, Brown, 1946.

8. Martin and Hannah Van Buren

Alexander, Holmes, *The American Talleyrand.* New York: Harper & Brothers, 1935.

Curtis, James C., *The Fox at Bay.* Lexington: University of Kentucky Press, 1970.

Lynch, Dennis T., *An Epoch and a Man.* Port Washington, New York: Kennikat reprint, 1970.

Morse, John T., Jr., *Martin Van Buren.* New York: AMS Press, 1922.

Niven, John, *Martin Van Buren.* New York: Oxford, 1983.

Remini, Robert V., *Martin Van Buren and the Making of the Democratic Party.* New York: Columbia University Press, 1959.

Sloan, Irving J., ed., *Martin Van Buren Chronology.* Dobbs Ferry, New York: Oceana, 1969.

9. William Henry and Anna Harrison

Cleaves, Freeman, *Old Tippecanoe.* New York: Scribner's, 1939.

Goebel, Dorothy B., *William Henry Harrison.* Indianapolis: Indiana Library and Historical Department, 1926.

10. John, Julia, and Letitia Tyler

Chidsey, Donald B., *And Tyler Too.* New York: Thomas Nelson, 1978.

Frazer, Hugh R., *Democracy in the Making.* Indianapolis: Bobbs-Merrill, 1938.

Morgan, Robert J., *A Whig Embattled.* Lincoln: University of Nebraska Press, 1954.

Seager, Robert II, *And Tyler Too.* New York: McGraw-Hill, 1963.

11. James and Sarah Polk

Morrell, Martha M., *Young Hickory.* New York: Dutton, 1949.

McCormac, Eugene I., *James K. Polk.* New York: Russell reprint, 1965.

Polk, James K., *Diary.* 4 vols. Chicago: McClurg, 1910.

Sellers, Charles G., *James K. Polk.* Princeton, New Jersey: Princeton University Press, 1957.

12. Zach and Peggy Taylor

Baur, Karl J., *Zachary Taylor*. Baton Rouge: Louisiana State University Press, 1985.

Hamilton, Holman, *Zachary Taylor*. 2 vols. Indianapolis: Bobbs-Merrill, 1941, 1951.

McKinley, Silas B., and Silas Bent, *Old Rough and Ready*. New York: Vanguard, 1946.

McLaughlin, Andrew C., *Silas Cass*. Cambridge: Riverside Press, 1891.

Nevins, Allan, *Ordeal of the Union*. New York: Scribner's, 1947.

Nichols, Edward J., *Zach Taylor's Little Army*. Garden City, New York: Doubleday, 1963.

Porter, Kirk H., and Donald B. Johnson, compilers, *National Party Platforms*. Urbana, Illinois: University of Illinois Press, 1961.

13. Millard and Abigail Fillmore

Brooks, Noah, "A Chapter of Condensed History," *Overland Monthly and Out West*, 1872.

Cluskey, Michael W., *The Political Text-book, or Encyclopedia*. Philadelphia: J. B. Smith, 1860.

"Contemporary Sayings," *Appleton's Journal*, 1874.

Greeley, Horace, *The American Conflict*. Vol. I. Hartford: O. D. Case, 1866.

Griffith, George, "A Chapter on Autographs," *The Ladies' Repository*, 1875.

Helper, Hinton R., *The Impending Crisis*. New York: A. B. Burdick, 1860.

Rayback, Robert J., *Millard Fillmore*. Buffalo: Henry Stewart, 1959.

Richardson, James D., ed., *Messages and Papers of the Presidents*. 5 vols. Washington: Government Printing Office, 1884–97.

Treadwell, Walcien, "The Rose of New England," *Appleton's Journal*, 1878.

Truman, Ben C., "Gossip About the Presidents," *Overland Monthly and Out West*, 1898.

14. Franklin and Jane Pierce

Nichols, Roy Franklin, *Franklin Pierce*. Philadelphia: University of Pennsylvania Press, 1931.

15. Old Buck and Rufus

Curtis, George T., *Life of James Buchanan*. New York: Harper, 1883.

Klein, Philip S., *President James Buchanan*. University Park, Pennsylvania: Pennsylvania State University Press, 1962.

McClure, A. K., *Our Presidents and How We Make Them*. New York: Harper, 1902.

Stuart, Graham H., *The Department of State*. New York: Macmillan, 1949.

16. Abraham and Mary Todd Lincoln

Angle, Paul M., ed., *Herndon's Life of Lincoln*. Cleveland: World, 1930.

Baker, Jean H., *Mary Todd Lincoln*. New York: Norton, 1987.

Barton, William E., *The Life of Abraham Lincoln*. 2 vols. Indianapolis: Bobbs-Merrill, 1925.

Basler, Roy P., *The Lincoln Legend*. New York: Houghton Mifflin, 1935.

Beveridge, Albert J., *Abraham Lincoln*. 2 vols. Boston: Houghton Mifflin, 1928.

Browne, Francis E., *The Everyday Life of Abraham Lincoln*. New York: Thompson, 1886.

Carpenter, Francis B., *The Inner Life of Abraham Lincoln*. Boston: Houghton Mifflin, 1887.

Clark, L. Pierce, *Lincoln: A Psycho-Biography*. New York: Scribner's, 1933.

Fehrenbacher, Don E., *Prelude to Greatness*. Stanford: Stanford University Press, 1962.

Hertz, Emanuel, *Abraham Lincoln: A New Portrait.* 2 vols. New York: Liveright, 1931.
_____, *The Hidden Lincoln.* New York: Viking, 1928.
Lincoln, Abraham, *Collected Works.* Roy P. Basler, ed. 9 vols. New Brunswick, New Jersey: Rutgers University Press, 1953–55.
_____, *Complete Works.* John G. Nicolay and John Hay, eds. 12 vols. New York: 1894.
_____, *The Lincoln Papers.* David C. Mearns, ed. 2 vols. Garden City, New York: Doubleday, 1948.
Nicolay, John G. and John Hay, *Abraham Lincoln: A History.* 10 vols. New York: Century, 1890.
Pratt, Harry E., *Abraham Lincoln Chronology.* Springfield: Illinois State Historical Library, 1953.
Shaw, Archer H., *The Lincoln Encyclopedia.* New York: Macmillan, 1950.
Shutes, Milton, *Lincoln's Emotional Life.* Philadelphia: Dorrance, 1957.

17. Andrew and Eliza Johnson

Barzman, Sol, *Madmen and Geniuses.* Chicago: Follett, 1974.
Beale, Howard K., *The Critical Year.* New York: Ungar, 1958.
Lomask, Milton, *Andrew Johnson.* New York: Farrar, Straus, 1960.
Nevins, Allan, ed., *The Diary of a President.* New York: Capricorn, 1968.
Stryker, Lloyd P., *Andrew Johnson.* New York: Macmillan, 1929.
Trefousse, Hans L., *Andrew Johnson.* New York: Holt, 1928.
Winston, Robert W., *Andrew Johnson.* New York: Holt, 1928.

18. Ulys and Julia Grant

Catton, Bruce, *Grant Moves South.* Boston: Little, Brown, 1960.
_____, *Grant Takes Command.* Boston: Little, Brown, 1969.
_____, *U. S. Grant and the American Military Tradition.* Boston: Little, Brown, 1954.
Frost, Lawrence A., *U. S. Grant Album.* New York: Bonanza, 1946.
Goldhurst, Richard, *Many Are the Hearts.* New York: Reader's Digest Press, 1975.
Grant, Julia Dent, *Memoirs.* Carbondale: Southern Illinois University Press, 1975.
Grant, Ulysses, *Personal Memoirs.* 2 vols. New York: Webster, 1892.
Grant, Ulysses S., III, *Ulysses S. Grant.* New York: Morrow, 1968.
Lewis, Lloyd, *Captain Sam Grant.* Boston: Little, Brown, 1950.
Woodward, W. E., *Meet General Grant.* New York: Liveright, 1928.

19. Rutherford and Lucy Hayes

Barnard, Harry, *Rutherford B. Hayes.* Newton, Connecticut: American Political Biography Press, 1954.
Eckenrode, H. J., *Rutherford B. Hayes.* New York: Dodd, Mead, 1930.
Hayes, Rutherford B., *Diary and Letters.* 5 vols. Columbus: Ohio State Archaeological and Historical Society, 1922.
Williams, Charles C., *The Life of Rutherford B. Hayes.* 2 vols. Columbus: Ohio State Archaeological and Historical Society, 1928.
William, T. Harry, ed., *Diary of a President.* New York: McKay, 1964.

20. James and Crete Garfield

Balch, William R., *The Life of James Abram Garfield*. Philadelphia: McCurdy, 1881.

Blaine, James G., *Eulogy on James Abram Garfield*. Boston: Osgood, 1882.

Boorman, Hendrik, *The Road to Respectability*. Cleveland: Western Reserve Historical Society, 1988.

Bundy, J. M., *The Life of Gen. James A. Garfield*. New York: Barnes, 1880.

Conwell, Russell, *The Life of James A. Garfield*. Portland, Maine: Stinson, 1881.

Garfield, James A., *Diary*. 4 vols. Harry J. Brown and Frederick D. Williams, eds. Lansing: Michigan State University, 1967–81.

Leech, Margaret, and Harry J. Brown, *The Garfield Orbit*. New York: Harper, 1978.

McCabe, James D., *Our Martyred President*. Philadelphia: National, 1881.

Peskin, Allan, *Garfield*. Kent, Ohio: Kent State University Press, 1978.

Ridpath, John C., *The Life and Work of James A. Garfield*. Cincinnati: Jones, 1881.

Smith, Theodore C., *The Life and Letters of James Abram Garfield*. 2 vols. New Haven: Yale University Press, 1925.

Taylor, John M., *Garfield of Ohio*. New York: Norton, 1970.

Thayer, William M., *From Log Cabin to White House*. London: Ward, Lock, 1882.

21. Chester and Nell Arthur

Howe, George F., *Chester A. Arthur*. New York: Dodd, Mead, 1934.

Reeves, Thomas, *Gentleman Boss*. New York: Knopf, 1975.

22, 24. Grover and Frances Cleveland

Bonnell, John S., *Presidential Profiles*. Philadelphia: Westminster, 1971.

Eaton, Herbert, *Presidential Timber*. New York: Free Press of Glencoe, 1964.

Lynch, Denis T., *Grover Cleveland*. New York: Liveright, 1932.

McElroy, Robert, *Grover Cleveland*. New York: Harper, 1923.

Nevins, Allan, *Grover Cleveland*. New York: Harper, 1932.

Tugwell, Rexford G., *Grover Cleveland*. New York: Macmillan, 1968.

23. Ben, Carrie, and Mame Harrison

Harrison, Benjamin, *This Country of Ours*. New York: Scribner's, 1897.

————, *Views of an Ex-President*. Indianapolis: Bowen-Merrill, 1901.

Pollard, James E., *The Presidents and the Press*. New York: Macmillan, 1947.

Sievers, Harry J., *Benjamin Harrison*. 3 vols. Vols 1-2, New York: University Publishers, 1952, 1959; vol. 3, Indianapolis: Bobbs-Merrill, 1968.

25. William and Ida McKinley

Gould, Lewis L., *The Presidency of William McKinley*. Lawrence, Kansas: Regents Press, 1980.

Leech, Margaret, *In the Days of McKinley*. New York: Harper, 1959.

McKinley, *Speeches and Addresses*. New York: Appleton, 1893.

Olcott, Charles S., *The Life of William McKinley*. 2 vols. Boston: Houghton Mifflin, 1916.

Spielman, William C., *William McKinley*. New York: Exposition, 1954.

26. Teddy, Alice, and Edith Roosevelt

Bishop, Joseph B., *Theodore Roosevelt and His Time: Shown in His Own Letters*. 2 vols. New York: Scribner's, 1920.

Brands, H. W., T. R., *The Last Romantic*. New York: Basic, 1997.

Burns, James M., *Roosevelt*. New York: Harcourt Brace Jovanovich, 1970.

Chessman, G. Wallace, *Theodore Roosevelt*. Boston: Little, Brown, 1969.

Hagedorn, Hermann, *The Roosevelt Family of Sagamore Hill*. New York: Macmillan, 1954.

McCullogh, David, *Mornings on Horseback*. New York: Simon and Schuster, 1981.

Morris, Edmund, *The Rise of Theodore Roosevelt*. New York: Coward, McCann, 1979.

Pringle, Henry F., *Theodore Roosevelt*. New York: Harcourt, Brace, 1956.

Roosevelt, Nicholas, *Theodore Roosevelt*. New York: Dodd, Mead, 1967.

Roosevelt, Theodore, *An Autobiography*. New York: Scribner's, 1920.

27. Will and Nellie Taft

Anderson, Donald F., *William Howard Taft*. Ithaca: Cornell University Press, 1973.

Anderson, Judith I., *William Howard Taft*. New York: Norton, 1981.

Kirk, Russell, and James McClellan, *The Political Principles of Robert A. Taft*. New York: Fleet Press, 1967.

Patterson, James T., *Mr. Republican*. Boston: Houghton Mifflin, 1972.

Pringle, Henry, *The Life and Times of William Howard Taft*. 2 vols. New York: Farrar & Rhinehart, 1939.

Roosevelt, Theodore, *Letters*; Elting E. Morison, ed. 7 vols. Cambridge: Harvard University Press, 1951–54

Ross, Ishbel, *An American Family, the Tafts*. Cleveland: World, 1964.

28. Woodrow, Ellen, and Edith Wilson

Baker, Ray Stannard, *Woodrow Wilson*. 6 vols. Garden City, New York: Doubleday, Doran, 1930–37.

Clements, Kendrick A., *Woodrow Wilson*. Boston: Twayne, 1987.

Hale, William B., *Woodrow Wilson*. Garden City, New York: Doubleday, Page, 1913.

Link, Arthur S., *Woodrow Wilson*. New York: Hill and Wang, 1962.

Miller, Nathan, *Theodore Roosevelt*. New York: Morrow, 1992.

29. Warren and Flossie Harding, and Company

Adams, Samuel G., *Incredible Era*. Boston: Houghton Mifflin, 1939.

Anthony, Carl S., *Florence Harding*. New York: Morrow, 1998.

Russell, Francis, *The Shadow of Blooming Grove*. New York: McGraw-Hill, 1968.

Sinclair, Andrew, *The Available Man*. New York: MacMillan, 1965.

30. Calvin and Grace Coolidge

Coolidge, Calvin, *Autobiography*. New York: Cosmopolitan, 1929.

McCoy, Donald R., *Calvin Coolidge*. New York: Macmillan, 1967.

White, William Allen, *A Puritan in Babylon*. New York: Macmillan, 1938.

31. Herbert and Lou Hoover

Burner, David, *Herbert Hoover*. New York: Knopf, 1979.

Emery, Anne, *American Friend*. Chicago: Rand McNally, 1967.

Hinshaw, David, *Herbert Hoover*. New York: Farrar, Straus, & Co., 1950.

Hoover, Herbert, *Memoirs*. 2 vols. New York: Macmillan, 1951–52.

Lyons, Eugene, *Herbert Hoover*. New York: Doubleday, 1964.

Nash, George H., *The Life of Herbert Hoover*. New York: Norton, 1983.

Smith, Richard N., *An Uncommon Man*. New York: Simon and Schuster, 1984.

32. FDR, Eleanor Roosevelt, and Their Playmates

Alsop, Joseph, *FDR*. New York: Viking, 1982.

Bishop, Jim, *FDR's Last Year*. New York: Morrow, 1974.

Burns, James M., *Roosevelt*. New York: Harcourt, Brace, and World, 1956.

Davis, Kenneth, *FDR*. New York: Putnam, 1972.

Perkins, Frances, *The Roosevelt I Knew*. New York: Viking, 1946.

Roosevelt, Eleanor, *This I Remember*. New York: Harper & Bros., 1949.

Roosevelt, James, and Sidney Shallett, *Affectionately FDR*. New York: Harcourt, Brace, 1959.

Schlesinger, Arthur M., *The Age of Roosevelt*. Boston: Houghton Mifflin, 1957.

Ward, Geoffrey, *Before the Trumpet*. New York: Harper & Row, 1985.

33. Harry and Bess Truman

Cochran, Bert, *Harry Truman*. New York: Funk & Wagnalls, 1973.

Donovan, Robert J., *Tumultuous Years*. New York: Norton, 1982.

Ferrell, Robert H., *Off the Record*. New York: Harper & Row, 1980.

Hillman, William, *Mr. President*. New York: Farrar, Straus, and Young, 1952.

Miller, Merle, *Plain Speaking*. New York: Berkeley, 1973.

Miller, Richard, *Truman*. New York: McGraw-Hill, 1986.

Poen, Monte M., *Strictly Confidential*. Boston: Little, Brown, 1982.

Truman, Harry S, *Letters Home*. New York: Putnam, 1983.

_____, *Years of Trial and Hope*. Garden City, New York: Doubleday, 1956.

Truman, Margaret, *Harry S Truman*. New York: Morrow, 1973,

34. Ike and Mamie Eisenhower, Plus "That Girl Kay"

Adams, Sherman, *First-Hand Report*. New York: Harper & Bros., 1961.

Ambrose, Stephen E., *Eisenhower*. 2 vols. New York: Simon and Schuster, 1983–84.

Beschloss, Michael R., *Eisenhower*. New York: Harper & Row, 1990.

Brendon, Piers, *Ike*. New York: Harper & Row, 1986.

Broadwater, Jeff, *Eisenhower*. Chapel Hill: University of North Carolina Press, 1992.

Brownell, Herbert, *Advising Ike*. Lawrence: University Press of Kansas, 1993.

Eisenhower, David, *Eisenhower at War*. New York: Random, 1986.

Eisenhower, Dwight D., *At Ease*. Garden City, New York: Doubleday, 1967.

_____, *Diaries and Selected Papers*. Baltimore: Johns Hopkins University Press, 1998.

_____, *Letters to a Friend*. Lawrence, Kansas: University Press of Kansas, 1984.

Eisenhower, John D., *Strictly Personal*. Garden City, New York: Doubleday, 1974.

Lyon, Peter, *Eisenhower*. Boston: Little, Brown, 1974.

Miller, Merle, *Plain Speaking*. New York: Berkeley, 1973.

Morgan, Kay Summersby, *Past Forgetting*. New York: Simon and Schuster, 1976.

Neal, Steve, *The Eisenhowers*. Garden City, New York: Doubleday, 1978.

35. JFK, Jackie, and Stable

Cassini, Oleg, *A Thousand Days of Magic*. New York: Rizzoli, 1995.

Clinch, Nancy G., *The Kennedy Neurosis*. New York: Grosset & Dunlap, 1973.

Collier, Peter, and David Horowitz, *The Kennedys*. New York: Summit, 1984.

Hamilton, Nigel, *JFK, Reckless Youth*. New York: Random, 1992.

Highman, Charles, *Rose*. New York: Pocket Books, 1995.

Kessler, Ronald, *Sins of the Father*. New York: Warner, 1996.

Klein, Edward, *All Too Human*. New York: Pocket Books, 1994.

Leamer, Laurence, *The Kennedy Women*. New York: Villard, 1994.

Manchester, William, *Portrait of a President*. Boston: Little, Brown, 1962.

Mills, Judie, *John F. Kennedy*. New York: Franklin Watts, 1962.

Reeves, Thomas C., *A Question of Character*. New York: Free Press, 1991.

Schlesinger, Arthur M., *A Thousand Days*. Boston: Houghton Mifflin, 1965.

Sorensen, Theodore C., *Kennedy*. New York: Smithmark, 1965.

Von Post, Gunilla, *Love, Jack*. New York: Crown, 1997.

36. LBJ, Lady Bird, and Ménage

Califano, Joseph A., *The Triumph and Tragedy of Lyndon Johnson*. New York: Simon and Schuster, 1991.

Caro, Robert A., *The Years of Lyndon Johnson*. 2 vols. New York: Knopf, 1983–90.

Conkin, Paul F., *Big Daddy from the Perdenales*. Boston: Twaine, 1986.

Cormier, Frank, *LBJ*. Garden City, New York: Doubleday, 1977.

Dallek, Robert, *Flawed Giant*. New York: Oxford, 1998.

————, *Lone Star Rising*. New York: Oxford, 1991.

Dugger, Ronnie, *The Politician*. New York: Norton, 1982.

Firestone, Bernard J. and Robert C. Vogt, *Lyndon Baines Johnson*. New York: Greenwood, 1988.

Goodwin, Doris K., *Lyndon Johnson and the American Dream*. New York: Harper & Row, 1976.

Harwood, Richard, and Haynes Johnson, *Lyndon*. New York: Praeger, 1987.

Joesten, Joiachim, *The Dark Side of Lyndon Baines Johnson*. London: Dawnay, 1968.

Johnson, Lady Bird, *A White House Diary*. New York: Holt, Rinehart, Winston, 1970.

Kearns, Doris, *Lyndon Johnson*. New York: Harper & Row, 1976.

McMaster, H. R., *Dereliction of Duty*. New York: HarperCollins, 1997.

Miller, Merle, *Lyndon*. New York: Putnam's, 1992.

Mooney, Booth, *The Lyndon Johnson Story*. New York: Farrar, Straus, 1964.

Muslin, Hyman L., and Thomas Jobe, *Lyndon Johnson*. New York: Insight, 1991.

Reedy, George, *Lyndon B. Johnson*. Kansas City, Missouri: Andrews McMeel, 1982.

White, William S., *The Professional Lyndon B. Johnson*. Boston: Houghton Mifflin, 1994.

37. Richard and Pat Nixon

Allen, Gary, *Richard Nixon*. Boston: Western Islands, 1971.

Ambrose, Stephen E., *Nixon*. 3 vols. New York: Simon and Schuster, 1987–91.

Barrett, Laurence I., *Gambling with History*. Garden City, New York: Doubleday, 1983.

Brodie, Fawn, *Richard Nixon*. New York: Norton, 1981.

De Toledano, Ralph, *One Man Alone*. New York: Funk & Wagnalls, 1969.

Eisenhower, Julie Nixon, *Pat Nixon*. New York: Simon and Schuster, 1986.

Emery, Fred, *Watergate*. New York: Random, 1994.

Larsen, Rebecca, *Richard Nixon*. New York: Franklin Watts, 1991.

Leamer, Laurence, *Make-Believe*. New York: Harper & Row, 1983.

Mazo, Earl, and Stephen Hess, *Nixon*. New York: Harper & Row, 1968.

Morris, Roger, *Richard Milhous Nixon*. New York: Holt, 1990.

Nixon, Richard, *In the Arena*. New York: Simon and Schuster, 1990.

_____, *Memoirs*. New York: Grosset & Dunlap, 1978.

Parmet, Herbert, *Richard Nixon*. Boston: Little, Brown, 1990.

Quigley, Joan, *What Does Joan Say?* Secaucus, New Jersey: Birch Lane, 1990.

Volkan, Vamik D., Norman Itzkowitz and Andrew W. Dod, *Richard Nixon*. New York: Columbia University, 1997.

White, Theodore H., *Breach of Faith*. New York: Atheneum, 1975.

Wicker, Tom, *One of Us*. New York: Random, 1991.

Witcover, Jules, *The Resurrection of Richard Nixon*. New York: Putnam, 1970.

38. Jerry and Betty Ford

Aaron, Jan, *Gerald R. Ford*. New York: Fleet, 1975.

Ford, Betty, *The Times of My Life*. New York: Harper & Row, 1978.

_____, *Betty—A Glad Awakening*. Garden City, New York: Doubleday, 1987.

Hersey, John, *The President*. New York: Knopf, 1975.

Sidey, Hugh, *Portrait of a President*. New York: Harper & Row, 1975.

TerHorst, Jerald F., *Gerald Ford and the Future of the Presidency*. New York: Third Press, 1974.

Vestal, Bud, *Jerry Ford*. New York: Coward, McCann, & Geoghegan, 1974.

Weidenfeld, Sheila Rabb, *First Lady's Lady*. New York: Putnam's, 1979.

39. Jimmy and Rosalynn Carter

Adler, Bill, ed., *The Wit and Wisdom of Jimmy Carter*. Secaucas, New Jersey: Citadel, 1977.

Ariail, Dan, and Cheryl Heckler-Feltz, *The Carpenter's Choice*. Grand Rapids: Zondervan, 1996.

Bourne, Peter G., *Jimmy Carter*. New York: Scribner's, 1997.

Carter, Jimmy, *Turning Point*. New York: Times, 1992.

_____, and Rosalynn, *Everything to Gain*. New York: Random, 1987.

Carter, Rosalynn, *First Lady from Plains*. Boston: Houghton Mifflin, 1984.

Glad, Betty, *Jimmy Carter*. New York: Norton, 1980.

Hargrove, Erwin C., *Jimmy Carter*. Baton Rouge: Louisiana State University Press, 1988.

Kucharsky, David, *The Man from Plains*. New York: Harper & Row, 1976.

Mazliosh, Bruce, & Edwin Diamond, *Jimmy Carter*. New York: Simon and Schuster, 1979.

Morris, Kenneth E., *Jimmy Carter*. Athens: University of Georgia Press, 1996.
Simmons, Dawn L., *Rosalynn Carter*. New York: Frederick Fell, 1979.
Slavin, Ed, *Jimmy Carter*. New York: Chelsea House, 1989.
Troester, Rod, *Jimmy Carter*. Westport, Connecticut: Praeger, 1996.
Wooten, James, *Dasher*. New York: Summit, 1978.

40. Ron, Jane, and Nancy Reagan, and Their Bunch
Adler, Bill, *Ronnie and Nancy*. New York: Crown, 1985.
Barrett, Laurence I., *Gambling with History*. Garden City, New York: Doubleday, 1983.
Boyarski, Bill, *Ronald Reagan*. New York: Random, 1981.
Cannon, Lou, *Reagan*. New York: G. P. Putnam's Sons, 1982.
Dugger, Ronnie, *On Reagan*. New York: McGraw-Hill, 1983.
Edwards, Anne, *Early Reagan*. New York: Morrow, 1987.
Kelly, Kitty, *Nancy Reagan*. New York: Simon & Schuster, 1991.
Leighton, Frances S., *The Search for the Real Nancy Reagan*. New York: Macmillan, 1987.
Mayer, Jane, and Doyle McManus, *Landslide*. Boston: Houghton Mifflin, 1988.
Morella, Joe, and Edward Z. Epstein, *Jane Wyman*. New York: Delacorte, 1985.
Reagan, Maureen, *First Father, First Daughter*. Boston: Little, Brown, 1989.
Reagan, Nancy, *My Turn*. New York: Random, 1989.
_____, *Nancy*. New York: Morrow, 1980.
Reagan, Ronald, *An American Life*. New York: Simon and Schuster, 1990.
_____, *Where's the Rest of Me?* New York: Duell, Sloan, and Pearce, 1965.
Smith, Hedrick, et. al., *Reagan*. New York: Macmillan, 1980.
Van der Linden, Frank, *The Real Reagan*. New York: Morrow, 1981.
Wallace, Chris, *First Lady*. New York: St. Martin's, 1986.
Wills, Garry, *Reagan's America*. Garden City, New York: Doubleday, 1987.

41. George and Barbara Bush
Bush, Barbara, *Barbara Bush—A Memoir*. New York: Scribner's, 1994.
Bush, George, *Looking Forward*. New York: Doubleday, 1987.
Duffy, Michael, and Dan Goodgame, *Marching in Place*. New York: Simon and Schuster, 1992.
Green, Fitzhugh, *George Bush*. New York: Hippocrene, 1989.
Hyams, Joe, *Flight of the Avenger*. New York: Harcourt Brace Jovanovich, 1991.
Kilian, Pamela, *Barbara Bush*. New York: St. Martin's, 1992.
Radcliffe, Donnie, *Simply Barbara Bush*. New York: Warner, 1989.
Spy magazine, Summer 1992.
Sullivan, George, *George Bush*. New York: Messner, 1989.
Trento, Susan B., *The Powerhouse*. New York: St. Martin's, 1992.

42 . Bill and Hillary Clinton, and a Few of Many
Allen, Charles E., and Jonathan Portis, *The Comeback Kid*. New York: Birch Lane, 1992.
Brock, David, *The Seduction of Hillary Rodham*. New York: Free Press, 1996.
Gallen, David, *Bill Clinton as They Knew Him*. New York: Gallen, 1994.
King, Norman, *Hillary*. New York: Birch Lane, 1992.

Maraniss, David, *First in His Class*. New York: Simon and Schuster, 1995.

Moore, Jim, *Clinton*. Fort Worth: Summit Group, 1992.

Osborne, Claire G., *The Unique Voice of Hillary Rodham Clinton*. New York: Avon, 1997.

Radcliffe, Donnie, *Hillary Rodham Clinton*. New York: Warner, 1993.

Taylor, Rebecca Buffum, *Clinton*. New York: Warner, 1992–93.

Walker, Martin, *The President We Deserve*. New York: Crown, 1996.

Warner, Judith, *Hillary Clinton*. New York: Signet, 1993.

II. The Presidency and Multiple First Families

Adler, Bill, *Presidential Wit*. New York: Trident, 1966.

The American Heritage Pictorial History of the Presidents of the United States. 2 vols. New York: American Heritage, no date.

Andrew, Christopher M., *For the President's Eyes Only*. New York: HarperCollins, 1995.

Anthony, Carl S., *America's Most Influential First Ladies*. Minneapolis: Oliver, 1992.

_____, *First Ladies*. New York: Morrow, 1990–91.

Bailey, Thomas A., *The American Pageant*. Boston: Heath, 1966.

Barclay, Barbara, *Our Presidents*. Pasadena: Bowmar, 1970.

Barzman, Sol, *The First Ladies*. New York: Cowles, 1970.

Boller, Paul F., *Presidential Wives*. New York: Oxford, 1988.

Caroli, Betty Boyd, *First Ladies*. New York: Oxford University Press, 1987.

Cawthorne, Nigel, *Sex Lives of the Presidents*. New York: St. Martin's, 1964.

Collins, Gail, *Scorpion Tongues*. New York: Morrow, 1998.

Colman, Edna M., *Seventy-five Years of White House Gossip*. Garden City, New York: Doubleday, Page, 1925.

Cunliffe, Marcus, *The American Heritage History of the Presidency*. New York: American Heritage, 1968.

DeGregorio, William A., *The Complete Book of U.S. Presidents*. New York: Wings, 1993.

Donovan, Robert J., *The Assassins*. New York: Harper, 1952.

Filler, Louis, ed., *The President Speaks*. New York: Putnam's, 1964.

The First Ladies: Martha Washington to Barbara Bush. New York: Greenwich, 1989.

Frank, Sid, and Arden D. Melick, *The Presidents*. New York: Crown, 1984.

Fromkin, David, *In the Time of the Americans*. New York: Knopf, 1995.

Fuller, Edmund, and David E. Green, *God in the White House*. New York: Crown, 1968.

Furman, Bess, *White House Profile*. Indianapolis: Bobbs-Merrill, 1951.

Goebel, Dorothy B. and Julius, *Generals in the White House*. Garden City, New York: Doubleday, Doran, 1946.

Gould, Lewis L., ed., *American First Ladies*. New York: Garland, 1996.

Graham, Frank, *Man's Dominion: The Story of Conservation in America*. New York: Evans, 1971.

Hagood, Wesley O., *Presidential Sex*. New York: Citadel, 1995.

Hay, Peter, *All the Presidents' Ladies*. New York: Viking, 1988.

Healy, Diana, *America's First Ladies*. New York: Atheneum, 1988.

Hicks, John D., et. al., *A History of American Democracy*. Boston: Houghton Mifflin, 1966.

Jacobson, Doranne, *Presidents and First Ladies*. New York: Smithmark, 1995.

Jensen, Amy L., *The White House and Its Thirty-two Families*. New York: McGraw-Hill, 1958.

Johnson, David E. and Johnny R., *A Funny Thing Happened on the Way to the White House*. New York: Beaufort, 1983.

Kane, Joseph N., *Facts About the Presidents*; 6th edition. New York: H. W. Wilson, 1993.

Kessler, Ronald, *Inside the White House*. New York: Pocket Books, 1995.

Klapthor, Margaret B., *The First Ladies*. Washington: White House Historical Association, 1981.

Kruh, David and Louis, *Presidential Landmarks*. New York: Hippocrene, 1992.

The Living White House. 2 vols. Washington: White House Historical Association, 1975.

Lorant, Stefan, *The Glorious Burden*. New York: Harper & Row, 1968.

————, *The Presidency*. New York: Macmillan, 1951.

Mayo, Edith P., general editor, *The Smithsonian Book of the First Ladies*. New York: Holt, 1996.

McClure, A. K., *Our Presidents*. New York: Harper & Bros., 1902.

McConnell, Jane and Burt, *Our First Ladies*. New York: Crowell, 1969.

Milhollen, Hirst D., et al., *Presidents on Parade*. New York: Macmillan, 1948.

Miller, Hope R., *Scandals in the Highest Office*. New York: Random, 1973.

Miller, Nathan, *Star-Spangled Men*. New York: Scribner's, 1998.

Paletta, Lu Ann, *The World Almanac of First Ladies*. New York: World Almanac, 1990.

Potter, John M., *Plots Against the Presidents*. New York: Astor-Honor, 1968.

The Presidents. Indianapolis, Indiana: Curtis, 1980.

Quinn, Sandra L., and Sanford Kanter, *America's Royalty*. Westport, Connecticut: Greenwood, 1983.

Roseboom, Eugene H., *A History of Presidential Elections*. New York: Macmillan, 1957.

Safire, William, *The New Language of Politics*. New York: Random House, 1968.

Seale, William, *The President's House*. Washington: White House Historical Association, 1986.

Sherman, John, *Recollections of Forty Years in the House, Senate, and Cabinet*. 2 vols. New York: Werner, 1895.

Small, Norman J., *Some Presidential Interpretations of the Presidency*. Baltimore: Johns Hopkins Press, 1932.

Stebben, Gregg, and Jim Morris, *White House Confidential*. Nashville: Cumberland House, 1998.

Stone, Irving, *They Also Ran*. Garden City, New York: Doubleday, 1966.

Taylor, Tim, *The Book of Presidents*. New York: Arno, 1972.

Tourtellot, *The Presidents on the Presidency*. New York: Russell and Russell, 1964.

Truman, Ben C., "Gossip About the Presidents," *Overland Monthly*, 1898.

Truman, Margaret, *First Ladies*. New York: Random House, 1995.

Tugwell, Rexford G., *How They Became President*. New York: Simon & Schuster, 1964.

Whitney, David C., *The American Presidents*. New York: Stewart, 1959.

Wilson, Woodrow, *History of the American People*. 4 vols. New York: Harper & Bros., 1901.

Young, Donald, *American Roulette*. New York: Holt, Rhinehart, Winston, 1965.

Index

Printed in the USA
CPSIA information can be obtained
at www.ICGtesting.com
JSHW022209140824
68134JS00018B/953

9 781581 820812